The Museum as a Cinematic Space

Edinburgh Studies in Film and Intermediality
Series editors: Martine Beugnet and Kriss Ravetto
Founding editor: John Orr

A series of scholarly research intended to challenge and expand on the various approaches to film studies, bringing together film theory and film aesthetics with the emerging intermedial aspects of the field. The volumes combine critical theoretical interventions with a consideration of specific contexts, aesthetic qualities, and a strong sense of the medium's ability to appropriate current technological developments in its practice and form as well as in its distribution.

Advisory board
Duncan Petrie (University of Auckland)
John Caughie (University of Glasgow)
Dina Iordanova (University of St Andrews)
Elizabeth Ezra (University of Stirling)
Gina Marchetti (University of Hong Kong)
Jolyon Mitchell (University of Edinburgh)
Judith Mayne (The Ohio State University)
Dominique Bluher (Harvard University)

Titles in the series include:

Romantics and Modernists in British Cinema
John Orr

Framing Pictures: Film and the Visual Arts
Steven Jacobs

The Sense of Film Narration
Ian Garwood

The Feel-Bad Film
Nikolaj Lübecker

American Independent Cinema: Rites of Passage and the Crisis Image
Anna Backman Rogers

The Incurable-Image: Curating Post-Mexican Film and Media Arts
Tarek Elhaik

Screen Presence: Cinema Culture and the Art of Warhol, Rauschenberg, Hatoum and Gordon
Stephen Monteiro

Indefinite Visions: Cinema and the Attractions of Uncertainty
Martine Beugnet, Allan Cameron and Arild Fetveit (eds)

Screening Statues: Sculpture and Cinema
Steven Jacobs, Susan Felleman, Vito Adriaensens and Lisa Colpaert (eds)

Drawn From Life: Issues and Themes in Animated Documentary Cinema
Jonathan Murray and Nea Ehrlich (eds)

Intermedial Dialogues: The French New Wave and the Other Arts
Marion Schmid

The Museum as a Cinematic Space: The Display of Moving Images in Exhibitions
Elisa Mandelli

Theatre Through the Camera Eye: The Poetics of an Intermedial Encounter
Laura Sava

edinburghuniversitypress.com/series/esif

The Museum as a Cinematic Space

The Display of Moving Images in Exhibitions

Elisa Mandelli

EDINBURGH
University Press

Edinburgh University Press is one of the leading university presses in the UK. We publish academic books and journals in our selected subject areas across the humanities and social sciences, combining cutting-edge scholarship with high editorial and production values to produce academic works of lasting importance. For more information visit our website: edinburghuniversitypress.com

© Elisa Mandelli, 2019, 2021

Edinburgh University Press Ltd
The Tun – Holyrood Road
12 (2f) Jackson's Entry
Edinburgh EH8 8PJ

First published in hardback by Edinburgh University Press 2019

Typeset in Garamond MT Pro by
Servis Filmsetting Ltd, Stockport, Cheshire

A CIP record for this book is available from the British Library

ISBN 978 1 4744 1679 5 (hardback)
ISBN 978 1 4744 8426 8 (paperback)
ISBN 978 1 4744 1680 1 (webready PDF)
ISBN 978 1 4744 1681 8 (epub)

The right of Elisa Mandelli to be identified as author of this work has been asserted in accordance with the Copyright, Designs and Patents Act 1988 and the Copyright and Related Rights Regulations 2003 (SI No. 2498).

Contents

List of Figures vii
Acknowledgements viii
Preface ix

Introduction 1

Part I Between History and Modernity: Films in Exhibitions in the Twentieth Century

1. Cinema, Museums, Memory and Education 17
   'The ocular evidence that is truthful and infallible par excellence': Cinema, museums and the preservation of memory 17
   The Educational Role of Cinema 20
   Cinema, Museums and the Demands of Modern Life 21

2. 'A dimly-lighted corner': Moving Images in Museums in the First Decades of the Twentieth Century 27
   Museums and Movies: Cinema at the Imperial Institute 27
   Films as Exhibits: Moving Images inside the Museums' Galleries 29
   An Archive for the Preservation of Films at the Imperial War Museum 31
   Trenches, Tanks and the Explosion of a Mine: Mutoscopes at the Imperial War Museum (1924–38) 35
   Exception or Rule? Debating the Use of Moving Images in Museum Galleries 40

3. Moving Images in Museums, World's Fairs and Avant-garde Exhibition Design 46
   Twentieth-century Avant-gardes and Exhibition Design 46
   'The paradise of the exhibitor': Museums and World's Fairs 51
   Films at the New York Museum of Science and Industry 55

4. The Multi-media Museum: The 1960s–70s 61
   Museums and Films from UNESCO to World's Fairs 61
   The exhibition as A Mosaic: Marshall McLuhan and Harley Parker 63
   Museums and the 'AV Revolution' 65

Part II The Museum as a Cinematic Space: Museums and Moving Images in the Twenty-first Century

5. From the Museum Experience to the Museum as an Experience 73
   From Objects to Visitors: The Virtualisation of the Museum 73
   Museums and the 'Experience Economy' 75
   Moving images and the Museum Experience 78

6. Audio-visuals in Exhibitions 82
   Archival Footage 82
   Documentaries 85
   Reconstructions and Fictional Films 86
   Video Testimonies 87

7. The Museum and its Spectres 91
   The Mirror and the Portrait: The Widespread Museum of the Resistance in Turin 92
   The 'Ghosts' of the Witnesses: The In Flanders Fields Museum 96
   Phantasmagoria 100

8. A Walk through Images 105
   Galleries, Projections and Cinematic Effects: The Trento Tunnels 106
   A film in space: *Peopling the Palaces* at Venaria Reale 110

9. New Interpretations of the Movie Theatre 115
   'A bit like a large cinema': The Big Picture Show at the Imperial War Museum North 116
   A Movie Theatre inside the Museum: The Historial Charles de Gaulle 119

10. Touching Images 124
    Touching, Browsing: Interactive Tables 125
    Rewriting space: The Museum Laboratory of the Mind 127
    Interactions/Interrelations 130

Conclusions 137

Bibliography 139
Index 157

Figures

7.1	Widespread Museum of Resistance: projections on the walls of the building	93
7.2	Widespread Museum of Resistance: the witnesses	95
7.3	In Flanders Fields Museum: the witnesses' display cases	97
8.1	Trento Tunnels: the black gallery	108
8.2	Trento Tunnels: figures of soldiers projected on tulle screens	109
8.3	Installation *Peopling the Palaces*: the kitchens	111
10.1	Widespread Museum of Resistance: the interactive table	126
10.2	Museum Laboratory of the Mind: the invisible wall	128
10.3	Museum Laboratory of the Mind: installation *Bearers of Stories*	132

Acknowledgements

This book first began as a PhD dissertation completed at the Ca' Foscari University and the IUAV (University of Venice Faculty of Architecture) in Venice, Italy. Many thanks to my supervisor, Giuseppe Barbieri, for his guidance and support. Former versions of this book greatly benefited from readings from Fabrizio Borin, Miriam De Rosa, Giacomo Manzoli, Emanuele Pellegrini, Valentina Re, Leonardo Quaresima, and Cosetta Saba, to whom I am profoundly grateful. I am indebted to the series editors, Martine Beugnet and Kriss Ravetto-Biagioli, for all their invaluable advice and help during the process of preparing the manuscript.

I am grateful to the archivists and curators who have been generous with their time and expertise, particularly those at the British Library, Churchill War Rooms, FilmWork Trento, Imperial War Museum London and Imperial War Museum North, In Flanders Fields Museum, Museo Diffuso della Resistenza, Museo Laboratorio della Mente, and Reggia di Venaria Reale.

I am deeply grateful to Leslie Gillian, the commissioning editor for Film Studies at Edinburgh University Press, who believed in this project from the very beginning, and to Richard Strachan, for all his kind assistance. I am thankful to Daniela Almansi, for her careful translations and proofreading.

Many thanks to my family and friends for their encouragement and support.

Former versions of parts of this book have appeared in different forms in the following publications: 'The Museum as a Cinematic Space: The Display of Moving Images in History Museums', *Cinéma & Cie. International Film Studies Journal*, 24, 2015, pp. 131–43; 'Spectacular Attractions: Museums, Audio-Visuals and the Ghosts of Memory', *Acta Universitatis Sapientiae, Film and Media Studies*, 11, 2015, pp. 77–92; 'Immagini della storia. Musei, audiovisivi e l'esperienza del passato', *Studi culturali*, XII, 2, 2015, pp. 235–47; 'Toute la vie et le mouvement du monde: le cinéma au musée dans les années 1920–1930', *1895. Revue d'Histoire du Cinéma*, 78, 2016, pp. 29–43; 'Il museo come spazio fantasmatico: le immagini in movimento al Museo Laboratorio della Mente di Roma', *Studi e ricerche. Dipartimento di storia, beni culturali e territorio dell'Università di Cagliari*, IX, 2016, pp. 203–11; *Esporre la memoria. Immagini in movimento nel museo contemporaneo* (Udine: Forum, 2017).

Preface

Moving images have become a common feature in museums, where visitors are now accustomed to finding a broad variety of projections and screens. But when did films start to be displayed in history, science, and natural history museums? How did visitors react to the transformation of static displays by means of moving images? And what are the current stakes of showing audio-visuals in exhibition spaces? *The Museum as a Cinematic Space* is an extensive investigation of the use of moving images in exhibition design outside the field of art. It explores how museums have incorporated films and audio-visuals in their displays from the beginning of the twentieth century up to the present.

From the beginning of the twentieth century, museum professionals have taken interest in the potential of the new cinematic medium, and have considered the possibility of using films as a means of exhibition. This has led over the decades to explore technological as well as conceptual solutions to integrate audio-visual devices in the gallery space. From the Mutoscopes used in the 1920s to the contemporary immersive projections, curators have had to deal with issues such as the relationship of moving images with museum objects, as well as the way in which visitor movement in space relates and intertwines with the movement of the images on the screen. Moreover, audio-visuals have repeatedly raised the problem of the balance between the serious and educational mission of the museum and the will to entertain the public, with an imbalance in favour of entertainment that today seems in many cases to define the very concept of museum.

In addition to describing the concrete solutions and strategies used by curators to exhibit films, my goal is to identify the practical, technical, and discursive conditions that enabled the use of moving images in museum galleries during the twentieth century and the twenty-first. My focus will be on the inclusion of cinematic elements (films, screens, projections, and so on) within the display. By opening itself to moving images, the exhibition becomes a place where cinema and museum spectatorships converge, reshaping the fixed relations between the public, the images, and the viewing space itself.

The book is divided into two parts. Part I traces a historical overview of the display of moving images in museums in the twentieth century, focusing on the earliest use of films in exhibition galleries and on their gradual diffusion into the 1970s. I examine how the rules and conditions defining the use of moving images in museums were negotiated during these crucial decades, as well as the kinds of images selected to be shown in the galleries and how they affected the visitors' experience.

In the first decades of the twentieth century, film was considered an ideal medium for the preservation of memory, and was rapidly included among the educational means used in museums. Although films were mainly projected in auditoriums, attempts were also made to include them in the galleries, alongside other exhibits. One of the best-documented cases of the use of moving images in museum spaces – albeit one that has not been fully studied prior to this book – is the Imperial War Museum in London, which, as early as 1924, began to exhibit war films from its archives in eight Mutoscope machines.

With reference to the 1930s and 1940s, the following discussion addresses the connections between museums, world fairs, and didactic exhibitions by European avant-garde artists, and then provides an overview of the spreading of film projections and other multi-media and interactive devices in museum galleries in the 1960s and 1970s, following the advent of video and technological innovations that rendered these machines more easily available, as well as the growing importance accorded to the visual design of exhibitions.

Archival research, together with the analysis of period magazines, has allowed me to bring to light and describe a set of practices related to the use of audio-visuals in museum spaces that were previously unknown or not adequately considered. Through these sources, the discussion proposed in Part I offers historical background, demonstrating that the use of moving images in museum galleries has a long history that is rooted in the first decades of the twentieth century. My goal is to identify and contextualise where and when continuities and breakthroughs took place.

Part II of the volume, instead, explores the use of films and videos in contemporary museum exhibitions through a series of analysis of relevant case studies. The exhibitions analysed throughout the chapters have been chosen after an extensive survey of contemporary museums' displays, in view of how efficiently they facilitate an effective discussion of the needs, problems, and practices of the use of moving images in museums. Some of these exhibitions have never been the object of critical analysis, while others are better known among scholars and curators, either because they interconnect with artistic practice (this is the case of Studio Azzurro's museums, or Peter Greenaway's installation at Venaria Reale, a historical site near Turin), or because they represent successful or indeed problematic examples of museography (such as the Imperial War Museum North in Manchester). In this volume, I investigate them paying attention specifically to the ways in which moving images are integrated in the display and affect the meaning of the whole exhibition.

The cases discussed include a sample of exhibitions in which projections of historical characters or testimonies appear, like spectres, to tell their story to visitors (as in the case of the Widespread Museum of Resistance in Turin, or the In Flanders Fields Museum in Ypres). I furthermore detail installations in which museum narrative could be compared to film narrative, not only because they both unfold in time following a 'script', but also because the exhibition employs, through its own media-specific means, filmic techniques such as montage, zooms, and close-ups, as well as a complex articulation of the story and characters (like in the Trento Tunnels, two former highway tunnels reconverted into a museum, and the Peter Greenaway installation at the Venaria Reale).

In other museums, architecture and exhibition design could be influenced by the 'classic' cinematic *dispositif* and its components (screen, dark room, projection, seated spectators), as in the Big Picture Show, an audio-visual show that takes place at the Imperial War Museum North, and in the cinema theatre at the Historial Charles de Gaulle in Paris. I also consider museums that utilise interactive devices, where visitors have to touch the moving images – rather than press-buttons – the surface of which acts as an interface between the spectator and the representation (as happens at the Museum Laboratory of the Mind in Rome, Italy).

Although the two parts of the book apply different research methodologies to the historical investigation and analysis of contemporary case studies, they are in no way disconnected. Although the works I look at follow in chronological order, the aim is not to provide a linear and exhaustive historical reconstruction. Rather, concentrating on some emblematic cases allows an in-depth discussion of the needs to which the moving images exposed in museums respond, the problems they raise, as well as the way in which they lead to a rethinking of the design of the exhibition space and the very idea of museum. I propose an analysis of the forms of negotiation between the exhibition and the cinematic *dispositif*, identifying four main recurring configurations. For each of them, I discuss the relationship between the moving images, the layout of the space and the visitor's position. The focus on contemporary history museums allows me to reflect on the specific means of historical representation and the preservation of memory implemented by museums, and on the role of moving images in this process.

The cross-comparison between the historical and the contemporary historical exhibition practices reveals a number of continuities and ruptures, showing that many apparently unprecedented issues have already been addressed in earlier phases of the history of the institution. The museum remains an interstitial space that establishes relations with the entertainment and even advertising industries. In fact, the analysis of audio-visuals in museum galleries provides a privileged point of view from which to consider the affinities and reciprocal influences between museums and entertainment venues, such as fairs, great exhibitions, and contemporary amusement parks. This approach reinforces the idea that the museum should not be considered as an isolated and out-of-time institution. Rather, its practices politics, and objectives are strictly connected to the broader cultural and leisure landscape, in a two-way exchange: one which the study of the display of moving images allows me to examine in depth.

Introduction

Today, art galleries and art, history, science, and cinema museums alike make extensive use of video loops, film installations, and projections, and an impressive amount of scholarly attention has been devoted to the investigation of this tendency. My approach to this phenomenon is both historical and critical. I begin by identifying the coalescence of three major modes of disseminating moving images in museums: the first group of exhibitions treat cinema as a technology or as a specific medium. This category comprises both cinema equipment shown in science and technology or film museums, and film-related objects (such as photographs, posters, or costumes) displayed in exhibitions that focus on the relations between art and cinema or on the work of film directors. Cinema has been used as a medium of visual display since the first decades of the twentieth century: in 1922, for instance, the inventor Will Day lent 500 items from his collection of cinematic apparatuses to the London Science Museum.[1] The Museum exhibited Day's equipment until 1959, when the items were purchased by Henry Langlois, director of the Cinémathèque Française.[2] It was also in the 1920s that intellectuals such as Ricciotto Canudo, Léon Moussinac, and Robert Mallet-Stevens organised pioneering exhibitions that aimed at legitimising cinema as an art form, such as those that took place in Paris at the *Salon d'Automne* (*Autumn Salon*) (1921, 1922, and 1923) and at the Musée Galliera (1924), where the exhibition *The Art in French Cinema* (*L'art dans le cinéma français*) included enlarged frames, set photographs, and costumes, and was accompanied by film screenings and lectures.[3] The exhibition of cinematic apparatuses remains common in cinema museums as well as in art galleries.[4]

The second group of cinema-related exhibitions includes contemporary art installations involving the use of films and moving images. The foremost examples of this category are cinematic installations created by artists or filmmakers[5] (the boundaries between which are sometimes very blurred), which became widespread in museums and art galleries from the 1990s. In these works, cinema is treated as the source of unlimited iconographic material, narrative techniques,[6] modes of productions, and reception.[7] This mode of display entails a broad series of large-scale collective exhibitions, frequently curated by artists or art critics, which relate more directly to the relationship between art and cinema. Often these exhibitions propose a general historical overview of the growing presence of moving images in museums and galleries, starting with avant-garde film and the use of video to document artistic performances in the 1960s and 1970s.[8] They differ significantly in their scope and approach and adopt a specific component of the cinematic *dispositif* (projection, for example) as the starting point to explore the migrations of images among various media and artistic domains.[9] Finally, the multifaceted interactions between cinema and contemporary art also include exhibitions curated by filmmakers, such as Agnès Varda's *L'île et elle*,[10] a site of fertile intersections between the director's installations and her cinematic universe, and Jean-Luc Godard's *Voyage(s) en utopie*,[11] which explored a complex web of issues, including the question of cinema's integration in the exhibition space.

While scholars have investigated these connections, the field still lacks a comprehensive understanding of a third form of penetration of moving images in museums, which is related to their role in museology and exhibition design.

Indeed, from the beginning of the twentieth century, and in a pervasive way in the contemporary landscape, moving images have been exhibited in a wide range of institutions such as natural history, science, or history museums, where video installations, projections, and screens occupy the domain traditionally inhabited by artefacts and artworks. Within these settings, films and audio-visual displays serve as tools for contextualisation, explanation, or visitor engagement. *The Museum as a Cinematic Space* focuses on this last mode of dissemination of moving images in exhibitions. In these pages I argue that moving images are far from being merely instrumental, as they deeply affect the strategies of museum exhibitions and the meanings that they convey.

THE MIGRATION OF MOVING IMAGES INTO MUSEUMS

At a first glance, cinema and museum exhibitions are clearly distinct, especially in terms of the reception and of the articulation of temporality and movement: the static viewer of moving images could be considered as the opposite of the visitor who moves across the museum space.[12] As Francesco Casetti explains,

> The rise of cinema at the end of the nineteenth century . . . created a clear-cut opposition between, on the one hand, spectacles based on images fixed in place and spectators free to move in space according to personal itineraries, as in the case of the panorama and the museum and, on the other hand, spec-

tacles based on mobile images (or at least quasi-mobile) and fixed spectators, gathered together in an audience in front of the screen, as in the theatre or the magic lantern show. Cinema's inclusion in the latter group inevitably led to the characterization of the first group as non-cinematic.[13]

Scholars have identified many other differences between cinema and exhibition spaces, such as dark versus light, sound versus silence, and disembodied versus embodied perception.[14] These differences are epitomised by the antithesis between the 'white cube' of the modernist art museum, a historically and culturally determined system, with its white walls and its allegedly neutral organisation,[15] and the components of the 'classic' cinema-viewing situation (dark room–projection–screen–motionless viewer) reproduced inside the galleries in the form of the so-called 'black box'.[16]

However, these distinctions are less rigid than they may appear, and the interpenetration between the forms of presentation and reception typical of the cinema or the museum are (and have been in the past) frequent and productive, both in the field of art (with video art, experimental cinema, moving-image installations) and in those of education and spectacle.

In the artistic context, scholars have proposed various definitions to name the multiple forms of penetration of moving images in museums, such as 'other cinema',[17] 'othered cinema',[18] 'cinema of exhibition',[19] and 'artists' cinema'.[20] The issue that lays at the core of the different terminology, which moreover continues to catalyse the debate, is the very definition of this type of artistic practices and artworks. Should the installations of moving images be considered a part of the territories of art or cinema? What is left of the cinema[21] when it migrates in the art museum? Can we still call it 'cinema'?

One of the most influential (albeit often contested) voices in that debate belongs to Raymond Bellour, to whom only the collective projection of a film in a darkened theatre is worth being called 'cinema'.[22] In this perspective, cinema is strictly opposed to the terrain of gallery-based film installation (what Bellour had in previous works defined as 'other cinema'[23]): despite the passages operating from one to the other, and vice versa, he firmly asserts that it is not acceptable to confuse the two experiences.

On the contrary, Philippe Dubois advocates for an expansion of the territories of 'cinema', to include the artistic forms that introduce in the museum components of the cinematic *dispositif* (such as screens, or projections) or refer to film history. More broadly, for Dubois cinema has produced an 'imaginary of the image', which has penetrated our thoughts and our way of looking at the world so deeply that it functions as a model that can stand for our relationship to all other contemporary images. So, to Dubois, cinema is not disappearing at all, but, on the contrary, it 'gains ground' in the diversity of its forms and practices.[24]

These are the two poles of a debate that, moving within these conflicts and polarisations, has led scholars to compose a rich and varied map of the forms of migration of moving images into the art museum.[25] However, the non-artistic domain remains mostly excluded from these analyses. Moving-images installations in non-artistic museums, such as those of history or science, have long been overlooked, or at most considered trivialised or degraded versions of experimentations conducted in artistic research.[26]

In order to challenge this attitude, in this volume I want to stress that the exhibition of moving images outside of the artistic context represents a rich and fertile terrain for enquiry. These instances illuminate one of the most multifaceted modes of the circulation on moving images and raise a variety of compelling questions, regarding the social role of the museum or the technological availability, maintenance, and obsolescence of images, memory, personal and collective history, and indeed our relationships with these elements.

Compared to artistic installations, the exhibitions I deal with present some peculiarities. In particular, they are not conceived as autonomous works of art: even when the aesthetic dimension plays an important role (as in the Studio Azzurro's museums), they are primarily intended to convey certain contents (whether historical, technical, or scientific), consistently with the broader educational and communication strategy of the museums in which they are installed. The solutions adopted are therefore developed in relation to a multiplicity of needs on the scientific, museological, and museographic levels, as well as those of communicator and even spectacle. However, I would stress that they do not play a merely instrumental role, but contribute to rewriting and redefining the contents proposed by the museum and the relation it establishes with visitors.

Moreover, this does not prevent exchanges with artistic solutions from being frequent and productive, nor that some of these installations can, even if indirectly, solicit a reflection on the relationship between the cinematic and museum viewing contexts (a particularly evident case being the Big Picture Show, analysed in Chapter 9). Likewise, in museums such as those of science, history, or natural history, we can identify interesting experimentations, more or less intentional, with the display of moving images, as well as with the variety of supports and formats, ranging from small screens to environmental projections.

Also, since I conceive the museum as an institution that is far from being closed, isolated, and timeless, I argue that the exhibitions I analyse here interact with the wider cultural and media landscape in which they are located. They must therefore be considered in the framework of the wider phenomena of the penetration of moving images in everyday spaces, from urban scenarios to domestic contexts.[27]

For these reasons, I begin my investigation discussing a matter that I consider crucial in the debates on the circulation of moving images outside the movie theatre: the question of the *dispositif*. In film studies, the issue was formulated by Jean-Louis Baudry in the 1960s–70s,[28] and has since experienced a renewed centrality in the debates on early cinema,[29] as well as in the field of investigations on cinema and contemporary art. In the latter field, to discuss the nature of the *dispositif* has become a crucial concern when theorising and analysing the multiple ways that moving images enter museums.[30]

In my investigation, I understand the *dispositif* on the basis of the well-known definition given by Michel Foucault, as a 'thoroughly heterogeneous ensemble', a 'system of relations' that can be established between a complex series of elements.[31] Foucault's definition was taken up by Gilles Deleuze, who conceives the *dispositif* as 'a multilinear whole . . . composed of lines of different natures . . . Each line is broken, subject to *changes in direction*, bifurcating and forked, and subjected to *derivations*.'[32] For Deleuze, studying this concept means 'preparing a map, a cartography, a survey of unexplored lands'.[33] This idea was already developed by Deleuze and Guattari in *A Thousand Plateaus*, where the notion of 'assemblage' (*agencement*) identifies, as Francesco Casetti aptly sums up, the 'heterogeneous elements that are stripped from former combinations, that enter into a new relation with one another, and that form a new general profile'.[34]

According to Casetti, Deleuze raises two important points: the 'sense of an opening'[35] and of continuous transformation, but also 'the presence of . . . a kind of comprehensive structure to which all these things make reference – despite the fact that the structure itself is mutable'.[36] From this perspective, Casetti proposes to conceive the dispositive (as he calls it)[37] as an 'assemblage', stressing the importance not only of the different components that it implies, but also of 'the reasons and the ways in which they find a mutual arrangement'.[38]

Casetti identifies a set of elements that characterise the 'cinema-assemblage', and what brings them together.[39] In his view, precisely because it has functioned as an apparatus, cinema maintains its identity despite the many transformations it faces: the history of cinema is marked by multiple experiments with new possibilities, but at the same time it always finds 'a configuration compatible with the habitual one'.[40]

In my view, conceiving the cinema as a *dispositif* in the sense of an assemblage enables not only to recognise of the multiplicity of its manifestations, but especially to focus on how it can intertwine with other *dispositifs*, such as the exhibition. In this book I will not only discuss how moving images have obtained a place in museum displays, but also how this migration has involved a constant renegotiation of narrative, presentation, and reception forms between the two apparently different *dispositifs* of the cinema and the exhibition.

Some of the exhibitions I describe throughout the book maintain a strong link with the cinematic *dispositif* (the projection, the collective spectacle, the immobile spectator), while others rewrite it in a more substantial way. To consider the museum as a 'cinematic space' thus enables underlining of how the very form of the museum display is questioned and reshaped by the elements of the cinematic *dispositif*, as well as identifying the new possibilities that the latter opens in the practices of exhibition design.

Together with the concept of *dispositif*, the expression 'moving images' deserves a brief explanation. This locution has several advantages. First, it is a broad term, which allows to account for heterogeneous forms of textuality. In this book, it is complemented by the terms 'audio-visual', which emphasises the integration of images and sounds, and 'film', which refers to more structured forms of textuality.

Also, and more importantly, as Catherine Elwes stresses in her *Installation and the Moving Image*, the expression 'moving images' 'emphasises the dynamic element of apparent motion'[41] that unifies the works she analyses. Albeit Elwes recognises that motion in film is given by a series of fixed frames, and that the movement is actually only apparent; she maintains that 'the impression of movement . . . is not diminished by the technology's structural stasis'.[42]

The centrality of motion is crucial to my argument: the films that have been projected in museums since the early decades of the twentieth century had, for the commentators of the time, the merit of bringing the movement (and, as one of them wrote, 'life')[43] into museum galleries. Also, it is precisely the dimension of movement that questions and disrupts the most consolidated museum display techniques, posing new challenges to curators and asking visitors to rethink the form of their visit.

BETWEEN FILM AND MUSEUM STUDIES

In order to investigate the display of moving images in museums, this book adopts a strongly interdisciplinary approach that combines theoretical and methodological tools drawn primarily from museum, film, and media studies. Following museum studies, I will pay attention not only to the way in which exhibition design can influence the meaning of the exhibits, but also to the type of relationship that the visitor establishes with the contents proposed by the institution. On the other hand, film and media studies offer methodological instruments to investigate the dissemination of moving images in a variety of contexts and situations outside the movie theatre, both in the past and in the contemporaneity.

Museum Studies

The so-called 'New Museology' trend that emerged in Britain in the 1970s and 1980s provide a set of indispensable methodological instruments towards a critical analysis of the whole system of organisation and transmission of knowledge inside museums.[44] The museum is in fact conceived as a non-neutral tool of consensus building, as a space for control and conflict between different cultures and social classes. New Museology investigates the functions, mission, needs, and developments of the museum, with a particular focus on its relations with visitors. This approach orients the most recent tendencies of museum studies, which extend their scope and strengthen their empirical and practical base.[45] If an exhibition is never neutral, museum scholars reaffirm that we cannot underestimate the multiplicity of levels and factors that contribute to museum communication.[46]

Museum studies are naturally multidisciplinary and interdisciplinary[47] and cross-pollinate with a variety of other fields, including cultural studies, sociology, anthropology, and art history, but also visual, memory, and media studies. At the intersection of museum studies and media studies, a fertile research field examines the use of media devices in the various areas of museum practice, from conservation to exhibition, teaching, and communication.[48] This is undoubtedly one of the most topical and prolific territories of museological investigation, as evidenced by the contributions collected in 2015 in one of the volumes of the *International Handbooks of Museum Studies* series, dedicated to *Museum Media* and edited by Michelle Henning.[49] The essays – many of which will be mentioned in this book – explore the different forms in which new media are included in museums, challenging their conventions and redefining their nature. Henning's volume offers a much-needed systematisation of a broad set of issues: the museum as a medium and its relations with other media; the emergence of immersion and interactivity as crucial concerns of contemporary museums; the increasing importance attributed to audio-visuals and moving images; the evolution of curatorial practices and design in relation to new media devices; and the circulation of contents outside the physical boundaries of the museum through various media, including the Web.

In recent years, some museum scholars have analysed moving-images installations in the context of wider discourses on the musealisation of issues such as traumatic memories. I found particularly interesting the works of Silke Arnold-de Simine, *Mediating Memory in the Museum*[50] and Steffi de Jong, *The Witness as an Object*.[51] Arnold-de Simine investigates the role of memory, trauma, empathy, and nostalgia in contemporary Western museums, discussing the forms in which memory is mediated in museums, and analysing – among other case studies – a series of audio-visual installations. Steffi de Jong focuses on Holocaust museums, and investigates the use of audio-visual testimonies in the museum narrative and in the exhibition design strategies.

These publications reveal a growing scholarly recognition of the importance of audio-visual media in contemporary museum practices, which my book intends to further encourage. However, albeit that there is a growing interest for contemporary museum audio-visual installations, museum studies still lack a wide-ranging investigation of their history.

Film and Media Studies

It is in the field of film studies that we find the first attempts to study the role of moving images in museums from a historical perspective. Haidee Wasson and Alison Griffiths analyse the use of film in museums in the first decades of the twentieth century, respectively in art institutions such as the Museum of Modern Art (MoMA) in New York and in science and natural history museums, including the American Museum of Natural History.[52] These works have inspired and oriented my research, suggesting new paths for further research on audio-visual media in exhibition design.

Although I will have the opportunity to return to these contributions – especially Griffiths' – on several occasions, let me briefly highlight here their main themes and relevance to my research. In *Museum Movies: The Museum of Modern Art and the Birth of Art Cinema*, Wasson focuses on the history of the Film Library at the MoMA and shows how the entrance of cinema into the 'temple' of modern art had transformed the common understanding of film, which came to be considered as an art form, placed under the authority of an elite institution. More broadly, Wasson demonstrates that MoMA was part of a wider set of discourses, practices, and institutional contexts that stressed the educational value of cinema. Moreover, she shows that museums embraced mass media for different purposes: to reach a broader and more popular public, due to the growing importance of their educational mission; to disseminate ideas, concepts, and meanings; and to secure a place in the emerging landscape of modern leisure.[53]

Alison Griffiths' *Shivers Down Your Spine* provides essential methodological references. Griffiths explores a wide range of immersive and interactive forms of spectatorship, such as those provided by medieval cathedrals, panorama, IMAX screens, as well as by science and natural history museums. Regarding the last two cases, Griffiths discusses the evolution of exhibition techniques in institutions such as the Science Museum in London, the Smithsonian Institution in Washington, and the American Museum of Natural History of New York. She focuses on the introduction of automatic, electronic, and then digital media in the twentieth and twenty-first centuries, with a focus on the 1920s, the 1970s, and the present time. Her analysis of the different forms in which cinema made its entrance in museum exhibitions has paved the way to a new field of enquiry, and has brought to the attention of scholars a hitherto neglected array of practices.

Both Wasson and Griffiths underline that audio-visual media cannot be considered as isolated, but should be considered in relation to other media such as print, radio, and later television. Similarly, throughout this book, audio-visual media in museums will be always (albeit implicitly) considered as a part of a 'media network' (*Medienverbund*), to use Thomas Elsaesser's words: 'a network of competing, but also mutually interdependent and complementary media or media practices, focused on a specific location, a professional association, or even a national or state initiative'.[54]

As exemplified by the work of Wasson and Griffiths, in film and media studies the research on the display of moving images is closely intertwined with other lines of investigation, focusing on forms of spectatorship other than the 'classic' theatrical reception, and on the uses of films beyond the context of the cinematographic institution.

Over the last few years, a growing number of scholars have been focusing on the so-called 'useful cinema' – a term that designates the circulation of educational, scientific, or industrial films in a wide range of contexts (including schools and museums, but also churches and prisons), outside the entertainment and art distribution systems.[55] This methodological approach emphasises the need to consider films in the framework of the practices, discourses, and *dispositifs* that are intertwined with the specific activities and goals of various institutions. It encourages to research, along with textual forms, the modes of production and reception, as well as the social practices connected with them.

Although privileging a historical perspective, the research on 'useful cinema' is strictly related to the contemporary digital scenario. Indeed, the advent of digital media has led to a proliferation of places and modes of film consumption, and the ensuing changes have encouraged scholars to investigate the precursors of the current situation in the past centuries.[56] This trend is exemplified by Thomas Elsaesser and by scholars of the so-called 'media archaeology'.[57] If, even before the advent of digital media and the current pervasiveness of moving images, there were other forms of film circulation outside the context of entertainment, according to Elsaesser the peculiarity of the contemporary media scenario strongly encourages a renewed look at the past:

> our idea – and maybe even our definition – of cinema has changed even without appealing to digitisation as a technology, which is nonetheless implicit as a powerful 'perspective correction' and thus counts as an impulse in this retrospective re-writing of the past.[58]

This approach invites us to relativise the supposed novelty of what is happening under the impulse of digitisation. Rather than a technological or aesthetic breakthrough, digitisation brought about an epistemic turn that revealed a series of already existing but hitherto neglected phenomena.

This book adopts a similar approach: the pervasiveness of moving images in contemporary museums suggests a new perspective from which we can question the past and pay attention to the previously overlooked penetration of audio-visual media into exhibition spaces. This does not mean that present and past overlap or that they are bound by a linear progress. I follow up on Elsaesser's suggestion – drawn from Foucault – to consider both continuities and ruptures by 'taking in the discontinuities, the so-called dead-ends, and by taking seriously the possibility of the astonishing otherness of the past'.[59] As Elsaesser writes,

> only a presumption of discontinuity (in Foucault's terms, the positing of epistemic breaks) and of fragmentation (the rhetorical figure of the synecdoche or the *pars pro toto*) can give the present access to the past, which is always no more than a past (among many actual or possible ones), since for the archaeologist, the past can be present to the present with no more than its relics . . . an archaeology respects the possible distance the past has from our present perspective, and even makes it the basis of its methodology.[60]

In the first part of the book I will underline how the museum aligned with the emerging trends of modernity through the use of cinema – one of modernity's emblematic forms – while in the second part I will observe how today pre-cinematic spectacular forms such as Phantasmagoria re-emerge at the intersection between moving images and museum exhibitions. In short, upon entering the museum, moving images alter the supposed linearity of the development of exhibition practices, technology, and media, opening up unexpected lines of transformation.

THE MUSEOLOGICAL DISCOURSES BETWEEN CONTINUITIES AND RUPTURES

Museology proves an extremely fertile ground for the dialectics between continuity and rupture. Alison Griffiths remarks that 'to a large extent, very little has really changed in the world of museums since the heyday of nineteenth-century exhibition culture'.[61] However, for this reason, she argues, 'as curators ponder the ontological status and pedagogical value of technology-dependent exhibits within the twenty-first-century museum, they might do well to consider what lessons can be learned from the enduring debates of the past'.[62] Griffiths's statement demonstrates that this rift between continuity and discontinuity that lies at the heart of current curatorial debates should be more accurately described as the debate over the relationship of education to entertainment. The use of media devices in museums and galleries has fuelled this debate, along with the ever-increasing need to make them popular, and therefore relevant to contemporary visitors. As I will show in the following chapters, while museum professionals are attracted by new technologies and their ability to appeal to a wider audience, they also worry about the possible challenge to the institution's accuracy in transmitting knowledge.

If Griffiths' perspective emphasises the often-overlooked historical dimension of the use of cinema and media in the museum, Kathleen McLean is far more critical, as she deplores a lack of progress in exhibition techniques from the 1960s to this day, as well as the inability of museum professionals to seize the opportunities to renew the institution in a profoundly changed scenario. Provocatively, when comparing the first issue of the journal *Curator* (1958) to the one published fifty years later,[63] McLean recognises 'a disconcerting similarity'[64] between the questions discussed in the two periods:[65]

> certainly, museums and their exhibitions have changed with the times to some extent, reflecting the changing values of the societies of which they are a part... But despite these changes, opportunities, and new understandings, exhibition professionals still seem to be saying the same things colleagues were saying 50 years ago, while thinking they are new ideas.[66]

Among these recurring matters, McLean identifies the tension between entertainment and education; the opposition between exhibitions based on material objects and those presenting abstract concepts; the plea for experimentation in display techniques; and concerns about visitors' comfort. Another recurring theme is the importance of media technologies as part of the museum's effort to keep up with the times, as well as the need to take inspiration from world's fairs, and more generally from exhibition venues outside the museum field.

These issues will emerge several times in the next chapters, showing how problems related to the use of moving images in museums are strictly connected to the definition of the identity and the purposes of the institution, as well as to its relationship with the public.

NOTES

1. Some institutional collections of cinematic equipment were established before Will Day's donation, for example, at the National Technical Museum in Prague, in 1908–11. See Trope, 'Le Cinéma pour le Cinéma'. However, the museum was not the first site where cinematic machines were exhibited: several items had been displayed at International Exhibitions and commercial fairs since the 1890s. For a brief overview, see Albera, 'Exposé, le cinéma s'expose'.
2. On Will Day's collection, see Aubert, et al. (eds), 'The Will Day Historical Collection of Cinematograph & Moving Picture Equipment'.
3. On these exhibitions, see Gauthier, *La passion du cinéma*, pp. 72–9.
4. One of the most well-known exhibitions is Païni and Cogeval (eds), *Hitchcock et l'Art: coïncidences fatales*, held on 6 June–24 September 2001 at the Centre Pompidou in Paris.
5. Such as Chantal Akerman, Tacita Dean, Stan Douglas, Harun Faroki, Douglas Gordon, Pierre Huygue, William Kentridge, Christian Marclay, Steve McQueen, and Shirin Neshat, to mention only a few.
6. Among the vast bibliography on this subject, see at least Autelitano (ed.), *The Cinematic Experience*; Balsom, *Exhibiting Cinema in Contemporary Art*; Bordina, et al. (eds), *Extended Temporalities*; Bruno, *Atlas of Emotion*; Bruno, *Public Intimacy*; Bruno, *Surface*; Connolly, *The Place of Artists' Cinema*; Dubois, et al. (eds), *Oui, c'est du cinéma/Yes, It's Cinema*; Dubois, et al. (eds), *Extended cinema*; Elwes, *Installation and the Moving Image*; Leighton (ed.), *Art and the Moving Image. A Critical Reader*; Noordegraaf, et al. (eds), *Preserving and Exhibiting Media Art*; Trodd (ed.), *Screen/Space*.
7. These issues are explored in Connolly, *The Place of Artists' Cinema*.
8. See, for example, Eamon and Douglas (eds), *Art of Projection*; Michalka (ed.), *X-Screen. Film Installation and Actions in the 1960s and 1970s*, exhibition held at the Museum Moderner Kunst Stiftung Ludwig Wien, 13 December 2003–29 February 2004.
9. See, for example, Michaud (ed.), *Le Mouvement des images*, exhibition held at the Centre Pompidou, 9 April 2006–29 January 2007; Van Assche, et al. (eds), *Passages de l'image. Films, vidéos, images de synthèse*, exhibition held at the Centre Georges Pompidou, 19 September–18 November 1990.
10. VV. AA., *Agnès Varda. L'Ile et elle. Regards sur l'exposition*, exhibition held at the Fondation Cartier pour l'art contemporain, 18 June–1 October 2006.
11. *Voyage(s) en utopie. JLG, 1946–1966. A la recherche d'un théorème perdu*, exhibition held at the Centre Pompidou, 11 May–14 August 2006.
12. See, for example, Groys, 'Media Art in the Museum'.
13. Casetti, *The Lumière Galaxy*, p. 71.
14. See Elsaesser, 'Entre savoir et croire', pp. 60–3.
15. See O'Doherty, *Inside the White Cube: The Ideology of the Gallery Space*.
16. See Uroskie, *Between the Black Box and the White Cube*.
17. Bellour, 'Of Another Cinema'.

18. Balsom, *Exhibiting Cinema in Contemporary Art*.
19. Royoux, 'Cinéma d'exposition > l'espacement de la durée'; Royoux, 'Pour un cinéma d'exposition'.
20. Connolly, *The Place of Artists' Cinema*.
21. As Jacques Aumont asks in his *Que reste-t-il du cinéma?*
22. Bellour, *La Querelle des dispositifs*, p. 14.
23. Bellour, 'Of Another Cinema'.
24. Dubois, 'Présentation', pp. 13–14.
25. For a synthetic bibliography, see notes 6 and 7 to this chapter.
26. See Albera, 'Exposé, le cinéma s'expose', pp. 202–8.
27. See at least Casetti, *The Lumière Galaxy*; De Rosa, *Cinema e postmedia*.
28. Baudry first refers to the idea of 'basic apparatus' (*appareil de base*) to subsequently discuss the notion of *dispositif* (translated in English as 'apparatus') from a Lacanian perspective. He suggests that the technical configuration of cinema (the camera and the projector, as well as the configuration projector–screen–dark room) has an ideological impact on the spectator's reception. Accordingly, the *dispositif* is a simulating machine that produces in the psychology of the spectator an artificial regression similar to the dream and the scene of the unconscious. Baudry's theories subsequently generated the so-called 'apparatus theory'. See Baudry, 'Ideological Effects of the Basic Cinematographic Apparatus'; Baudry, 'The Apparatus: Metapsychological Approaches to the Impression of Reality in Cinema'.
29. See Maule (ed.), 'Representational Technologies and the Discourse on Early Cinema's Apparatus'; Gaudreault, et al. (eds), *The Cinema, A New Technology for the 20th Century*.
30. See Federici, *Cinema esposto*.
31. Foucault, 'The Confession of the Flesh'. See also Foucault, *Discipline and Punish: The Birth of the Prison*. As mentioned above, we prefer here the translation 'dispositive' to the term 'apparatus' used in the English translations of Foucault's text.
32. Deleuze, 'What is a Dispositif?', p. 338. See also Casetti's discussion of Deleuze's thesis in *The Lumière Galaxy*, pp. 78–81; italics in the original.
33. Deleuze, 'What is a Dispositif?', pp. 338–9.
34. Casetti, *The Lumière Galaxy*, p. 81; Deleuze and Guattari, *A Thosuand Plateaus*.
35. Casetti, *The Lumière Galaxy*, p. 79.
36. Ibid. p. 80.
37. Casetti proposes to use the term 'dispositive' to distance from the traditional 'apparatus theory' and to connect to theories such as Foucault's (see *The Lumière Galaxy*, pp. 233–4, note 1). For the use of the term 'dispositive', see also Bussolini, 'What Is a Dispositive?'
38. Casetti, *The Lumière Galaxy*, p. 81.
39. Ibid. pp. 81–7.
40. Ibid. p. 96.
41. Elwes, *Installation and the Moving Image*, p. 5

42. Ibid. p. 5.
43. See Chapter 2.
44. See Vergo (ed.), *The New Museology*.
45. See Macdonald (ed.), *A Companion to Museum Studies* and the four volumes of the series edited by Sharon Macdonald and Helen Rees Leahy, *The International Handbooks of Museum Studies*.
46. See Hooper-Greenhill, *Museums and the Shaping of Knowledge* and Hooper-Greenhill, *Museums and the Interpretation of Visual Culture*.
47. See Macdonald, 'Expanding Museum Studies'.
48. See at least Cameron and Kenderdine (eds), *Theorizing Digital Cultural Heritage*; Kalay, et al. (eds), *New Heritage. New Media and Cultural Heritage*; Kidd, *Museums in the New Mediascape*; Parry (ed.), *Museums in a Digital Age*; Thomas and Mintz (eds), *The Virtual and the Real*.
49. Henning (ed.) *Museum Media*. See also Henning, *Museums, Media and Cultural Theory*.
50. See Arnold-de Simine, *Mediating Memory in the Museum*.
51. de Jong, *The Witness as Object*. See also Shandler, *Holocaust Memory in the Digital Age*.
52. Wasson, *Museum Movies*; Wasson, 'Big, Fast Museums/Small, Slow Movies'; Griffiths, *Wondrous Difference*; Wasson, *Shivers Down Your Spine*; Wasson, 'Film Education in the Natural History Museum'.
53. Wasson, *Museum Movies*, p. 69.
54. Elsaesser, 'Archives and Archaeologies', p. 22.
55. The phrase 'useful cinema' has been utilised in the title of the volume edited by Charles R. Acland and Haidee Wasson, *Useful Cinema*. See also Hediger and Vonderau (eds), *Films that Work*; Orgeron, et al. (eds), *Learning with the Lights Off*.
56. Acland and Wasson, 'Introduction: Utility and Cinema', in Acland and Wasson (eds), *Useful Cinema*, pp. 1–14.
57. See Huhtamo and Parikka, *Media Archaeology. Approaches, Applications, and Implications*; Parikka, *What is Media Archaeology?*; Strauven 'Media Archaeology: Where Film History, Media Art, and New Media (Can) Meet'.
58. Elsaesser, 'The New Film History as Media Archaeology', p. 86. See also Elsaesser, *Film History as Media Archaeology*.
59. Elsaesser, 'Early Film History and Multi-Media', p. 20.
60. Id., 'The New Film History as Media Archaeology, pp. 103–4.
61. Griffiths, *Shivers Down Your Spine*, p. 161. See also Griffiths, 'Media Technology and Museum Display'.
62. Ibid. p. 384.
63. It is important to note that McLean considers a less extended chronological period than Griffiths.
64. McLean, 'Do Museum Exhibitions Have a Future?', p. 110.
65. See also Pardo, 'Audiovisual Installations as a Strategy for the Modernisation of Heritage Presentation Spaces'.
66. McLean, 'Do Museum Exhibitions Have a Future?', p. 118.

Part I

Between History and Modernity:
Films in Exhibitions
in the Twentieth Century

CHAPTER ONE

Cinema, Museums, Memory and Education

'THE OCULAR EVIDENCE THAT IS TRUTHFUL AND INFALLIBLE PAR EXCELLENCE': CINEMA, MUSEUMS AND THE PRESERVATION OF MEMORY

In *The Culture of Cities*, published in 1938, Lewis Mumford proclaims the death of the monument.[1] According to the well-known critic and historian of architecture, monuments not only fail to keep memory alive, but also prevent the development of new life in the place where they are erected. To Mumford, monuments belong to the past: they are 'a contradiction in terms'[2] for modern society, which is oriented towards a constant process of renewal. To be truly modern, cities should be dynamic entities, constantly adapting to new needs and lifestyles. To this aim, the memorial function must be delegated to institutions specifically created for this purpose, namely museums: 'by confining the function of preservation to the museum, we thus release space to the rest of the city for the fresh uses of the living'.[3] Museums are functional to the full development of modern society precisely because they represent a well-delimited place where 'memorials of culture' can be preserved without overwhelming people.[4] However, they should not strive to preserve everything, but carefully select the items, and to ensure the regular rotation of the exhibits.

In Mumford's view, along with museums, mechanical media contribute to storing the memory of the past and thereby create space for the continuous renewal of life: 'what cannot be kept in existence in material form, we may now measure, photograph in still and moving pictures, record in sounds, and summarise in books and papers'.[5] This process of selection should take place 'while the life is still present',[6] in order to obtain 'not merely a fragment of the original shell, but a working knowledge'[7] of the object to be preserved. In *Technics and Civilization*, published a few years before *The Culture of Cities*, Mumford had already claimed that mechanical media share the mission of museums, since they give

> modern civilization a direct sense of the past and a more accurate perception of its memorials than any other civilization had, in all probability, had. Not

alone did they make the past more immediate: they made the present more historic by narrowing the lapse of time between the actual events themselves and their concrete record. For the first time one might come face to face with the speaking likenesses of dead people and recall in their immediacy forgotten scenes and actions.[8]

According to the author, film, being able to capture the 'flux of time', is more effective than photography in preserving the memory of the past:

> [I]n a world of flux and change, the camera gave a means of combating the ordinary processes of deterioration and decay, not by 'restoration' or 'reproduction' but by holding in convenient form the lean image of men, places, buildings, landscapes: thus serving as an extension of the collective memory. The moving picture, carrying a succession of images through time, widened the scope of the camera and essentially altered its function; for . . . it could keep in steady focus events which could not otherwise be held in consciousness with the same intensity and fixity.[9]

The idea that the filmic medium could 'capture' and reproduce reality already circulated at the end of the nineteenth century. In 1898, the Polish photographer and film pioneer Bolesław Matuszewski described cinema as a powerful means for the preservation of history, and as a scientific and educational tool. In his well-known pamphlet 'A New Source of History', published in Paris, he claims that 'animated cinematography' should aim to document rather than entertain. By allowing the operator to record events as they happen, it offers a direct insight into the past: the celluloid film constitutes not only a historical document, but also a part of history in its own right, 'history which has not died and whose revival does not require a genius'.[10] According to Matuszewski, 'a ray of light cutting through a lens in the darkness'[11] is enough to reawaken past events: in a kind of spectral apparition, 'a cinematographic picture, . . . which is created between the source of light and the whiteness of the screen, makes it possible that the dead come to life and the absent come back'.[12]

In a context permeated by the rhetoric of photographic objectivity,[13] Matuszewski believed that the cinema's capacity to reproduce movement made it more able than photography to truly capture reality. On the one hand, a single photograph could be easily retouched and was therefore at higher risk of giving a falsified image of reality. On the other hand, Matuszewski was certain of the impossibility to modify the many frames of a reel, which ensured, in his view, the integrity of the represented events.[14] If such a statement may today sound quite naïve, it was not uncommon at the time. For instance, in the article 'The Cinematographic Archives', published in 1911, Morgan Fredy wrote that, if one could effortlessly alter a photograph, 'who would dare undertake the retouching of 1200 frames that make up a film?'[15]

Confident in the transparency of filmic representation and in its total adherence to reality, Matuszewski argues that what 'the cinematograph ... does show is indubitable and constitutes absolute truth ... Animated photography is characterized by authenticity, accuracy and precision which are not present anywhere else. It is the eyewitness par excellence, reliable and infallible.'[16] In the author's view, thanks to its objectiveness, the cinematograph could correct the failings of the human eye in the recollection of historical events, and cinematography can be considered as the most reliable source of history.[17]

Matuszewski drew two consequences from his own claim. First, film can be used as an effective didactic tool in a variety of fields. In an article titled 'Animated Photography: What It Is, What It Should Be', published a few months after 'A New Source of History', Matuszewski proposed to use animated photography as a source of information and as a teaching tool in industry, science, and history.[18] Second, Matuszewski was aware that moving images needed to be properly stored and suggested to use the depositories of well-known institutions, such as the French National Library or the Historical Museum of Versailles.[19]

In the same years, many others proposed to establish film archives and to preserve film reels in museum storages.[20] For instance, in 1896, the film pioneer Robert Paul proposed to the British Museum to include moving pictures in its collections. Stephen Bottomore has shown that, due to different reasons, only one film was preserved for a limited time.[21] However, the question was debated for many years among museum professionals, who considered it 'of really urgent importance'.[22] The main problem was the dangerousness of nitrate:

> there can be no question that the preservation of film of permanent value and their exhibition to the future generations would be a clear national asset ... Unfortunately, the high [sic] inflammable nature of the film material renders such a scheme impracticable.[23]

As films were difficult to preserve, they were considered ephemeral compared to the centuries-old museum objects:

> the other [difficulty] was the fact that the life of cinematograph film is limited to a few years. We are quite unaware whether there has been any improvement as regards permanency in the material of which the films are made. If there has been, we should be glad to be informed.[24]

At the time, the idea that moving pictures could preserve memory was strictly intertwined with the problem of preserving the memory of moving pictures.

The Educational Role of Cinema

In the July 1923 issue of the University of Illinois' Educational Department bulletin, dedicated to the role of cinema in visual education, Frederick D. McClusky wrote the article 'Place of Moving Pictures in Visual Education', where he stated that 'visual education [is] not new'. As he wrote,

> the recent emphasis upon visual education has created the impression in the minds of many persons that the movement is very new. This is not true. Slides and stereographs have been used in schools for over two decades and such visual aids as charts, models, diagrams, pictures and museum exhibits for a much longer period.[25]

However, McClusky continued, the developments in photography and mostly in film opened up new opportunities in this field, sparking the educators' enthusiasm to the point that visual education as such came to be identified with the cinema.[26] In the educational field, not only cinema was therefore a consolidated tool, but its impact was so innovative that it was even considered the instrument of visual education par excellence. Although McClusky believed that the role of cinema in education needed to be critically examined, he could not help acknowledging the prevalence of film among the instruments available to teachers and educators, in both formal and informal contexts.

A case in point noted by McClusky was the extraordinary diffusion of magazines dedicated to visual education in which cinema had a privileged role, as well as the sections devoted to educational issues in cinema magazines, such as the column 'Educational Department' in *Moving Pictures World* (1907–27). From 1910 to 1930, a growing number of publications were entirely devoted to the use of film in schools and other educational contexts: to mention only a few, *Reel and Slide* (1918–19), which later became *Moving Picture Age* (1919–22), and converged with *Educational Screen* (1922–62); *Educational Film Magazine* (1919–22); *The Screen* (1921–2); and *Visual Education* (1920–4). The last one was the official publication of the American Society for Visual Education, whose foundation in 1919 sanctioned the institutional recognition of visual education in the United States.

The discourses, practices, and institutions that stressed the role of film in education were at the time widespread. Chronologically, as we have seen, the educational significance of film had already been acknowledged by Matuszewski and others at the end of the nineteenth century and the beginning of the twentieth. Many, including Matuszewski, were convinced that films would eventually replace textbooks.[27] In his *The Art of the Moving Picture*, Vachel Lindsay writes: 'the motion pictures will be in the public schools to stay. Text-books in geography, history, zoology, botany, physiology, and other sciences will be illustrated by standardized films.'[28]

Institutions and activities related to visual education spread in the United States as well as in Europe. In Great Britain, the Commission on Educational and Cultural Films was founded in 1929 as an unofficial organisation funded by grants from private trusts and local authorities, in order to undertake an extensive investigation on film in education. In 1932 it published the report *The Film in National Life*, which strongly recommended the use of film within the education system.[29] The Commission worked closely with museum professionals to integrate the use of film in museum activities, and was also involved, together with the British Institute of Adult Education, in the organisation of the *Exhibition of Mechanical Aids to Learning*, held at the London School of Economics on 4–6 September 1930.[30] The exhibition brought together some of the principal mechanical inventions used in the service of education, including, as stated in the catalogue, television, 'talkies', broadcasting, films, lanterns, epidiascopes, gramophones, and so on. Manufacturers gave demonstrations of their devices, and educational experts gave lectures and classroom demonstrations. The *Museums Journal* recommended museum professionals, 'in view of the growing importance of the cinema in museum work', to take part in the event.[31]

In France, between the two world wars, the Offices of Educational Cinema (Offices du cinéma éducateur) set up a network of education, teaching, and propaganda through film.[32] In Germany, the Cinema Reform Movement (Kinoreformbewegung) played a key role in the dissemination of educational cinema, also thanks to the journal *Der Kinematograph* (1907–35).[33] The League of Nation promoted an International Institute for Educational Cinematography, which was established in Rome and operated from 1928 to 1937, publishing, from 1929 to 1934, the influential *International Review of Educational Cinematography*.[34] What is important to note here is the sheer number of practices and discourses focused on the film's potential as an effective tool for education and teaching. This fact, however, was acknowledged only gradually and not without criticisms, particularly among museum professionals.

CINEMA, MUSEUMS AND THE DEMANDS OF MODERN LIFE

At the time of the end of the nineteenth century and the beginning of the twentieth, a new understanding of museums and of their role gradually emerged. Museums began to be conceived as institutions devoted not only to the advancement of research in various fields, but also to the transmission of knowledge to a wider public. This evolution spanned over several decades, and in many respects varied from one institution to the other.

According to this new understanding of the role of museums, they sought to expand their public beyond the narrow circle of scholars and connoisseurs. For instance, the main issue of the Mannheim conference on 'Museums as Places of Popular Culture' in 1903 was to establish how museums could attract the lay public.[35] The ensuing debates are emblematic of the concerns of museum workers of the time. Many speakers expressed the need to deeply rethink the display in order to distinguish between research areas (for scholars) and education areas (for non-specialist visitors). The latter needed to be better organised, avoiding any cluttering of objects,[36] creating labels and guide sheets, and using popular media such as photography to increase the public's interest.[37]

These issues continued to be addressed by museum professionals in the following decades. They were extensively discussed in the international journal *Mouseion*, official magazine of the International Office of Museums (Office International des Musées (OIM)), established in 1926 by a decision of the International Commission for Intellectual Cooperation (CICI), League of Nations. In the April 1929 issue, the journal published the report of the meeting of the OIM's committee of experts, held that same year in February.[38] Among the questions debated, there was again the necessity to reorganise the display, separating the study collections from a selection of items displayed for the general public. Also, the committee advanced the proposal to display some maps of the museum, with the aim to help the visitor to orient him or herself in the building.[39] These innovations tried to provide a solution to the problem of the non-specialist, disoriented museum-goers.

Children became one of the main target audiences, and museums started regularly collaborating with schools by organising guided tours and conferences especially conceived for a younger public.[40] Conference rooms or auditoriums equipped for lantern (and later film) projections became increasingly present in museums. Lantern projections and films not only made it easier to explain the museum items or artworks, but they also undoubtedly exerted a great appeal, helping to attract a larger number of visitors. It is no coincidence that the use of magic lanterns or projections was always highlighted in lecture announcements. The importance of cinema in the education of the public continued to be recognised in the following decades. In 1934, an article published on the journal *Mouseion* emphasises the value of cinema in facilitating the general public in the understanding of museums' artworks and objects.[41] Films would in fact help in situating items in their own artistic, historical, or natural context, as well as showing the conditions for their manufacture and use.

Other practices were aimed at extending the scope of museums beyond their own walls, through travelling exhibitions or special collections circulating in schools and other educational institutions. The task of reaching and educating a vast and popular audience was carried out through a wide range of didactic means, including the newest media: photography and cinema, as well as press, radio,[42] and, later, television.[43] Such a complex network of educational activities, based on the use of various media, fostered the acceptance of film in museums, both on a practical and conceptual level. Film, however, was not merely grafted on a pre-existing structure, but brought about a number of changes or innovations.[44]

From the beginning of the twentieth century, museums created audiovisual collections through the purchase or direct production of films, organised illustrated conferences or screenings, or circulated films in schools and other educational institutions, as I will illustrate in the next chapter through the case of the Imperial War Museum.

Despite persistent criticism about the educational value of film, mostly prompted by the fear that it might distract the audience from the 'authentic' objects and from the nobler educational purposes of the institution, cinema was increasingly recognised as an effective tool for museums to attract visitors. It thus became one of the solutions adopted by museums to reach a broader and more popular public, to achieve a wider dissemination of ideas, concepts, and meanings, and to establish themselves in the emerging landscape of modern entertainment, while also reaffirming their position of cultural authorities.[45]

Both Lewis Mumford and Bolesław Matuszewski believed that films and museums were linked by their relationship with history and their common memorial function: films and museums stored the vestiges of the past and could serve as repositories of memory. However, if we consider the question from a different perspective, we could argue that moving images were also a means to root museums in the present and to assert its vitality – thereby addressing the widespread scepticism about its capacity to respond to the demands of contemporaneity.

As it is well known, in the decades of transition between the nineteenth and twentieth centuries, public museums were increasingly reproached to be inadequate to meet the new needs of modernity. As pointed out by Michelle Henning, the criticism was mostly directed at their 'obsession with the past',[46] which led to an accumulation of huge collections, amassed in storehouses or displayed in crowded galleries. Museums were thus considered unable to communicate to the public, especially to non-specialists. Such vehement condemnations came from different directions. Paul Valéry, for instance, described the museum institution as 'a wax-floored solitude, savouring of temple and drawing room, of cemetery and school'.[47] Anti-museum rhetoric was a leitmotiv of twentieth-century avant-gardes: from the futurist Filippo

Tommaso Marinetti to the suprematist Kazimir Malevich, many compared museums to cemeteries, describing them as repositories of dead bodies.[48] As discussed above, curators and museum professionals were also increasingly aware that previous museum standards were defective in relation to the new educational mission that a modern institution was supposed to promote.

Films responded to the museum's need to keep up with the times and to show that it was a 'living' organism, attentive to the demands of a modern and urban public and ready to fit in the dynamics of city life, with its growing number of attractions and forms of entertainment.[49] In this context, as we will see, cinema was considered to be able to provide a picture of the past that was characterised as 'alive' for its capacity to grasp the tensions and requirements of the current times.

NOTES

1. Mumford, *The Culture of Cities*, p. 438.
2. Ibid.
3. Ibid. p. 446.
4. Ibid.
5. Ibid.
6. Ibid.
7. Ibid.
8. Mumford, *Technics and Civilization*, pp. 244–5.
9. Ibid. p. 243.
10. Matuszewski, 'A New Source of History', p. 27.
11. Ibid.
12. Ibid.
13. See Lebart, 'Archiver les photographies fixes et animées'.
14. Matuszewski, 'A New Source of History', p. 27.
15. Cited in Bottomore, '"The Sparkling Surface of the Sea of History"', p. 87.
16. Matuszewski, 'A New Source of History', p. 27.
17. A similar statement was made a few years earlier, in 1894, by the British inventor and filmmaker William K.-L. Dickson, who wrote that 'instead of dry and misleading accounts, tinged with the exaggerations of the chroniclers' minds, our archives will be enriched by the vitalized pictures of great national scenes, instinct with all the glowing personalities which characterize them' (cited in Bottomore, '"The Sparkling Surface of the Sea of History"', p. 86).
18. Matuszewski, 'Animated Photography: What it is, What it Should Be'.
19. Matuszewski, 'A New Source of History', pp. 28–9.
20. See Houston, *Keepers of the Frame*; Slide, *Nitrate Won't Wait*.
21. Bottomore, '"The Collection of Rubbish"'.
22. 'Cinematograph Films in Museums', p. 115.
23. 'Kinema Films for Posterity', p. 336.

24. 'Cinematograph Films in Museums', p. 115.
25. McClusky, 'Place of Moving Pictures in Visual Education', p. 3.
26. Ibid.
27. Matuszewski, 'A New Source of History', p. 26.
28. Lindsay, *The Art of the Moving Picture*, p. 253. In 1915, David W. Griffith imagined the public library of the future as populated by moving images rather than books: 'instead of consulting all the authorities, wading laboriously through a host of books, and ending bewildered, without a clear idea of exactly what did happen and confused at every point by conflicting opinions about what did happen, you will merely seat yourself at a properly adjusted window, in a scientifically prepared room, press the button, and actually see what happened. There will be no opinions expressed. You will merely be present at the making of history.' Griffith, 'Some Prophecies', p. 35.
29. See *The Film in National Life*.
30. See the catalogue of the exhibition: *Exhibition of Mechanical Aids to Learning*.
31. 'Exhibition of Visual and Aural Aid to Education', p. 65. See also Griffiths, *Shivers Down Your Spine*, p. 248.
32. See Borde and Perrin, *Les Offices du cinéma éducateur*.
33. See Schorr, *Die Film und Kinoreformbewegung*.
34. See Taillibert, *L'Institut International du Cinematographe Educatif*.
35. 'The Mannheim Conference on Museums as Places of Popular Culture'.
36. Ibid. p. 108.
37. Ibid. p. 106.
38. 'Réunion de la Commission consultative d'experts de l'Office International des Musées (8 et 9 Février 1929)'.
39. Ibid. pp. 78–9.
40. 'The Mannheim Conference on Museums as Places of Popular Culture', p. 106.
41. 'La cinématographie au service des Musées et des Monuments d'art', p. 157.
42. See Griffiths, '"Automatic Cinema" and Illustrated Radio'.
43. See Spigel, *TV by Design*.
44. The concrete applications of film to various museum activities since the first decades of the twentieth century have been brought to light by scholars like Alison Griffiths, who describes how films were adopted at the American Museum of Natural History, not without difficulties and contradictions (Griffiths, *Wondrous Difference*; Griffiths, *Shivers Down Your Spine*). Another scholar, Theresa Scandiffio, has reconstructed how the Field Museum of Natural History of Chicago integrated cinema in the framework of a wider and more coherent exhibition, communication and educational project aimed at attracting and educating a vast and differentiated audience, which included both the elites and the popular classes (Scandiffio, *'Better'n Any Circus That Ever Come To Town'*). Regarding art museums, Haidee Wasson not only described the establishment of the film library of the Museum of Modern Art (Wasson, *Museum Movies*), but also pointed out that by 1925, the Metropolitan Museum of Art in New York was already producing films about its own galleries and artworks. These films

provided a cinematic staging of the museum's collections that aimed both to make them more accessible and attractive to the public and to strengthen their authority by offering an officially sanctioned and therefore 'correct' reading of the collections (Wasson, *Big, Fast Museums/Small, Slow Movies*).
45. See Wasson, *Museum Movies*, p. 69.
46. Henning, *Museums, Media and Cultural Theory*, p. 38.
47. Valéry, 'The Problem of Museums', p. 203. See also Henning, *Museums, Media and Cultural Theory*, p. 41.
48. See Groys, 'The Struggle Against the Museum'; Henning, *Museums, Media and Cultural Theory*, pp. 38–43.
49. See Wasson, *Museum Movies*, pp. 68–109.

CHAPTER TWO

'A dimly-lighted corner': Moving Images in Museums in the First Decades of the Twentieth Century

Museums and Movies: Cinema at the Imperial Institute

In April 1930, the British *Museums Journal* devoted a section to the theme 'Museums and Movies', publishing the transcripts of two lectures given at the museology conference in Worthing in July 1929: 'The Panorama and the Cinema at the Imperial Institute', by William T. Furse, and 'The Cinema in Museums', by Edwin E. Lowe.[1] They address the relationship between musem and cinema from various angles and provide a kind of 'state of the art' of the use of film in museums during the 1920s and 1930s. The articles point to the idea that cinema was the ideal answer to a number of questions on the professional agenda of the time. According to the anonymous, enthusiastic author of the introduction, cinema was even more effective than dioramas, dramatic reconstructions, and even *tableaux vivants* in making museums more 'lively', due to its ability to bring 'the whole life and movement of the world on to a few square feet in one little room'.[2] The two essays that followed acknowledged the importance of moving images for the modernisation of museums, but presented two different points of view on how they should be used: in the exhibition galleries or in auditoriums.[3]

The first article was signed by the director of the Imperial Institute, a research institute founded in 1887 as the National Memorial of Queen Victoria's Jubilee to promote the economic development of British colonies. The Imperial Institute's exhibition galleries featured items from all the British Empire, with the aim to show to the public its vastness, richness, and diversity.[4] The institution was mentioned several times in the *Museums Journal* as a particularly successful example of balance between education and entertainment.[5]

In accordance with the latest museological views, William Furse organised the galleries in order to avoid the cluttering of objects, and privileged the use of what he called 'panoramas' (also known as 'dioramas') to illustrate life scenes and industries from the various nations of the Empire.[6] The Imperial Institute dioramas were three-dimensional models, half-way between painting and sculpture, mounted on a platform raised one metre above the floor and enclosed in a wooden structure with a glass panel on the front and a border of about twenty centimetres, electrically lit. The front edge not only had the practical purpose of hiding the electric bulbs, but it also framed the representation, creating an illusionistic effect similar to the one provided by cinema or photography. At the Imperial Institute, dioramas were used to draw the visitors' attention and to give more interest to exhibits (industrial products, food, artefacts from the colonies), which were not always particularly appealing on their own.[7]

As stated in the Institute's *Annual Report*, cinema was deemed as 'a valuable supplement to the static exhibits',[8] and Furse considered it useful in making the museum more captivating to the public and to increase the number of visitors to the galleries.[9]

In 1927, the Imperial Institute opened a cinema auditorium of about 400 places. It hosted screenings for schools and the general public and showed industrial and trade films, as well as films showing life scenes from the territories of the Empire. These films were usually provided by the Colonies and Dominions, by official or commercial bodies, or by the Empire Marketing Board. Great emphasis was placed on the educational value of films, which depicted life and customs from different countries, and could therefore arouse the interest of younger and general audiences. As claimed in the 1936 *Bulletin*, the Imperial Institute claimed to have played 'no small part in the conversion of educationists to the use of the Cinema as a means of visual instruction and in encouraging the production of educational films'.[10]

As evidenced by the figures in the annual reports, the screenings had a high attendance, which grew at an increasing rate: in 1927 the total attendance amounted to 135,545 people, in 1928 to 214,830, in 1929 to 243,914, and in 1930 to 370,451 people.[11] In 1929, there were more than 1,000 programmes of one hour and a half, each composed of approximately five films, and often repeated in the course of the day. In 1936, while the educational field still relied on silent films (some teachers believed them to be more appropriate to the concentration skills of their pupils, and appreciated the fact that they could be easily commentated during the projection), the Imperial Institute was already experimenting with the 'talkies'.[12] Moreover, the *Annual Report 1929* announces that 'a modern film store, with cutting, distributing and inspection rooms is being constructed close to the cinema'. However, as the same report attests, the main problem was finding suitable educational movies:

> while some countries such as Canada, Australia and New Zealand are continually bringing their film up-to-date and introducing new subjects, the films of other Empire countries are in the same conditions as when made some years ago. From some countries there are no films at all. There is an urgent

need for modern well-taken and intelligently arranged films of several parts of the Empire'.[13]

In Furse's view, films not only had strong educational potential, but, just like dioramas, they were also capable of attracting visitors, stirring up their curiosity and inviting them to explore the objects more closely. Cinema was included in a set of strategies designed to make the museum and its exhibitions more appealing to an audience accustomed to the new stimuli of modern life.

FILMS AS EXHIBITS: MOVING IMAGES INSIDE THE MUSEUMS' GALLERIES

Furse's contribution to the *Museums Journal* section 'Museum and Movies' was followed by an essay by Edwin E. Lowe, curator of the Leicester Museum.[14] Like many of his colleagues, Lowe was convinced that cinema provided the most appropriate answer to the problem of developing an effective educational model for museums, capable of attracting a non-specialised public. However, Lowe's proposal was different. Instead of creating a cinema auditorium separated from the exhibition rooms, he suggested to integrate moving images into the exhibition itself:

> [M]y idea is, not that we should have a separate cinema hall or room in the building, but that in at least one of the more dimly-lighted corners with which most museums are provided we should fix up a projection apparatus which a visitor could start into action just as he [*sic*] starts a machinery model moving in the Science Museum, by pressing a button or switch. The screen would be small but of sufficient size to be visible in dull daylight to twenty or thirty people, if so many had foregathered.[15]

The dim lighting of the exhibition rooms would provide, according to the curator, an ideal compromise between the darkness of a movie theatre and the bright lighting of a museum. The visitor-operated apparatus would capture the interest of the public by showing five-minute moving pictures on various subjects 'supplementary to the museum collections':[16] placed next to the objects, the animated images would make them 'alive' in a more immediate and effective way than if the projections were isolated from the rest of the exhibition. Individually or during museum tours, visitors would shift their attention back and forth between the motionless and decontextualised exhibits and the moving images representing their environment or functioning.

Lowe argued that, in order to maintain the visitors' attention and to stimulate their curiosity, the films would need to be replaced every month. The movement of the cinema, and the possibility to constantly renew the images on display made their way into museums as effective antidotes against the dustiness and immobility of which, as stressed in Chapter 1, they were so often accused.

The equipment described by Lowe allowed viewers to manually start the projection. This was mostly a practical means to avoid having to continuously operate the devices. However, the need for the visitors to set in motion the apparatus by themselves also suggests a willingness to encourage the active involvement of the public. This was already the case at the Science Museum in London, where visitors could touch and activate many of the devices on display. Significantly, the Science Museum was mentioned in the introduction of the 'Museums and Movies' section as a 'splendid exception' among contemporary museums, which revealed 'by contrast the[ir] essential dullness'.[17]

Since 1922, the Science Museum has been hosting one of the richest film collections in the world, donated by the collector and inventor Will Day. Film apparatuses were placed inside display cases as part of an evolutionary narrative about the technological progress in the field of cinema.[18] Lowe's proposal went in a different direction: the cinematographic equipment that he proposed to install in the galleries was not meant to illustrate a given stage in technical progress or mechanical functioning of the apparatus. Rather, it was destined to breathe 'life' into the objects on display by showing them in movement.

Thanks to the help of a Kodak technician, Lowe offered to his colleagues a demonstration of 'an improvised cinema projector and screen which seem adaptable to . . . museum use':[19] the Kodascope, a small 16 mm portable projector, used mainly for commercial demonstrations.[20] The annual reports and other archival documents of the Leicester Museum do not provide any information about the actual use of film projectors in the museum's galleries. We know, however, that Lowe used projection devices during the museum's weekly conferences, which were illustrated by magic lanterns, a microscope with a projector, and later by an epidiascope – an optical instrument that allowed texts or magnified images of objects or texts to be projected onto a screen.[21]

In 1931, the *Museums Journal* published the news that the American Museum of Natural History in New York had installed in its rooms an automatic projector called 'Dramagraph'.[22] It consisted of a projector placed inside a wooden cabinet with a glass screen and a button on the front. When the visitors pressed the button, the electrical mechanism was activated, and a 16 mm film of about four and a half minutes began to run. At the end of the projection no rewind was needed, and the film was immediately ready to start again. This case has been discussed by Alison Griffiths,[23] who has stressed that due to the costs associated with maintenance and with subject replacement, the museum, which had borrowed six machines in 1928, decided two years later to return them to the producing firm.[24]

In his article in the *Museums Journal*, Lowe mentions two problems in connection with his proposal: the first was a technical one, and the second was related to the difficulty of finding films. This second obstacle was addressed by encouraging the collaboration between museums and other cultural and educational institutions for the realisation and circulation of films. The technical problems were also considerable. Until the first half of the twentieth century, many practical or economic issues made it quite difficult to install projectors in exhibition galleries – and this solution was therefore very rare. These complications, however, did not discourage the most enterprising museum professionals: for instance, as we will see in the following chapter, at the Imperial War Museum in London films had already found their place in the galleries some years before the publication of the above-mentioned issue of the *Museums Journal*.

AN ARCHIVE FOR THE PRESERVATION OF FILMS AT THE IMPERIAL WAR MUSEUM

The First World War represented for many countries a decisive event that consecrated the role of films as a means of historical testimony and renewed the interest in their preservation. Back in 1916, an article in *The Times* stated:

> [N]ow that the greatest events in world history is transpiring, so to speak, before our cameras, the historians are offered their first extraordinary opportunity to establish archives of film records, to preserve into the indefinite future the exact replicas of today's actions.[25]

What interests me here is not the cinematic representation of war as such, but the emphasis on the cinema's memorial function in relation to twentieth-century war events. In other words, it is noteworthy that cinema was invested with the same task (the preservation of the past and the reinforcement of national identity) that was assigned to museums.[26]

In Britain, the establishment of a National War Museum, subsequently named the Imperial War Museum, was officially approved by the British War Cabinet on 5 March 1917, and was formally sanctioned by a parliamentary law on 2 July 1920. Settled in London, the institution had the mission of preserving the memory of the still on-going events of the First World War. It collected trophies, books, maps, posters, paintings, and other material related to the military conflict. The intention was to gather testimonies of all of the subjects involved in the war, including civilians.[27]

The museum collections included a number of propaganda war movies, provided by the Ministry of Information, which were considered 'of unique historical interest'.[28] The Imperial War Museum's film archive was one of the first film libraries to be ever established, and remains to this day one of the most important ones. The collecting and cataloguing activities started in 1919, about twenty years after the publication of Matuszewski's pamphlet. This case study is particularly noteworthy as it reveals how film archives found their way into museums and were believed to share many of the latter's functions and objectives. It allows me to consider in more detail the development of discourses about film as a historical record and about the need of preserving it. The case of the Imperial War Museum also helps me investigate the use of films in museum practice and its display inside the galleries.

The fourth annual report of the Imperial War Museum (1920–1) records the acquisition of 'certain of the cinematograph films for the War Office, Admiralty and Air Force and those films produced by other Departments during the War'.[29] Since the museum was not yet hosted in a permanent building, a storage vault and a small exhibition room were placed in the War Office headquarters. Edward Foxen Cooper, Cinematograph Adviser to His Majesty's Customs, was in charge of managing the films, together with a representative of the Foreign Office.[30]

As shown by Roger Smither and David Walsh, under the guidance of Foxen Cooper, the Board of Directors started selecting the films that were considered to be of genuine historical value and therefore worth preserving.[31] In order to choose among the 600 and more films that they received, the materials were submitted to officers from the various army departments. The titles of the first films received reveal the most common themes: battles (*Battle of the Somme, Battle of Arras, Offensive on the Cambrai Front*); official ceremonies (*Investiture of the War Heroes at Hyde Park, British Horse Shows in Italy, Royal Visit to France*); descriptions of army departments and of their activities (*Life of a Munition Maker, With the Flying Corps, Preparing for a Bombing Raid*); and missions in foreign countries (*British Troops in India, South African Artillery in Action, Ruined Villages in France*).[32]

As Smither and Walsh point out, the application of strict criteria of historical accuracy influenced not only the selection of films, but also the way in which they were preserved. Surprisingly, keeping films in their integrity was not the main concern. Indeed, it was considered more important to select the sequences that appeared to have a historical value, and to eventually cut them off from other scenes that were considered unfaithful to the actual events.[33] Such an interest in individual fragments rather than in the totality of the film also emerged when films were shown inside museum galleries.

The establishment of the film archive represented one of the 'conditions of possibility' for the cinema to enter in the Imperial War Museum galleries. Not only was it an easily available source of materials, but its richness confronted museum professionals with the problem of showing films to the audience. Films would in fact reinforce the institution's mission to preserve the memory of the conflict and to guide the visitors in the understanding of war events.

How to Show Film Footage? Showing the Imperial War Museum Film Collection

Since its foundation, the Imperial War Museum faced the problem of finding suitable spaces to show its collections. The museum was officially established in 1917, and items started being collected despite the lack of a suitable space to store them. In those years, a few temporary and itinerant exhibitions were organised.[34] From 1920 to 1924, the museum was hosted at the Crystal Palace in the south of London; from 1924, it was transferred to two galleries that formerly belonged to the Imperial Institute in South Kensington. Only in 1936 was the museum transferred to its current location at Lambeth Road, Southwark, in the former Bethlem Royal Hospital building. Until the establishment of a permanent seat, the film collection was stored at the War Office headquarters.

Even after finding a provisional seat at the Crystal Palace, the museum continued to circulate materials among other educational or military institutions: photographs, memorabilia, and artworks were later complemented with magic lantern slides, whose loan generated a notable income.[35] In addition to collection and preservation, the film department was also in charge of dissemination, mostly for educational purposes:[36] the films were hired by schools, private lecturers, and various sections of the army.[37] Museum footage was also used for the realisation of educational movies about the war, often through collaborations with film producers such as the British Instructional Films.[38]

The museum received many requests to use its footage in movies or newsreels. Its dissemination policies, however, were quite rigid: materials from the museum collections could be used only for educational purposes, and should not be combined with fictional scenes, except in accurately documented battle reconstructions:[39] 'the Trustees refuse applications for the use of war films in conjunction with fictitious war scenes or in commercial films the interest of which is purely sentimental'.[40] In addition, printed frames from films were provided for publication in books, newspapers, and magazines.[41]

The need to preserve the documentary value of films was the basic principle that regulated their circulation: one the one hand, the museum's authority guaranteed the truthfulness of the footage; on the other, the institution exercised a close control over its use, so as to avoid any inappropriate manipulation. In short, the widespread recognition of the cinema's educational and documentary value determined its use in the Imperial War

Museum practice but was in turn reaffirmed by the museum's prescription to use films as 'veridical' historical records.

Unlike other museums that provided free loan services,[42] the circulation of films and photographic materials was a source of revenue for the Imperial War Museum. In 1934–5 the film office received forty-one applications for the use of film for instructional, historical, commercial, or private purposes. Each application was subject to the approval of the museums Trustees.[43] That year only three applications were rejected, and the total incomes amounted to £992.[44] Curators were aware of the importance of disseminating their materials, and made sure that the price for the loan of copies remained low, so as to encourage their use.[45]

Films were frequently borrowed for instructional lectures at service colleges and by branches of the British Legion.[46] Sometimes they were also projected in commercial movie theatres: for instance, in 1927, *The Battle of Arras* was screened at the Tivoli Theatre in London to celebrate Armistice Day (11 November).[47] The loan always generated revenues for the museum, and showed that

> there is a considerable latent demand to see these films, and it is to be regretted that there is no means of making their existence more widely known, the best of which would undoubtedly be the provision of a small cinema theatre in the Museum in which they could be shown to the visiting public.[48]

This statement reveals that one of the main problems faced by the Imperial War Museum was the impossibility of showing its increasingly rich collection of films inside its own walls. Almost paradoxically, while museums equipped with a projection space often had considerable difficulties finding suitable films, the Imperial War Museum had no place to show the many films that it owned.

The creation of a cinema theatre inside the museum, even limited to a hundred places or so, had always been considered the most appropriate solution, especially on the brink of a new world conflict: 'there is little doubt that the public showing of films recording the Britain effort in the Great War would have been particularly opportune when the country is again been [*sic*] called to national service'.[49]

However, due to the lack of space and economic means, the museum cinema could not be realised until 1966. From then on, daily projections were organised, finally offering 'the best means of exhibiting the collection to the Museum visitors'.[50]

TRENCHES, TANKS AND THE EXPLOSION OF A MINE: MUTOSCOPES AT THE IMPERIAL WAR MUSEUM (1924–38)

Many years before the creation of the museum cinema theatre, the curator and secretary of the Imperial War Museum, Major Charles ffoulkes, was already looking for a way to show the films from the museum's collection, as they 'would be of great educational value in showing certain details of war films connected with our exhibits'.[51] In ffoulkes' view, the ideal device would operate according to the 'penny-in-the-slot' principle, and could be placed in daylight, in order to adapt to the viewing conditions of the museum galleries.

In the summer of 1923, he charged his assistant, Captain J. Murray Kendall, to find automatic devices to present the films inside the museum galleries. Kendall got in touch with Will Day, whose pioneering collection of film apparatuses was on display at the Science Museum, near the galleries of the Imperial War Museum in South Kensington. Kendall's attention was initially attracted by a machine that Day was developing, which allowed one viewer at the time to screen a film at the desired speed, a feature that could be useful when examining war films.

ffoulkes and Kendall also considered the Autoscope, an automatic projector used at the Wembley fair to show advertising films, which could be used both in daylight or in the darkness. After each twenty-minute projection, the film in the Autoscope would rewind itself automatically and the projection would resume. However, negotiations with the producing firm to create a smaller version of the device were dropped due to high costs.[52]

Finding a suitable device for the museum turned out to be quite difficult. After a year of research, Major ffoulkes decided to adapt a Mutoscope, an individual vision device patented in 1894 by Biograph, and that he called 'MUTASCOPE [sic.] machine'. Having carefully enquired about patent issues and having made sure that the patent had expired, in 1924 he commissioned the technician Mr Moy to create a similar machine for the museum. An old but operating Mutoscope was bought from one of the amusement venues that still used it, and was reconditioned to fit the curator's requests.

Mutoscopes were originally intended for commercial purposes (for example, they were often used in demonstrations of articles on sale). Also, the British Biograph created a series of *Animated Illustrated Journals*, a kind of moving-image version of daily newspapers. During the Second Boer War (started in 1899), it produced numerous war movies, which circulated among sister companies around the world.[53] However, Mutoscopes gained popularity as entertainment devices. In Great Britain, they were mostly presented in three kinds of places: specially dedicated venues, fairs and sporting events, and railway stations. The individual vision allowed by the peephole fostered the spread of forbidden and obscene (when not explicitly pornographic) subjects.[54] Mutoscopes were thus associated with leisure or even private vice, and were often considered a threat to morality.[55] ffoulkes himself was well aware of it, having noticed their great popularity in entertainment venues when conducting his research to install the devices in his museum.

In ffoulkes' correspondence with Moy, we can infer that the curator was anxious to see the device at work, and hoped to be able to place it in the galleries for the Armistice Day, on 11 November 1924.[56] The Mutoscope was probably already in operation by October 1924, when Major ffoulkes asked the Treasury to provide him with funds to buy seven more, which were acquired and placed in the galleries. The press described the use of Mutoscopes in a museum as a true innovation: 'a new feature, exhibited for the first time in any museum'.[57] The reporter, just like ffoulkes, probably ignored that, by 1911, the New York Post Office Museum (at the time just a small exhibition arranged inside the post office) was already using thirty Mutoscopes to illustrate its various services, from shipment to delivery.[58]

The Mutoscope was based on the 'flip-book' principle:[59] a series of photographic prints on flexible cards were attached to a circular core, and when the latter was turned rapidly through a crank, the images appeared to become animated and simulated motion.

In order to be shown, images needed to be transferred from the film reel to cards: as Foxen Cooper wrote to Major ffoulkes,

> [I]t will not be merely printing from the complete negative, but selective pictures will have to be first taken, and these will have either to be enlarged or as you say printed direct, and the magnifying glasses would in the latter instance give the desired size of picture to the observer.[60]

This change of support reverses what is commonly understood as the transition from pre-cinema (the flip book) to cinema, and suggests that the relationship between the two was never as unidirectional as it seemed. The entrance of films in the museum reveals how the evolution of devices for presenting moving images does not necessarily proceed in a linear way, but is made of different practices that coexist and intertwine.

To activate the mechanism, viewers needed to insert a penny and turn a handle. Thanks to a magnifying glass, they could then look at war images through a peephole. Significantly, ffoulkes repeatedly insisted that the device should be made for individual rather than collective viewing. He considered this requirement to be crucial, and continued to emphasise it several years later, when looking for new projection devices to replace the Mutoscopes.

One of the main reasons was that, as the device was operated through a coin, the individual use ensured higher incomes: 'these machines will . . . be exhibits which should earn an appreciable amount of revenue'.[61]

Each device showed one roll at the time, but Major ffoulkes and Edward Foxen Cooper had a number of different subjects prepared to ensure a regular rotation. In a letter to Foxen Cooper, ffoulkes describes the first set of scenes for the Mutoscopes:

1. Some good trench scenes, possibly in the battle of Arras.
2. Tanks. I believe that in one film 'Crème de Menthe' is shown.
3. The King's Visit to the Front.
4. Torpedo boat destroyers. I think a similar subject is shown in the Zeebrugge Film. I should like especially destroyers steaming towards the spectator.
5. Explosion of a mine. You may remember that this subject was criticised at one of our meetings as possibly being taken behind the lines.
6. Turret guns of a Battleship. (? Queen Elizabeth) In this picture the guns slowly elevate and turn from right to left.[62]

Trenches, tanks, torpedo boats, weapons, the explosion of a mine . . . The Mutoscopes were intended to present 'classic' war subjects, with a certain emphasis on the spectacular dimension: 'I should like especially destroyers steaming towards the spectator',[63] wrote ffoulkes, probably thinking about the impact that the scene would have on visitors peeking at them through the peephole.

The Mutoscopes would show visitors the various aspects of war: by land, by sea, or by air. In the choice of subjects, great emphasis was obviously placed on artillery and war equipment: in a subsequent list of subjects, ffoulkes included, for instance, 'Destroyers firing', and 'Man using a rifle grenade'.[64] ffoulkes and Foxen Cooper selected scenes that could have a more striking effect on the spectators thanks to the movement of the images, such as 'Scottish Regiment on the March', 'Infantry marching through a road cutting waving helmets', and 'Horses carrying ammunition moving from the front of the picture over to the horizon'.[65] Spectators were, thanks to the Mutoscopes, immersed 'in the heart of the action'.

As viewers looked through a peephole, moving images were isolated from the rest of the objects exposed in the museum, which remained out of sight for the duration of the unfolding of the images. The collective museum experience was temporally converted into an individual one.[66] However, the scenes displayed in the Mutoscopes were in close relation with other museum exhibits, such as photographs, posters, and paintings, as well as medals and uniforms. The museum also had a collection of model boats and planes, as well as artillery and other pieces of military equipment.[67] The archival materials do not show any evidence on where the eight Mutoscopes were placed, but we know that they were considered 'exhibits in every sense of the word'.[68]

In 1920–1, a few years before the installation of the machines, the attitude of the public in the galleries was carefully studied. The survey revealed that non-labelled objects did not attract the attention of the average visitor. On the other hand, the public showed great interest in objects accompanied by explanatory information, a map of the territory where the objects were used, or a photograph showing them in action.[69] These strategies made it possible to contextualise the exhibits, to show their concrete use, and thus to make them alive: objects could be considered as testimonies of a very recent war rather than simple museum pieces. The animated images achieved the same result in a more effective way, since the films preserved by the museum showed real objects during real war actions. ffoulkes himself was aware that the visitors' interest in the Mutoscopes depended on the possibility to see 'many of our actual exhibits in action under War conditions'.[70]

As noted by the enthusiastic author of an article published in 1927 in *The Times*, 'after looking at a big gun one can walk aside to see a little machine, drop in a penny, and see, as in a peep-show . . . some gun in action in France. Relevancy again!'[71] Moreover, thanks to the Mutoscopes, the Imperial War Museum itself became a great attraction: as *The Times* stated, 'it's pretty safe to say that with the possible exception of the Science Museum, The Imperial War Museum strikes the most attractive place in London'.[72]

A few years after the installation of the Mutoscopes in the Imperial War Museum, the above-mentioned Edwin E. Lowe proposed to place cinematographic machines in the 'dimly-lighted corners' of museums. On the contrary, ffoulkes explicitly ordered to put the machines in full light. This difference is, of course, due to practical reasons: the projector proposed by Lowe was equipped with a screen, which required a dark environment to ensure visibility, while this did not apply to the Mutoscopes' peephole, which allowed them to be placed even in luminous galleries. However, the curator's insistence on the importance of avoiding dimly lit corners is noteworthy. To ffoulkes, it was probably important to ensure that the Mutoscopes were placed in the same conditions as the other exhibits. At the same time, we can assume that he wanted to avoid creating the shady and transgressive atmosphere often associated with peephole devices.

The Mutoscopes increased visitors' curiosity for the exhibition and for the museum as a whole, and, thanks to the penny-in-the-slot method, they ensured considerable economic gain. On the other hand, their position in the galleries had to be carefully negotiated, due to the institution's aims of civic and moral elevation. However, the boundary between the seriousness of the represented events and the spectacular appeal of the presentation has always characterised the Imperial War Museum, and the Mutoscope significantly contributed to this ambivalence.

The Mutoscopes between Novelty and Obsolescence

From 1924 to 1930, ffoulkes and Foxen Cooper continued to prepare new subjects for the Mutoscopes in order to maintain the interest and curiosity of the public and to give visibility to the museum's growing collection of films. However, the printing of photograms and the handling of the machines became increasingly complicated, due to numerous technical problems: 'the lights are continually failing, the locks are very insecure and the reel itself tend to get warped and the prints cut, etc.'[73] Unfortunately, when Mr Moy died in November 1926, nobody seemed to be able to solve these problems. In February 1928, ffoulkes wrote to Will Day to find out if there was still someone who could print the Mutoscope cards and eventually repair the machines, but Day himself confirmed that no one could take care of them.[74]

The obsolescence of machines had been a problem almost since their installation. Already in the 1925 annual report, we read: 'they are of a type long since obsolete and it is impossible to replace them. At best they show unsatisfactorily brief extracts from films.'[75] In 1930–1, ffoulkes tried to find new devices for the museum's galleries. He got in touch with several firms operating in the flourishing sector of portable projectors: the Continuous Projectors and the W. Vinten Ltd Cinematograph Engineers, which produced the 'Moviola cinematograph machine'. A few years later, in 1936 and 1938, when ffoulkes had already resigned, other retailers were approached: among them De Brunner & Lang-Sims, who proposed their 'Filmograph' Film Projector and Auto-projection Company Ltd, which had in its catalogue a device with headphones for sound, as well as a kind of television cabinet already used at the Glasgow exhibition in 1938. However, the Mutoscopes were not replaced, due to the impossibility of sustaining the cost of new devices. In 1936, when the museum moved to its new location in Southwark, the machines were again exhibited in the galleries, as they continued to attract visitors' curiosity, and hence to generate income.

The economic importance of the Mutoscopes for the Imperial War Museum should not be underestimated. A total of £200 was spent buying the eight machines, each equipped with a roll made at a cost of eight pounds each. The figures provided by the annual reports show that this amount was amortised in about a year. From November 1924 to March 1926, the museum earned £270.[76] The following year (April 1926–March 1927), when a general strike caused a decrease in the museum's attendance, the earnings amounted to £164.[77] In 1927–8, they were about £240.[78] In 1929–30, the revenue increased again to £362.[79] As Roger Smither and David Walsh point out, even in 1938, when the devices were explicitly defined as 'obsolete', it was at the same time noted that they generated the remarkable profit of £2,700.[80] The machines were used until the beginning of the Second World War, and then stored in a warehouse and abandoned in the 1970s.

The Mutoscopes of the Imperial War Museum represent a kind of paradox: in 1924 they were a novel addition to museum's exhibition, but at the same time there were already obsolete machines. In this way, the Imperial War Museum acted like a film museum, preserving throughout the years an old cinematic device.

EXCEPTION OR RULE? DEBATING THE USE OF MOVING IMAGES IN MUSEUM GALLERIES

For several years, the use of films inside museum galleries remained limited and often overlooked by British museum professionals. In November 1924, ffoulkes was contacted by a Hull Municipal Museum officer in order to obtain information on where to buy and how to install a Mutoscope machine. An article in the *Museums Journal* reveals that the machine was actually installed in the Hull museum in 1925 to show films about the process of seed crushing.[81] In 1927, it was ffoulkes' turn to contact the curator of the Commercial Museum for advice on the maintenance of the machines. He hoped to find other competent technicians, but he was informed that the Hull museum was working with the same manufacturer, Mr Moy.

The innovative use of projectors in the Imperial War Museum and the Hull museum galleries had a limited follow-up in the professional debate of the time. Commenting on the above-mentioned 1930 *Exhibition of Mechanical Aids to Learning*, an editor wrote in the *Museums Journal*:

> [O]ur representative visited the exhibition in the hope of finding there a cinematograph instrument of the press-the-button type suitable for use in museums. There were, it is true, at least two types of continuous cinematograph on exhibition, but, alas! there were difficulties connected with both which render their use in museums out of the question at present.[82]

Despite the great interest of the curator in the possibility of showing films in the galleries, the lack of an appropriate technology eventually put an end to the project. In 1934, in the 'Letters to the Editor' section, the *Museums Journal* published a request by the British Film Institute, which was investigating the use of 'automatic cinematograph projectors or "mutoscope" machines' in museums and other educational institutions. Curators were asked to answer a series of questions about projection timing, visitor interaction, the type of machine utilised and their effectiveness, as well as the kind of subjects.[83] The survey demonstrates the institutional acceptance of this practice in museums,[84] as well as the interest in its dissemination, but to my knowledge the results of the research were never published. However, in those years, the British Film Institute carried out several surveys on the use of film in educational contexts. In September 1934, the Institute published a document entitled *Survey of Situation Regarding Non-Theatrical Cinematograph Apparatus and Films*,[85] which aimed to provide an overview of the types of projectors available on the market, so that each educational institution could assess the one best suited for its specific needs. However, the report does not specifically mention the use of films in museum galleries.

In the United Kingdom, the Second World War marked a turning point in the use of film in museums. Indeed, the Ministry of Information considered national museums as an essential resource for its propaganda activities and, from the end of 1941, provided them with free projectors so that they could show films about the war. The noteworthy aspect of this operation is that, though museums were forced to show the films provided by the Ministry on the prescribed dates, on the remaining days they could project films on cultural or educational subjects.[86] For the institutions participating in the operation, the initiative had the advantage not only of increasing the number of visitors but also of revealing to museum professionals the educational potential of moving images: 'many have gained practical experience not only in operating the apparatus but in the technique that should be employed in this relatively new aid in visual education'.[87]

However, this did not stimulate the debate on the use of moving images inside museum galleries. We find a few considerations on this topic in a 1945 issue of the *Museums Journal*, in the context of a discussion on the importance of film in museum activities. The curator of the Reading Museum proposed that, in parallel with the screening of films in auditoriums, museums should also show moving images in the galleries, in natural or artificial light, so that the 'exhibition room can be a great success'.[88] But nothing came out of this proposal, and it seems that in those years museums did not extensively experiment with the exhibition of moving images in their galleries. By 1956, another author had returned to the subject in the same journal, observing that the press-button film sequences had hitherto been used in museums only on an occasional basis.[89]

Even though curators considered films effective educational tools, the screening of moving images in museum galleries remained for several decades a problematic option, due to various technological and economic limitations. Yet, the experimentation with Mutoscopes at the Imperial War Museum remains a remarkable page in the history of curatorial practices, which paved the way to the circulation of films outside the movie theatre. Apparently, it took several decades for moving images to find, from the 1960s and 1970s, a stable and increasingly important place in museum galleries, as I will discuss in Chapter 4. However, in the 1930s and 1940s museums were already experimenting with various solutions to enrich their exhibitions with moving images (see Chapter 3).

Notes

1. These articles have been discussed also in Griffiths, *Shivers Down Your Spine*, pp. 242–8.
2. 'Museums and Movies', p. 334.
3. See Griffiths, *Shivers Down Your Spine*, p. 247.
4. See 'The Imperial Institute', p. 1; Longair and McAleer (eds), *Curating Empire*.
5. See, for instance, the note on the *Museums Journal*, 'Imperial Institute': 'The Imperial Institute at Kensington ... has waked from its dreams of the last century and become, almost as if by the wave of a magician's wand, a Wembley in little and one of the most "live" and interesting exhibitions in London – an educational object lesson and an eloquent advertisement for inter-Imperial trade'.
6. Furse, 'The Panorama and the Cinema at the Imperial Institute', p. 337.
7. 'The Imperial Institute Exhibition Galleries', p. 195.
8. Imperial Institute, *Annual Report 1927*, p. 2.
9. See Furse, 'The Panorama and the Cinema at the Imperial Institute', pp. 338–9; see also Furse's note about the cinema at the Imperial Institute, *Annual Report 1926*, p. 41.
10. Imperial Institute, *Bulletin of The Imperial Institute*, p. 222.
11. Imperial Institute, *Annual Report 1927*, p. 26; Imperial Institute, *Annual Report 1930*, p. 45.
12. Imperial Institute, *Bulletin of The Imperial Institute*, p. 222; see also Linsday, 'Visual Instruction at the Imperial Institute', pp. 292–3.
13. Imperial Institute, *Annual Report 1929*, p. 46.
14. Lowe, 'The Cinema in Museums'.
15. Ibid. p. 343.
16. Ibid.
17. Ibid.
18. See Trope, 'Le Cinéma pour le Cinéma', pp. 33–4.
19. Lowe, 'The Cinema in Museums', cit., p. 343.
20. The circulation of films outside movie theatres was facilitated by the introduc-

tion of small-gauge formats such as 16 mm and 8 mm, respectively in 1923 and 1932, and of portable and automatic projectors that used non-flammable films or rear-projections to allow images to be seen in the light. Films were shown not only in museums and other educational institutions, but also in department stores, private clubs, and fairs. Haidee Wasson provides an excellent outline of this scenario, especially with regard to the American context, in *Museum Movies*, pp. 32–67 (Chapter 2, 'Mannered Cinema / Mobile Theaters. Film Exhibition, 16mm, and the New Audience Ideal').

21. City Museum Leicester and Art Gallery, *Twenty-sixth Report of the Committee 1929–1930*, pp. 5–6 and City Museum Leicester and Art Gallery, *Twenty-seventh Report of the Committee 1930–1931*, p. 7.
22. 'The Dramagraph'.
23. See Griffiths, *Shivers Down Your Spine*, pp. 244–7.
24. Ibid. p. 245.
25. Cited in Bottomore, '"The Sparkling Surface of the Sea of History"', p. 92.
26. See Kaplan (ed.), *Museums and the Making of Ourselves*; Kaplan, 'Making and Remaking National Identities'.
27. Kavanagh, 'Museum as Memorial'.
28. Imperial War Museum (IWM), *Third Annual Report of the Imperial War Museum 1919–1920*, p. 28.
29. IWM, *Fourth Annual Report of the Imperial War Museum, 1920–1921*, p. 4.
30. Ibid. On Foxen Cooper see Smither and Walsh, 'Unknown Pioneer'.
31. Smither and Walsh, 'Unknown Pioneer'.
32. IWM, *Fourth Annual Report of the Imperial War Museum, 1920–1921*, pp. 37–8.
33. Smither and Walsh, 'Unknown Pioneer', p. 190.
34. IWM, *Second Annual Report of the Imperial War Museum, 1918–1919*. See also Kavanagh, 'Museum as Memorial', pp. 89–90.
35. IWM, *Twelfth Annual Report of the Imperial War Museum, 1928–1929*.
36. IWM, *Eightieth Annual Report of the Imperial War Museum, 1924–1925*, p. 9.
37. IWM, *Seventeenth Annual Report of the Imperial War Museum, 1933–1934*, p. 16.
38. IWM, *Sixth Annual Report of the Imperial War Museum, 1922–1923*, p. 16.
39. Smither and Walsh, 'Unknown Pioneer', pp. 194–6.
40. IWM, *Seventeenth Annual Report of the Imperial War Museum, 1933–1934*, p. 16.
41. IWM, *Eighteenth Annual Report of the Imperial War Museum, 1934–1935*, p. 11.
42. For example, the American Museum of Natural History. See Fisher Ramsey, *Educational Work in Museums*.
43. IWM, *Eighteenth Annual Report of the Imperial War Museum, 1934–1935*, p. 9.
44. Ibid. p. 10.
45. Ibid. p. 10.
46. IWM, *Seventeenth Annual Report of the Imperial War Museum, 1933–1934*, p. 16.
47. Smither and Walsh, 'Unknown Pioneer', p. 198.
48. IWM, *Twenty-first Annual Report of The Director-General to the Board of Trustes, 1938–1939*, p. 2.
49. Ibid. p. 2.

50. IWM, *Annual Report 1986–1988*, p. 17.
51. Curator and Secretary to The Director, Messrs The Autoscope Company Ltd, 16/06/1924.
52. Correspondence between Major ffoulkes and Director, Autoscope Company Ltd, June–July 1924.
53. See Brown and Anthony, *A Victorian Film Enterprise*, pp. 188–214.
54. See Ibid. pp. 81–2, 222–3.
55. See Dulac and Gaudreault, 'Dispositfs optiques et attraction', p. 101.
56. Major ffoulkes to Mr Moy, 12 September 1924.
57. *Daily Chronicle*, 8 November 1924, cited in Smither and Walsh, 'Unknown Pioneer', pp. 193–4.
58. See 'A Chat With Uncle Sam's Trusted Mail Service Men', *The Washington Herald*, 15 January 1911.
59. On the flip-book, see Gunning, 'The Transforming Image'.
60. Edward Foxen Cooper to Major ffoulkes, 13 August 1924.
61. Major ffoulkes to the Secretary H.M. Treasury, 17 October 1924.
62. Major ffoulkes to Edward Foxen Cooper, 24 November 1924.
63. Ibid.
64. Major ffoulkes to Mr Moy, 30 January 1925.
65. Ibid.
66. See Griffiths, *Shivers Down Your Spine*, pp. 245–6.
67. See Foster, 'The Imperial War Museum'.
68. Major ffoulkes to the Secretary H.M. Treasury, 17 October 1924.
69. IWM, *Fourth Annual Report of the Imperial War Museum, 1920–1921*, p. 19.
70. Major ffoulkes to C.C.A. Monro, Esq., British Museum (Natural History), 21 March 1928.
71. *The Times*, 5 March 1927.
72. Ibid.
73. Mr Foster (Photo Record) to Major ffoulkes, 19 January 1927.
74. Mr Day to Major ffoulkes, 18 February 1928.
75. IWM, *Twentieth Annual Report of the Imperial War Museum, 1937–1938*, p. 14.
76. Major ffoulkes to C.C.A. Monro, Esq., British Museum (Natural History), 21 March 1928.
77. IWM, *Tenth Annual Report of the Imperial War Museum, 1926–1927*.
78. IWM, *Eleventh Annual Report of the Imperial War Museum, 1927–1928*.
79. IWM, *Thirteenth Annual Report of the Imperial War Museum, 1929–1930*.
80. Smither and Walsh, 'Unknown Pioneer', p. 194
81. 'A Commercial Museum', p. 167.
82. 'Exhibition of Mechanical Aids to Learning', p. 206. See also Griffiths, *Shivers Down Your Spine*, p. 248.
83. Crow, 'The Film in the Museum'.
84. See Griffiths, *Shivers Down Your Spine*, p. 247.
85. *Survey of Situation Regarding Non-Theatrical Cinematograph Apparatus and Films*.
86. 'Ministry of Information: Films and Projectors', p. 32.

87. 'Ministry of Information Films in Museums and Art Galleries', p. 4.
88. Smallcombe, 'Films in Museums'.
89. W.E.S, 'The Cinema and the Museum', p. 301.

CHAPTER THREE

Moving Images in Museums, World's Fairs and Avant-garde Exhibition Design

TWENTIETH-CENTURY AVANT-GARDES AND EXHIBITION DESIGN

During the 1920s and the 1930s, the artistic avant-gardes experimented with various cinematic and exhibition *dispositifs*. Persuaded of the interpenetration between art and life and of the necessity to overcome the practice of art for art's sake, avant-garde artists such as El Lissitzky, Frederick Kiesler, and László Moholy-Nagy, as well as Bauhaus members such as Herbert Bayer, Walter Gropius, and Mies van der Rohe, were active in a variety of sectors such as typography, graphic or furniture design, advertising, and exhibition design.[1]

These artists and architects designed not only museum galleries, but also and especially educational exhibitions that began to flourish in Germany in the 1920s.[2] Janet Ward speaks of an 'exhibition mania',[3] an economic and symbolic desire to show to the international community the new modern face of Germany. An *Ausstellungspolitik* (exhibition policy) was established, which led to the creation of a great number of exhibitions, in Berlin and throughout Germany, on the most heterogeneous topics related to technology, industry, or the needs of social life: cars, clothing, furniture, radio, photography and cinema, hygiene and health.

Although didactic exhibitions belonged to the nineteenth-century tradition of fairs and universal exhibitions, their main concern was not so much to present singular objects as to communicate ideas, composing, as Olivier Lugon states, 'argumentative or narrative structures, logical developments or emotional sequences in which each exhibit had to find its place'.[4] Working in these contexts, avant-garde artists were free from the institutional codes and regulations of the art field, and developed some of the most interesting and ground-breaking solutions in exhibition design.

The contribution of avant-garde artists was two-fold. First, they tested new ways of integrating moving images with other display solutions, such as diagrams, charts, lights, photographs, and panels. Second, they contributed to rethinking the exhibition as a complex and dynamic system articulated across multiple media. Such a system was supposed to be able to attract visitors by means of visual effects, orchestrate their perception and movements by means of its spatial arrangement and, if necessary, elicit a direct interaction.[5] Significantly, scholars such as Lugon have noted that even when films were not included in the exhibitions, the spatial configuration of avant-garde exhibition displays was animated by an intrinsically cinematic and dynamic principle.[6] As Lugon points out, many commentators of the time also emphasised the parallel between exhibitions and cinema, the latter being considered an example of democratic art for the masses, but also 'the very incarnation of modern perception characterised by mobility and dynamism. The exhibition ought thus to take it as a model and incorporate a veritable kinetic dimension.'[7] These exhibitions therefore represent an important piece of the puzzle that is the history of the integration of cinema and audio-visual media in museum galleries.[8]

The Cinematism of the Exhibition Space: El Lissitzky

The displays created by Soviet artist El Lissitzky are undoubtedly among the most eloquent instances of avant-garde exhibition design, providing a unique example of the interpenetration between museum institutions and exhibition fairs. El Lissitzky's first exhibition room, the *Proun Room (Prounenraum)*, was designed in 1923 for the *Great Berlin Art Exhibition (Große Berliner Kunstausstellung)*. It was followed by the *Room for Constructive Art (Raum für konstruktive Kunst)* at the International Art Exhibition in Dresden. During 1927 and 1928, upon request of Alexander Dorner, director of the Hannover Provincial Museum,[9] the latter display was reproduced inside the museum's *Abstract Cabinet (Kabinett der Abstrakten)*, dedicated to abstract art.

These landmark installations brought into the spotlight two fundamental principles: first, the exhibition space was to be considered as the theatre of a dynamic tension triggered by its very configuration; and, second, the relationship between exhibition and audience needed to be rethought in order to elicit a deeper involvement of the spectator. The cinematic principle created a strong interconnection between these two facets. In the *Abstract Cabinet*, for instance, the walls were covered with thin laths of steel, black and white on the sides and grey on the front, so that their colour appeared to change as the visitor moved across the room, creating what El Lissitzky defined an 'optical dynamic' (*optische Dynamik*).[10] Also, a system of casings with black perforated partitions moving on runners allowed visitors to reveal or conceal the paintings, prompting a direct interaction: as stated by El Lissitzky, the viewer was physically forced to interact with the exhibited objects.[11] As Maria Gough points out, the structure with two vertical casings and three tiers evokes the cinematic motif of the film strip.[12] The *Abstract Cabinet* had an intrinsic cinematic quality, since the movement of the visitor generated an unfolding principle similar to the running of photograms in a film reel. Olivia Crough argues that El Lissitzky's design of the so-called 'Demonstration Rooms' (the *Room for Constructive Art* and the *Abstract Cabinet*) demonstrates 'cinema without filmic projection'.[13]

Pavle Levi has proposed to define 'cinema by other means', 'the practice of positing cinema as a system of relations directly inspired by the workings of the film apparatus, but evoked through the material and technological properties of the originally non filmic media'.[14] Crough proposes to consider the 'Demonstration Rooms' as an example of 'cinema by other means'. Even though no moving images are presented in El Lissitzky's room, the organisation of the space, the lighting solutions, the arrangement of the display cases and of the objects and artworks 'demonstrate an unexpected cinematic operation'.[15] For El Lissitzky, as for many other twentieth-century avant-garde artists, cinema went far beyond the simple dimension of film projection.[16]

Besides being indirectly influenced by the kinetics of cinematography, El Lissitzky also included actual films in his installations. In 1928, he worked for the Soviet pavilion of the *Pressa Exhibition* in Cologne (the better-known name of the *Internationale Presse-Ausstellung des Deutschen Werkbund*), dedicated to the latest innovations in the fields of printing, publishing, and advertisement. El Lissitzky proposed to include films in two forms: on a large screen in a specially dedicated room, and on smaller devices placed along the exhibition itinerary.[17] Only the first project was realised, with the installation of a small movie theatre at the centre of the pavilion. As the theatre was inside the exhibition space, visitors could access it during their visit. However, as is often the case in such installations – artistic or not –, the sense of continuity between the two venues was downplayed by the shift in the reception mode (from movement to immobility, from light to darkness, and so on).

More generally, the spatial configuration of the *Pressa* display was permeated by a cinematic dimension, whereby multiple means and solutions, from lighting to graphics and mobile elements, were exploited to achieve a dynamic effect. A 24-metres long and 4-metres high photomural, titled *The Task of the Press is the Education of the Masses*, was structured in such a way as to have its composition 'set to motion' by the visitor's own movement, so that the montage of images of different sizes and with different subjects changed depending on the viewer's perspective.[18] In an essay eloquently titled 'Display that has Dynamic Force', typographer Jan Tschichold comments:

> [I]n place of a tedious succession of frameworks, containing dull statistics, [El Lissitzky] produced a new, purely visual design of the exhibition space and its contents, . . . by bringing a dynamic element into the exhibition by means of continuous films, illuminated and intermittent letters and number of rotating

models. The room thus became a sort of stage on which the visitor himself [*sic*] seemed to be one of the players.[19]

The idea of a cinematic reading of the exhibition space, which would later be taken up by scholars such as Benjamin Buchloh and Margarita Tupitsyn,[20] was already present in the catalogue created by El Lissitzky: the images of the installation were reproduced on a Leporello booklet (a single strip of paper folded into an accordion-pleat style), defined by El Lissitzky himself as a 'typographic cine-show'.[21] Thus, the cinema's intrinsically dynamic nature not only served as a reference for the exhibition's spatial configuration, but also as a point of connection between the exhibition design and typography.[22]

The following year, El Lissitzky curated the Soviet display of the exhibition *Film und Foto* in Stuttgart (1929, also known as *Fifo*).[23] Although the exhibition took stock of the latest progress in the fields of photography and film, the two media were mostly kept separate: photographs were hung on the walls of rooms organised by theme and nationality, while films were screened in a movie theatre according to a programme curated by the artist and filmmaker Hans Richter.[24] The Soviet room constituted an exception to this rule, as it included three projectors showing a selection of the most representative films of Soviet cinema, including Sergei Eisenstein's. A back-projection system allowed the viewers to watch the films while standing up and in a fully illuminated space.

Also, photographs and film frames by soviet artists such as Dziga Vervov were arranged around the screenings on a light and flexible structure of wooden pillars that organised the space into several levels of depth and height. As François Albera noted, the display 'offers the structure of a non-linear path that resembles the succession of the different shots of the film with its different rhythms, its changes of scale'.[25] The dynamic dimension of the cinema shattered the exhibition's spatial integrity into a multiplicity of plans and dimensions, while also integrating the alternative temporality of film loops. The spectator/viewer was in charge of recomposing these multiple dimensions and of carrying out, by moving across the space, an actual montage of the images.

Cinema and the Dynamism of Modern Life: Moholy-Nagy's Room of the Present

Hungarian artist László Moholy-Nagy made similar attempts to include moving images in the exhibition space. In 1930, he took part in the preparation of the German section of the *Salon of Artist-Decorators* (*Salon des artistes décorateurs*) in Paris, alongside other former Bauhaus members, such as

Walter Gropius, Herbert Bayer, and Marcel Breuer. The aim of the exhibition was to highlight the connection between industry, architecture, and design in contemporary Germany.[26] Moholy-Nagy designed a small projection room inside its part of the exhibition, and furnished it with two rows of seats closed on three sides by plastic walls. On one of these walls, an automatic projector showed a looping slide show of documentary photographs about the social life and industrial design of post-war Germany (the so-called *Deutschland-Reportage*). Although the images remain still their sequencing and emplacement within the exhibit (a dark room with a row of seats placed in front of a rectangular screen) evoked a movie theatre.

However, the evocation of the movie theatre was only partial, an attempt to negotiate between the cinema and the exhibition space. As there was no fourth wall opposite to the projection wall, the room was not clearly separated from the rest of the exhibition: significantly, half of the room's surface was left free for standing visitors who merely wanted to stop by before getting on with their visit.[27]

Like El Lissitzky, Moholy-Nagy experimented with possible exchanges and cross-pollinations between fair exhibitions and museum institutions. He was also commissioned by Alexander Dorner to recreate the display of the *Salon of Artist-Decorators* in the last room of the Hannover Provincial Museum, known as *Room of the Present (Raum der Gegenwart)*. Although the room was never completed, Moholy-Nagy's preliminary projects give us insights into the solutions that he planned to adopt.[28] In addition to the slide projector used for the *Salon of Artist-Decorators*, he had thought of back-projectors placed inside display cases that the viewers could activate by pushing a button. They would show the latest experiments in cinematography, including those of Viking Eggeling, Sergei Eisenstein and Moholy-Nagy himself.

These devices had the peculiarity of being equipped with a black mask placed in front of the screen, with a circular opening, as if to create a membrane separating the exhibition space from the film-viewing space.[29] This was certainly not the first back-projection device to include panels or other means to reduce the lighting near the screen, however, its configuration was quite unique: while the visitors was physically anchored in the exhibition space, their eyes were invited to dive into the dark space surrounding the projected images, as if to recreate, starting from the contrast between light and darkness, a separation – however ambiguous and reversible – between the exhibition and the viewing device.

In a wider sense, the running of the film was designed as part of a pervasively dynamic exhibition space, characterised by reels, sliding panels, and slide shows. Noam Elcott describes the *Room of the Present* as the 'first modern multi-media exhibition space',[30] arguing that the 'cinematic theme' gains a literal centrality in its display.[31] The room also contained the light projector of Moholy-Nagy's own design, the well-known Light Prop for an Electric Stage (or Light-Space Modulator), which the artist used in 1930 to create the film *Lightplay: Black/White/Gray* (*Lichtspiel: schwarz-weiß-grau*).[32] The device was housed in a square box with a circular opening on one side, creating a number of lighting and cinematic effects. If the Light-Space Modulator could be considered 'a film projector without film',[33] Elcott stresses that 'the square box functions as a portable movie theatre or expanded cinema. For in the absence of a darkened space, the interior of the box itself must function as the white screens onto which the coloured light-and-shadow play unfolds.'[34]

The room was explicitly dedicated to the latest scientific and technological developments and to the most topical aspects of contemporary life. The dynamic tension between the different components of the room aimed to express the vitality of the contemporary world. The cinema therefore found its place inside museums both as an expression of modernity and as a dynamic component of the display: in other words, its role was to align the museum – an institution traditionally associated with the past – with the dynamics of contemporary life.

'THE PARADISE OF THE EXHIBITOR': MUSEUMS AND WORLD'S FAIRS

The avant-garde artists' contribution to exhibition design was crucial in establishing a link between the history of museums and the history of world's fairs.[35] Both are based on the exhibition of objects and artefacts and share a concern for issues of display and interaction with the public, as well as the necessity to attract and interest visitors, manage their circulation and facilitate their visit.

From 1935 to 1938, Bauhaus members such as Bayer, Gropius, Mies van der Rohe, and Moholy-Nagy migrated to the United States, where they continued their research. The figure of Herbert Bayer is particularly important, as he crosses distant geographic and disciplinary areas: his activity as exhibition and graphic designer started in the 1920s and continued after he moved to the United States.[36] Besides fairs and commercial displays, he was also invited to work on several temporary exhibitions at the MoMA in New York, where he was able to put into practice the principles he had developed over the years: *Bauhaus 1919–1928* (1938), *Road to Victory* (1942), *Airways to Peace* (1943), and *Power in the Pacific* (1945).

Bayer's work had a direct influence on the curatorial debate and museum exhibition practice in the United States.[37] The journal *Curator* published his essay 'Aspects of Design of Exhibitions and Museums',[38] where he argues that exhibitions should combine different means of visual communication, such as 'visible printing or as sound, pictures as symbols, paintings, and photographs, sculptural media, materials and surfaces, color, light, movement (of the display as well as the visitor), films, diagrams, and charts'.[39] Bayer's article traces a history of the experimental practices of exhibition design, outlining a connection between the large international fairs of the second half of the nineteenth century, the European avant-gardes of the 1920s and 1930s, and their commercial, educational, and propaganda developments in the United States.

In *The Birth of the Museum*, Tony Bennett has underscored the deeper, ideological connection between the museums and world's fairs, especially in the second half of the nineteenth century and starting from the 1851 *Crystal Palace Exhibition*.[40] Bennett states that museums and expositions are part of a wider 'exhibitionary complex', including 'history and natural science museums, dioramas and panoramas, ... arcades and department stores'.[41] All of these institutions contribute to the construction of modern national identities. They are 'technologies of progress'[42] in a sense that indicates 'the different ways in which these representations were organised as performative resources which programmed visitors' behaviour as well as their cognitive horizons'.[43] The exhibitionary complex had a role of 'cultural governance of the populace':[44]

> a self-monitoring system of looks in which the subject and object positions can be exchanged, in which the crowd comes to commune with and regulate itself through interiorizing the ideal and ordered view of itself as seen from the controlling vision of power – a site of sight accessible to all.[45]

Tony Bennett also examines how great exhibitions and museums contributed to the emergence of a new public that brought together middle- and working-classes[46] through a number of regulation, education, and reform activities.[47] The deep connection between museums and expositions led to multiple exchanges at various levels. The transfer of objects and professionals between the two contexts, for instance, soon became a common practice. As noted by Robert W. Rydell, expositions accumulated a large number of artefacts that would later find a permanent accommodation inside museums.[48] The foundation in 1852 of the Victoria and Albert Museum in London, was a direct consequence of the *Crystal Palace Exhibition*,[49] which also influenced the nearby Science Museum, founded in 1857. Likewise, the San Diego Museum of Man, the Field Museum of Natural History, and the Chicago Museum of Science and Industry all originated from the Century of Progress Exposition of 1933–4.[50]

The two kinds of exhibition venues also exchanged display solutions: great expositions, less bound by institutional and economic obligations, were more open to experimental forms of display, although the proposals often came from museum professionals.[51] On the other hand, curators looked at great expositions to gain information about the trends in display and the most up-to-date exhibition techniques. A case in point are the 1939 international expositions of San Francisco (*Pageant of the Pacific*) and New York (*The World of Tomorrow*), which raised the interest of two museum directors, Carlos E. Cummings, head of the Buffalo Museum of Science, and Robert P. Shaw, from the New York Museum of Science and Industry.

The displays of the two exhibitions were analysed and considered for their potential application inside museums. The initiative led to two publications: *East is East and West is West*,[52] curated by Cummings and presented as 'some observations on the World's Fairs of 1939 – by one whose main interest is in museums',[53] and *Exhibition Techniques: A Summary of Exhibition Practice Based on Surveys Conducted at the New York and San Francisco World Fairs of 1939*, curated by Shaw.[54] As the latter wrote, the exhibitions were considered landmarks in display techniques:

> [W]ith the opening of the New York World's Fair it was at once apparent that here was the paradise of the exhibitor, with 150 million dollars spent in every conceivable way to present the most effective exhibits possible to entertain, educate, publicize and promote a vast array of governmental, scientific, industrial and other organizations and activities throughout the world, to show the American public and foreign visitors the achievements of the past, the developments of the present, and a glimpse of the future.[55]

Without neglecting the differences in aims, resources, and audience size, both authors firmly believed that museums could take a few pointers from expositions, which reputedly encompassed the best display techniques from the past as well as the most recent innovations in the field.[56]

Expositions provided museum staff with a 'school of exhibition design having no equals in the world',[57] and addressed a demand that had emerged in the 1930s and 1940s among American and European museums: that of combining their scientific rigour and educational mission with the urgent need to increase the entertainment value of their displays in order to attract a wider audience. In this respect, world's fairs were a goldmine of exemplary practices aimed at 'educating while entertaining'.[58]

Scholars like Karen A. Rader and Victoria E. M. Cain have noted that the relation between museums and world fairs found its clearest expression in science museums, despite a number of problems and contradictions. This is particularly true of the United States, where science museums proved extraordinarily open to the new display techniques that had been developed in the 1920s and 1930s in order to address the needs of a new media landscape where film, broadcasting, and advertisement played a crucial role.[59] In the words of Rader and Cain, 'reformers hailing from the worlds of retail, entertainment, and journalism had an easier time building new kinds of life science displays in these years . . . The wealthiest of them established museums of science and industry to house these creations.'[60]

Following the model of European industrial museums and world's fairs, these museums set aside scholarly research to focus on education, exploring 'biomedicine, industrialized agriculture, and other applications of life sciences in ways that seemed breathtakingly new to American museum goers'.[61] One of the priorities mentioned by Shaw along with the 'entertainment value,' is 'the story', that is, the dramatic value of the exhibit, and its relation to the concrete life of visitors.[62] Cummings appears to share this opinion:

> [T]here may be and doubtless are hard-boiled pedants who will stand as firm as the Rock of Gibraltar in their assertions that the purpose of a museum case is education, and education, and still more education, and that entertainment is in no sense a desideratum in a serious display or even anywhere in the whole institution. With these good folks we shall have no argument, only reiterating for their benefit the belief that the main and only idea of installing an exhibit is to get people to look at it; if they do not, it is no longer an effective display but merely a lifeless accumulation of more-or-less-valuable specimens.[63]

Shaw claimed that the best way to create a striking display was to appeal to the public's emotion: 'beauty, sentiment, thrills: the Fairs merely emphasized again how much mankind is moved by them – by color, light, music, dreams, hopes, fears, wonder, awe, amazement, surprise, admiration, delight, laughter'.[64]

Motion pictures provided effective and entertaining displays in national and international fairs. The trend started with the Paris Universal Exhibition of 1900 and culminated with the International Exposition of Arts and Techniques in Modern Life of 1937, also in Paris, which led to the inauguration of the French science museum Palais de la découverte.[65] Haidee Wasson observes that the New York World's Fair of 1939 made use of 'a whole range of projection technologies illuminated mannequins, multi-screened installations, and large improvisational screens such as ceilings'.[66] The fair also featured Chrysler's big screen with three-dimensional motion pictures, an official movie theatre and dedicated auditoria, and the cinematic component of the Futurama or of the panoramic screen with eleven projectors at the Kodak Hall of Colour.[67]

Moving images appeared in a variety of settings: in specially dedicated screening rooms, inside the exhibitions, on screens of various sizes, running in a loop, or activated by visitors or operators, silent or with sound, in black and white or colour, in illuminated or dark spaces, isolated or combined with other media. Whatever the setting, they contributed to reconfiguring the space and the visit, orienting visitors in a given direction or conveying them towards a specific pole of attraction.[68]

To museum professionals, great expositions proved a fruitful testing ground for the use of moving images in displays. As noted in the 1950s by Grace L. McCann Morley, director of the San Francisco Museum of Modern Art:

> exhibitions and fairs provide considerable services to museums by facilitating the invention and testing of audio-visual aids. Museums can rarely afford to use this kind of material with such prodigality. They are forced to make a careful choice; they look at all the possibilities offered by the material they are going to use and they know how to take advantage of it with ingenuity and precision that cannot be demonstrated by those who have to use it to attract large undifferentiated crowds.[69]

These close-knit exchanges between apparently distant worlds show that museums, far from being isolated and timeless institutions, were able to intercept the latest developments in display techniques. Museums used audio-visuals not only for educational purposes and to preserve and transmit memory, but also to attract a wider public and to keep up with the ever-moving and dynamic nature of modernity.

FILMS AT THE NEW YORK MUSEUM OF SCIENCE AND INDUSTRY

The New York Museum of Science and Industry, whose display was reorganised in 1936, is emblematic of the use of audio-visual devices in museum exhibitions of the time. Described by its director Robert Shaw as 'a laboratory of modern exhibition practice',[70] the museum was closely linked to the industrial world, offering a space where 'many industries bring the stories of their contributions to American living'.[71]

The museum presented the operation of machines according to methods not dissimilar to those used in fairs and trade exhibitions, also with the sponsorship of the same firms. Shaw emphasised the importance of an 'effective presentation'[72] of the contents: 'here these developments of science and industry are translated into exhibitions which reveal them in some of their most interesting and significant aspects'.[73] The museum made extensive use of industrial films in its galleries, experimenting with a few innovative solutions. The films allowed to improve and enrich the display, conveying to visitors a great deal of information about the exhibits, their origins and scope, as well as their functioning.

For instance, moving pictures were part of the display on the manufacture of *rayon*: the main structure consisted of a long showcase divided into three sections containing raw materials, parts of machineries (some of which in action), and photographs. On top of the central section, a film was shown on a small hooded screen. Visitors were invited to carefully observe the showcase in its entirety, and then to sit down comfortably and watch the five-minute film, enticingly titled *The Romance of Rayon*. In the director's view, the film brought 'the whole exhibit alive and [gave] it unity and significance',[74] through 'a series of animated diagrams, as entertaining in their way as Mickey Mouse cartoons'.[75] Moving images were thus considered a valid means to make the display not only more effective and efficient, but also more entertaining. Such an animated diagram was, according to Shaw, an ideal type of industrial film, since

> it covers the desired ground comprehensively and yet briefly; it strips the subject of technical mysteries and puts it into understandable language for the layman; and it does all this with a light touch that has an entertainment value all its own.[76]

As with the Imperial War Museum, the attractiveness of its films was largely due to their ability to show machines that, for obvious practical reasons, could not be on display in a museum, and to show them in operation. Significantly, films were often exhibited alongside equipment. In the section of the museum dedicated to the historical development of locks and keys, alongside demonstrative exhibits operated by visitors, a movie was shown on a small screen, presenting the safety systems used in a bank:

> [I]nstead of an animated diagram, this picture presents the people of the bank going about their business in connection with the vault. Close-ups of the mechanism of the lock's operation are shown, and when the two-minute film has run itself out, those who have been watching it have a pretty good idea of what a vault means to a bank and how it operates.[77]

Like the locks on display, the film was activated by visitors pressing a button. Also, visitors could restart the film if they wished to watch it a second time. In another section devoted to the operation of the punched card for electrical accounting, a film was shown alongside the machine itself:

> [I]n the exhibit, the visitor sees the machine methodically turning out the cards; in the picture, he sees what actually goes on inside the machine itself as it does its work, enabling it to count, sort, punch in the proper places, and otherwise virtually 'think like a man'.[78]

Thanks to the possibility of showing objects or situations that could not otherwise be exposed within the galleries, films were important tools for accompanying and enriching the museum presentation. The solutions studied by curators to display audio-visuals aimed to create a close integration between them and the other components of the exhibition, such as objects and diagrams. The cinematic language (details, overall views, editing) became complementary to other exhibits, 'dramatising' the whole exhibition.

An even more innovative display solution was used in a section dedicated to the digestive system, where two small screens were embedded in a wooden human figure, corresponding to the various organs, and showing their functioning. There were also films running in a loop, as well as a small projection room. In the corridor of the section devoted to stainless steel, visitors witnessed a demonstration during which four short films were projected. Then they arrived at a small theatre, where a sound 16 mm motion picture in colour was shown, leading them almost literally inside the factory where stainless steel was produced. Moving images, combined with the use of colour, created a kind of climax that astonished and captivated visitors.

The New York Museum of Science and Industry also presented a series of machineries on its front doors – a strategic position to capture the attention of passers-by. Films were also shown, and they proved to be very effective in attracting the attention of the crowd:

> [I]t had not been showing half an hour before the operating department of the building called up to ask if it could not be turned off as the lobby was so crowded with people watching the film that it was difficult to pass through.[79]

Due to the crowding, films could not be operated continuously, and the museum had to leave intervals between the projections to allow people to move on. According to the museum director, the film's success depended on its subject: the automobile, an object of almost universal interest, was presented in a spectacular escape from accident.[80] The movement of images allowed by cinema was thus married with the mobility of one of the modern transportation means par excellence. Moreover, the cinema was placed at the very heart of urban mobility – not isolated in a projection room or in the galleries, but on the museum's threshold – and came into direct contact with the crowd, stopping its movement and even regulating its flow. The film acted as a connection between the museum and the passers-by, mediating the first contact between the institution and the public. Museums, cities, and forms of modern mobility were closely linked through the means of film, which contributed to modernising the institution and keeping it up to date.

Notes

1. See Henning, 'Legibility and Affect: Museums as New Media'; Staniszewski, *The Power of Display*; Witkovsky (ed.), *Avant-Garde Art in Everyday Life*.
2. Lugon, 'Dynamic Paths of Thought', pp. 117–18.
3. Ward, *Weimar Surfaces*, p. 49.
4. Ibid. p. 118.
5. See Lugon, 'Dynamic Paths of Thought'.
6. Ibid.
7. Ibid. p. 128.
8. See Henning, 'Legibility and Affect: Museums as New Media'.
9. On Alexander Dorner, see Cauman, *The Living Museum*; Flacke-Knoch, *Museumskonzeptionen in der Weimarer Republik*; Ockman, 'The Road Not Taken'.
10. El Lissitzky, 'Exhibition Rooms'.
11. Ibid.
12. Gough, 'Constructivism Disoriented', p. 105.
13. Crough, 'El Lissitzy's Screening Rooms', p. 229.
14. Levi, *Cinema by Other Means*, p. 27.
15. Crough, 'El Lissitzy's Screening Rooms', p. 234.
16. See Elder, *Harmony and Dissent*; Levi, *Cinema by Other Means*.
17. Rjasanzew, 'El Lissitzky und die "Pressa" in Köln 1928', pp. 72–81.
18. On the *Pressa* photomural, see Buchloh, 'From Faktura to Factography'; Lugon, 'Entre l'Affiche et le monument'.
19. Tschichold, 'Display that Has Dynamic Force', p. 22.
20. Buchloh, 'From Faktura to Factography', pp. 106–7; Tupitsyn, 'Back to Moscow', p. 36.
21. El Lissitzky, *Union der Sozialistischen Sowjet-Republiken: Katalog des Sowjet-Pavillons*.
22. On El Lissitzky's typographic work, see Bois, 'El Lissitzky: Reading Lessons'.
23. The catalogue was reprinted in 1979: Steinorth (ed.), *Internationale Ausstellung des Deutschen Werkbundes Film und Foto: Stuttgart, 1929*.
24. Richter, *Filmgegner von Heute - Filmfreunde von Morgen*. The programme of the screenings has been reconstructed in Eskildsen and Horak (eds), *Film und Foto der zwanziger Jahre*, pp. 198–201.
25. Albera, 'Les Passages entre les arts', p. 26 (our translation).
26. See the exhibition catalogue: Bayer, *Exposition de la société des artistes décorateurs: Section allemande*.
27. This kind of black box *ante litteram* was taken up, a few decades later, in multi-channel video installations and in contemporary moving images installations that re-interpret the 'classical' cinematic *dispositifs* in order to develop new relationships between the viewer and the projected images.
28. A close description of the room is in Flacke-Knoch, *Museumskonzeptionen in der Weimarer Republik*, pp. 77–99. The room was reconstructed in 2009, following the original plans and drawings, by Jakob Gebert and Kai-Uwe Hemken. See Gebert

and Kai-Uwe Hemken, 'Raum der Gegenwart: Die Ordnung von Apparaten und Exponaten'.
29. For an elaboration on this aspect, see Elcott, 'Rooms of Our Time'.
30. Ibid. p. 31.
31. Ibid. p. 33.
32. Moholy-Nagy described the *Light-Space Modulator* in 'Lichtrequisit einer elektrischen Bühne'.
33. Elcott, 'Rooms of Our Time', p. 40.
34. Ibid.
35. See Rydell, 'World Fairs and Museums'.
36. On Herbert Bayer see Cohen, *Herbert Bayer: The Complete Work*.
37. See Samson, 'La Trame narrative, le multimédia et l'Exposition Universelle', p. 126.
38. Bayer, 'Aspects of Design of Exhibitions and Museums'.
39. Ibid. p. 258.
40. Bennett, *The Birth of the Museum*.
41. Ibid. p. 59.
42. Ibid. p. 10.
43. Ibid.
44. Ibid. p. 21.
45. Ibid. p. 69
46. Ibid. pp. 73–4.
47. Ibid. pp. 99–102.
48. Rydell, 'World Fairs and Museums', p. 143. See also Rydell, *World of Fairs: The Century-of-Progress Expositions*.
49. See Wainwright and Gere, 'The Making of the South Kensington Museum II'.
50. See Rydell, 'World Fairs and Museums', p. 136.
51. See ibid.
52. Cummings, *East is East and West is West*.
53. Ibid. p. i.
54. Shaw, *Exhibition Techniques*.
55. Ibid. p. 11.
56. Ibid. p. 7.
57. Ibid. p. 12.
58. Ibid. p. 16.
59. Rader and Cain, *Life on Display*, pp. 91–135.
60. Ibid. p. 113.
61. Ibid.
62. Shaw, *Exhibition Techniques*, p. 37.
63. Cummings, *East is East and West is West*, p. 80.
64. Shaw, *Exhibition Techniques*, p. 12.
65. See Morettin, 'Universal Exhibitions and the Cinema: History and Culture'; Riou, 'Le Cinéma à l'Exposition internationale de 1937'.
66. Wasson, 'The Other Small Screen', p. 92.

67. Ibid. p. 93.
68. Ibid. p. 92. See also Gagnon and Marchessault (eds), *Reimagining Cinema*; Friedberg, 'Trottoir roulant: The Cinema and New Mobilities of Spectatorship'; Gunning, 'The World as Object Lesson'.
69. McCann Morley, 'Présentation des expositions éducatives', p. 84 (our translation).
70. Shaw, *Exhibition Techniques*, p. 4.
71. Ibid.
72. Ibid. p. 5.
73. Ibid.
74. Shaw, 'Visualizing the Industrial Exhibit', p. 33.
75. Ibid. p. 30.
76. Ibid. p. 33.
77. Ibid.
78. Ibid.
79. Ibid. p. 46.
80. Ibid.

CHAPTER FOUR

The Multi-media Museum: The 1960s–70s

MUSEUMS AND FILMS FROM UNESCO TO WORLD'S FAIRS

Some of the activities promoted from 1958 to 1962 by UNESCO and the International Council of Museums (ICOM), the worldwide association of museum professionals founded in 1946, testify to the growing importance of films and audio-visuals in museums. This question was discussed during a conference of 'Museum, Film and Television Experts', held on 8–11 July 1958 at the United Nations Pavilion of the Brussels International Exhibition. In those years, museums had become fully conscious of their educational role, and were directing their efforts towards finding new and more effective ways to communicate with the public. The inspiring idea was that museums should not be considered only repositories of antiquities, but living organisms able to reach the public with modern appealing methods. One of the pivotal ideas of the seminar was that both film and television 'are destined, especially so far as their cultural programs are concerned, to exercise an increasing influence in the realm of museums'.[1] In this view, both media would help museums stay up to date and reach out to a wider audience.

The main goal of the conference was to increase awareness about technical issues and to promote collaboration between museum professionals and film and television producers.[2] Experts from both fields discussed how film and television could serve the museum as a whole, addressing topics such as the relationship between original works of art and their audio-visual representation, as well as the forms and contents of films and programmes for museums. As a confirmation of the effectiveness of audio-visual communication for museums, the film *Museum of Art*, which presented works from twenty American art museums, was shown at the American Pavilion of the Exhibition.[3]

A few months later, at the 1958 UNESCO Regional Seminar on the Educational Role of Museums in Rio de Janeiro, museum professionals recognised that films and television were museums' richest educational means, as they could be effectively employed in different ways.[4] According to the seminar report, films could be used at the beginning of guided tours, 'to prepare members of the group for the tour, by the use of different methods than those used in the museum display'.[5] Films should not replicate the exhibits and their spatial arrangement, or merely describe what visitors would see a few minutes later. Instead, what made films an attractive option was the possibility to communicate a great deal of supplementary information about the exhibition's contents, so as to adequately introduce them to visitors. Another kind of film could be used to inform teachers about the museum's educational resources, in general or in specific fields. Also, museums could organise the projection of documentary films about the museum's programme.[6]

As in the previous decades, museum professionals remained strongly interested in the possibility of showing educational films in auditoriums attached to their institutions. In 1962, UNESCO and ICOM launched a joint survey, 'The Use of Cultural and Scientific Films in the Museums of the World', coordinated by Jacques Durand.[7] More than 4,000 museums in 115 countries were interviewed about the type of equipment at their disposal and its present use. The main goal of the study was to explore the potential market for an international distribution system of scientific, historical, ethnographic, or art films.[8]

The survey investigated several topics: the role of the projection room (its permanent or temporary position in the museum, or whether it was loaned from another institution); the nature of the projector (permanent or borrowed); the number of available seats and the number of spectators; and the conditions of admission (free or charged). The final report revealed that 'out of a hundred museums possessing equipment, half [were] located in Europe, thirty in the United States of America, and only twenty in the rest of the world'.[9] On the whole, the survey showed that film screenings represented 'only a small part of the activities of museums',[10] despite the importance attributed by many professionals to their educational value.

Scepticism about the very principle of film screenings was still rampant among museum professionals.[11] Museums planning to install some kind of projection equipment encountered a number of obstacles, such as competition from television, lack of space, and technical difficulties. Above all, they suffered from lack of funds. Among the survey's respondents, few had film stocks, and many deplored the financial difficulties in purchasing or borrowing movies, as well as the latter's scarcity and poor quality. The proposal to set up an international distribution system was therefore positively received by most institutions.[12] These debates and surveys reveal a strong interest in how films projected in auditoriums could help in illustrating the museums' collections or subjects of interest, but do not focus on the use of audio-visuals in the galleries. However, the latter field also underwent a few changes in the framework of broader transformations.

Museum professionals continued to look with interest at international exhibitions. One of the first issues of the journal *Curator* published a report about the Brussels Expo of 1958, stating that it offered 'a unique opportunity for comparison and evaluation of international design trends'.[13] In the following decades, world's exhibitions continued to represent an ideal experimental field for 'expanding'[14] cinema's boundaries beyond the classic context of the movie theatre. Exhibition designers and experimental filmmakers such as Charles and Ray Eames[15] or Stan VanDerBeek,[16] to mention only a few, designed pavilions or attractions at the 1964–5 New York World Fair and Expo 67 in Montreal. Multi-screen presentations, 70 mm screens, immersive environments, kaleidoscopic presentations, combinations of films and live shows: as Monika Kin Gagnon and Janine Marchessault stress, this led to rethink 'the aesthetic and affective parameters of the cinematic'[17] and challenged 'the cinema production technology of the day, modes of screening, and audience reception, as well as received wisdom as to what cinema was or could be'.[18]

In the same years, the diffusion of video and electronic technologies not only transformed the art world, with the emergence of video art, but also offered more practical and economic ways for museums to create their own audio-visual materials, opening new opportunities for museum professionals.

Moreover, museum curators started to cooperate more closely with designers to make exhibitions attractive to a wider public.[19] In light of the increasing awareness about the educative role of museums, displays required effective communicative strategies in addition to scientific rigour. Some museum professionals remained sceptical of this strategy, but they were severely criticised by the most progressive curators, such as Albert E. Parr, director of the American Museum of Natural History. To Parr, 'the aesthetic success of the exhibit depends entirely upon the designer and the preparator's execution of the design, just as the intellectual success depends upon the curator, and the educational success upon the happy integration of the efforts of both'.[20]

THE EXHIBITION AS A MOSAIC: MARSHALL MCLUHAN AND HARLEY PARKER

The balance between scientific contents and design was discussed in a seminar curated by the communication theorist Marshall McLuhan and the artist, designer, and curator Harley Parker, held in October 1967 at the Museum of the City of New York and titled *Exploration of the Ways, Means, and Values of Museum Communication with the Viewing Public*.[21]

In McLuhan and Parker's view, the museum was not an isolated institution, but its identity was shaped by emerging technologies such as television and electronic media. Recognising the importance of placing the public at the centre of museum activities, McLuhan advocated the necessity of understanding its needs in terms of participation and emotional involvement. Museums should be able to communicate with people whose attitudes and interests were modelled by new media such as television. According to the speakers, museums should not function as mere repositories of items, but should instead be able to respond to the public's need to understand the context of the objects and the culture that produced them. Films were considered valuable tools to reach this goal, and proved even more effective than written labels when it came to conveying information about the artefact's environment, as well as to triggering the visitor's curiosity and participation.

To McLuhan and Parker, films and multi-media went beyond the linear narrative model that they saw as typical of printed books, in which the artefacts serve as illustrations of a story-line, and where the visitor follows a predetermined itinerary. Likewise, exhibitions adhering to the linear model prearrange for the public a unique path that proceeds straight from a concept to the following. Instead, McLuhan and Parker advocated for a completely different model, in which no exclusive links between the objects are provided by curators, but visitors are free to experiment with new ways of going through the display and its meanings.

The two speakers encouraged curators to understand the museum as a unique medium and to explore its potential in terms of display. According to McLuhan and Parker, the linear narrative needed to be replaced by a 'mosaic'-like narrative.[22] Without moving away from three-dimensional objects, display techniques should test multi-screen projections accompanied by sound recordings and other multi-sensory effects, in order to experiment with innovative ways of engaging visitors.[23]

McLuhan and Parker sparked debate between museum professionals. The lecturers' perspective was considered unorthodox from the point of view of museology, and challenged most of the curators' assumptions about the role of museums and their relationships with visitors. The transcription of the seminar reveals a palpable tension between new ideas about exhibition design and the persistence of established convictions, and helps us understand that the adoption of innovative solutions was prevented not only by practical and economic constraints, but also by opposing views.

To illustrate his and McLuhan's theories, Harley Parker designed an experimental exhibition for the permanent Dutch Gallery of the Museum of the City of New York. The room contained a fifteen-minute long multi-media presentation with an automatically controlled sight-and-sound sequence. It included color slides of Dutch scenes ..., along with scenes of New York as it looks today; a movie in black and white showing New York street scenes ...; sound tapes which contrasted 17th Century Dutch music with the sounds of contemporary New York; Strobe-lighted manikins of a Dutch boy and girl; and a few artifacts.[24]

The display of the gallery involved simultaneous projections of films and slides, multi-tape recordings, and other devices addressing not only vision but also sound, touch, and smell. The film and multi-media presentation avoided predetermined itineraries, inviting visitors to orient themselves among a variety of heterogeneous stimuli.

McLuhan and Parker's refusal to control the visitor's movements was consistent with the educational and commercial trends of the 1950s and 1960s. Noting the public's weariness of imposed itineraries, Oliver Lugon observed that 'many designers tried to find non-linear forms of didactic presentations that would give visitors a greater sense of liberty'.[25] However, this view was not shared by all the museum professionals, most of whom remained attached to the linear narrative model. Additionally, as in the case of the Imperial War Museum, many technical problems hindered the adoption of such display techniques.

MUSEUMS AND THE 'AV REVOLUTION'

In those years, many curators and designers recognise the opportunities that new audio-visual technologies offered new opportunities to renovate the displays. Like McLuhan and Parker, William Kissiloff claimed that museums needed to align themselves with contemporary trends by adopting 'mixed media':

> [M]ixed-media presentation is among the most widely discussed and highly publicized of contemporary phenomena. It has been the number one crowd-pleaser in every recent world's fair and the single most important new wrinkle in public education. It is the dominant trend in all the arts from dance to modern sculpture ... Why are not museums ... using this compelling communications tool?[26]

Kissiloff described mixed media as 'far more than the sum of their parts':[27] 'every element in mixed media adds a unique ingredient to the overall mix depending on that element's physical properties',[28] and 'the cumulative effect of film, slides, live actors and other diverse elements far outweigh the expected total'.[29] According to Kissiloff, the ideal setting for multiple media was the 'black box', or, alternatively, a 'total environment', which would separate the visitors from the outside world and intensify their involvement.[30]

Similarly, M. Malík advocated for a full integration between the different media used in the exhibition, on the model of films:

> the synthesis of the elements . . . must be subordinated to the same principles that govern *film editing* . . . Length of illumination time, movement, projection, and background sound should be graded in accordance with the chief basic subject of the matter that is being explained. In many cases we speak of dramatization of the subject.[31]

Along with slides, illuminated transparencies, and loop or story-line films, videotapes started to emerge as useful – and cost-effective – means to renew museum displays.[32] A survey conducted in 1972 by the American Association of Museums revealed that about 20 per cent of responding museums owned video equipment and used it not only for documentation, internal communication, and community relations, but also for 'creative expression and media exploration', and 'exhibition reinforcement or display enhancement'.[33]

Television monitors powered by videotape playback units started replacing continuous loop film projectors, because they proved more reliable, economic, and flexible.[34] Other technological innovations such as videodiscs and microprocessors, used to control audio-visual programmes, started being used by curators and designers to improve the attractiveness of exhibitions.[35] In 1973, William Fagalay, Gilbert Wright, and Frederick Dockstader wrote in *Museum News* that museums were undergoing an 'AV revolution',[36] characterised by a great use of films and videos, as well as other solutions such as slides and recorded sounds. The following year, the same journal dedicated its first special issue to audio-visual media.[37]

Film and other media were already being used in museum galleries in the previous decades, with all the difficulties that I described in the previous chapters. However, in the 1960s and especially in the 1970s, they achieved an unprecedented pervasiveness, accompanied by an increasing awareness of their functioning and of their potential effects on the public. Debates about their advantages are reminiscent of some of the arguments we already encountered when discussing previous uses of audio-visuals in exhibitions.[38] For instance, in 1976, Josef Beneš mentioned that their educational effectiveness surpassed that of static displays, and that they allowed museums to keep up with the times, satisfying the visitors' taste for modern technology:

> [I]f museums fail to use these media, they may find themselves superseded by other cultural institutions and relegated to the position of a backward and outmoded institution which has relinquished its important role in cultural life.[39]

The relationship between 'classical' forms of display, based on the primacy of objects, and the possibilities offered by new multi-media technologies, was one of the most controversial topics in the curatorial field. Audio-visual devices, according to the most sceptical curators, were highly distracting, and their entertainment value threatened the educational potential of the exhibitions.[40] In a 1974 issue of *Museum News*, Joseph Shannon condemned the use of audio-visual and other modes of presentation that divert the attention from the object, arguing that museums should set themselves apart from entertainment venues.[41] Conversely, on the same issue, Thomas Radford claimed that audio-visuals should almost completely replace labels and other written texts, as they provide 'multisensory experiences that stimulate active responses'.[42]

Eventually, more balanced views allowed curators to experiment with audio-visual technologies without totally rejecting the role of the objects or of other elements of the display. In 1979, George S. Gardner praised the newly designed permanent exhibition of the Hall of Earth History at the American Museum of Natural History, which included film loops and slide stories, as an ideal means to describe the continuously changing nature of Earth.[43] Curators and designers avoided packing up their galleries with artefacts and specimens; to create a more interesting environment for visitors, they introduced audio-vusuals along with large-scale and moving models, dioramas, and demonstrative scientific equipment.

At the Hall of Earth History, motion pictures, slides, and stereophonic sound were combined in an introductory room to immediately catch the visitors' attention with multiple stimuli, as well as to convey a great deal of information in a short time.[44] An entire glass wall was employed as a rear-projection screen, divided into five smaller portions. A twelve-minute long 16 mm film was at the heart of the presentation, and four smaller Carousel slide projections complemented and illustrated its contents. The film was shown in the lower right corner of the wall, at the height of the spectators' eyes. It combined raw material from various sources, selected to create a storyline that illustrated the history of the planet. The soundtrack mixed sound effects with an especially arranged musical score.

How did this multi-projection room relate to the rest of the exhibition? Physically, it was a separate environment that ensured a total immersion. However, connections were carefully created between the film and the slides presentations, as well as with the materials presented in the rest of the galleries. The slides both contributed to the film's contents and showed images of the exhibits, which the visitors could examine at a later stage.[45] The continuity of the display was thus emphasised, in an attempt to fully integrate audio-visuals with artefacts and other didactic devices. The 'multi-media show' had an undeniably spectacular component, aimed at impressing visitors and implicitly demonstrating the museum's ability to appropriate the latest media techniques:

> [T]he attempt was to create a very powerful experience ... We built visual effects that would give the illusion of gases in space, rather ethereal and formless, which collapse and condense into a fantastically dense mass, which explodes in a blinding flash of light (accompanied by suitable sound effects on the track).[46]

Still, the focus remained on the objects: audio-visual techniques were included

> into a museum experience that added to the overall impact of a hall made up mostly of artifacts and specimens ... The designer ... has options that permit him to orchestrate sound and light in ways that explain the collections and make their stories clearer and more exciting.[47]

These choices reflect the opinions of most museum professionals of the time, to whom audio-visual techniques were meant to complement the artefacts, without replacing them: technology had to maintain an auxiliary role. Echoing a broader museological assumption, Joseph Beneš stated:

> [I]n a museum, there can be no question of fancy effects or eye-catching gimmicks which do not increase the communication potential of the object on display but, with their surface allurements, distract visitors' attention from the information to be conveyed.[48]

Even the most progressive curators thought that audio-visual presentation strategies, while useful in contextualising objects and in contributing to the museum's communication strategy, should not compromise the artefacts' primacy. For example, George S. Gardner asserted:

> '[L]et the technique fit the subject' could be a guide to designers in the future. The controlled, skilled use of a visual image, whether it be slide, film, or video, combined with sound, scent, or animation can in many instances reinforce the message that the object is meant to convey.[49]

These concerns were part of a wider discussion on the growing popularisation of museum presentation, and reflected the fear that entertainment would prevail over education. In the 1980s and 1990s, the turn toward 'edutainment'[50] and the so-called 'disneyfication' of museums[51] were at the centre of an intense debate among curators.[52] As they renewed their display methods and rethought their relationship with the public, museums faced issues that remain topical and controversial to this day. I will examine them in more detail in the second part of the volume.

Notes

1. 'Conference on Museum, Film and Television Experts at Brussels', p. 32.
2. Ibid. The relationship between museums and television was highly debated in those years. See, for instance, Schoener, 'An Art Museum's Experiment in Television'; Miller, 'A Scientific Museum's Experiment in Television'; Dierbeck, 'Television and the Museum'; Burns, 'Should Museums Try TV?'; Johnstone, 'Museums and Television'. For the use of television at the Museum of Modern Art (MoMA) in New York, see Spigel, *TV by Design*.
3. See '"Museum of Art" to be Made Available in 34 Languages', p. 23.
4. See Rivière, *UNESCO Regional Seminar on the Educational Role of Museums*, p. 30.
5. Ibid. p. 31.
6. Ibid.
7. Durand, 'The Use of Cultural and Scientific Films in the Museums of the World'.
8. See Ibid. pp. 102–3.
9. Ibid. p. 104.
10. Ibid. p. 107.
11. Ibid. p. 106.
12. Ibid. pp. 108–10.
13. Witteborg, 'Curator Look at "Expo 58"', p. 41.
14. See Youngblood, *Expanded Cinema*.
15. On Charles and Ray Eames, see Albrecht, *The Work of Charles and Ray Eames*; Colomina, 'Enclosed by Images: The Eameses' Multiscreen Architecture'.
16. See Sutton, *The Experience Machine*.
17. Gagnon and Marchessault, 'Introduction', p. 3.
18. Ibid.
19. See, for example, Fine, 'The Role of Design in Educational Exhibits'.
20. Parr, 'The Time and Place for Experimentation in Museum Design', p. 37. The problem was debated in a number of contributions to the same journal. See, for instance, Id., 'Some Basic Problems of Visual Education by Means of Exhibits'; Id., 'The Arrogance of Artlessness'; Dandridge, 'The Value of Design in Visual Communication'; Burns, 'Museum Exhibition: Do-It-Yourself or Commercial?'
21. McLuhan, et al., *Exploration of the Ways, Means, and Values of Museum Communication with the Viewing Public*. McLuhan and Parker were the main speakers during the seminar, while Barzun was asked to address the concluding remarks. A well-known communication theorist, McLuhan had already published seminal volumes such as *The Gutenberg Galaxy* and *Understanding Media*.
22. The same term was applied by McLuhan to the Montreal Expo of 1967, which he described as a 'mosaic of discontinuous items in which people took an immersive satisfaction precisely *because* they weren't being told anything about the overall pattern or shape of it, but they were free to discover and participate and involve themselves in the total overall thing'. McLuhan, et al., *Exploration of*

the *Ways, Means, and Values of Museum Communication with the Viewing Public*, p. 3; emphasis in the original.
23. Ibid. p. 32.
24. Ibid. p. 37.
25. Lugon, 'Dynamic Paths of Thought', p. 138.
26. Kissiloff, 'How to Use Mixed Media in Exhibits', p. 83.
27. Ibid. p. 95.
28. Ibid. p. 85.
29. Ibid. p. 95.
30. Ibid. pp. 92–3.
31. Malík, 'Principles of Automation in Museum Exhibitions', p. 262; emphasis in the original.
32. See Kissiloff, 'How to Use Mixed Media in Exhibits', pp. 85–7.
33. Katzive, 'Museums Enter the Video Generation', p. 22.
34. See Gardner, 'The Shape of Things to Come', pp. 15–16.
35. Ibid. pp. 16–17.
36. Fagalay, et al., 'Thoughts on the Audio-Visual Revolution'.
37. *Museum News*, 52, 5, 1974.
38. See Griffiths, 'Media Technology and Museum Display'.
39. Beneš, 'Audiovisual Media in Museums', p. 121.
40. See Lovey, 'Museum av: Cultural Affairs', p. 12.
41. Shannon, 'The Icing Is Good but the Cake Is Rotten'.
42. Radford, 'From A to V.', p. 37.
43. Gardner, 'The Shape of Things to Come', pp. 6–8.
44. Ibid. p. 10.
45. Ibid. p. 11.
46. Ibid.
47. Ibid. p. 12.
48. Beneš, 'Audiovisual Media in Museums', p. 122.
49. Gardner, 'The Shape of Things to Come', p. 18.
50. See Mintz, 'That's Edutainment'.
51. See, for instance, Walton Smith, 'Planet Ocean: Applying Disneyland Techniques at a Science Museum'; King, 'Never Land or Tomorrow Land?'; Postman, 'Love Your Machine'. Alan Bryman described a more general process of 'disneyization' of the society: see *The Disneyization of Society*.
52. On these debates see Roberts, *From Knowledge to Narrative*, Chapter 1, 'Education as Entertainment', pp. 15–45.

Part II

The Museum as a Cinematic Space: Museums and Moving Images in the Twenty-first Century

CHAPTER FIVE

From the Museum Experience to the Museum as an Experience

FROM OBJECTS TO VISITORS: THE VIRTUALISATION OF THE MUSEUM

The last two centuries have seen museums gradually opening to a wider audience. Since the 1960s, the social role of museums has been increasingly questioned – criticising in particular museum elitism and conservatism – while the public has acquired an unprecedented centrality in the institution's activities.[1] Many researches in museum studies maintain that today visitors can no longer be considered as passive recipients; they are, instead subjects capable of actively engaging with the exhibits and with the information provided by the institution, and of discussing and negotiating values and meanings.[2] Thus, the emergence of a new paradigm, alternative to the Modernist one, is now widely acknowledged.[3] Among the scholars who noted this radical transformation of museum institutions, Eilean Hooper-Greenhill uses the term 'post-museum' to describe an emerging museum model, which in her view has many positive features, and that she describes as a process or an experience. The post-museum concentrates on the use of objects, rather than on their accumulation, and the exhibition ceases to be the core of museum activities, becoming one among other forms of communication, such as events, discussions, workshops, and performances. The new museum described by Hooper-Greenhill is a venue of exchange where objects are invested with multiple meanings, introducing the possibility of various interpretations and viewpoints, including those of the visitors.[4] As noted by Hooper-Greenhill, such a perspective implies shifting the focus from objects to visitors and their viewing experience: 'it is generally expected that audiences wish to be much more active and physically involved in museums today. The age of the passive visitor has passed, to be superseded by the age of the active and discriminating "consumer" or "client".'[5]

History museums fully incarnate this increased attention for the visitor, and offer a privileged point of view to investigate the processes that affect contemporary museology and curatorial practice, as well as the role of moving images in exhibition design. Indeed, the transformations they went through changed dramatically not only the role of the artefacts, but also the display format and the strategies of attribution of meaning. The last decades have seen a marked increase in history museums and memorials devoted to particularly traumatic events of the (even recent) past, and a corresponding influx of visitors. History museums traditionally selected objects less for their aesthetic or material value than for their capacity to convey the material traces of the past, and since the 1970s they have considerably diversified their exhibits to include items used in everyday life and by traditionally marginalised groups. The so-called 'New Social History' gave a significant impulse in that direction, by focusing on the experience of hitherto neglected figures, such as women, immigrants, and ethnic minorities.[6]

Along with these changes, we can observe a tendency to set the spotlight on the stories and memories of individuals, and a massive inclusion of personal accounts – often recorded in audio-visual form – in museum collections and exhibitions.[7] Oral sources acquired a growing importance for museums. 'Oral history' has been institutionally recognised as a discipline since the 1940s, thanks to the collections of witness accounts from the Second World War carried out by Allan Newins at the Columbia Oral History Research Office, and gained in popularity during the 1960s and 1970s.[8] Alongside oral accounts, audio-visual ones started being regularly collected from the end of the 1970s, in the wake of a renewed interest in the stories of Holocaust survivors, later extended to those involved in other recent traumatic events. This trend causes society to become saturated with thousands of individual accounts that are necessarily partial and inaccurate, due to their reliance on memory and their tendency to replace objectivity with experiential authenticity.

Museums thus gradually opened to the notion of intangible heritage, which UNESCO defines as the group of representations, practices, and expressions, as well as the knowledge and skills that communities, groups, or individuals recognise as part of their cultural heritage.[9] The intangible heritage has been included in ICOM's official definition of the museum:

> [A] museum is a non-profit, permanent institution in the service of society and its development, open to the public, which acquires, conserves, researches, communicates and exhibits the tangible and intangible heritage of humanity and its environment for the purposes of education, study and enjoyment.[10]

As video testimonies and audio-visual reconstructions become complementary or even alternative to objects and material evidences, contemporary museums exhibitions are subject to a process of 'virtualisation': the displays become immersive and environmental, privilege experience, and tend to recreate a 'virtual world' that the viewer is invited to enter and explore.[11] Such exhibition formats became widespread in contemporary memorial museums, as Paul Williams argues: 'precisely because the high stakes associated with the content of memorial museums can produce drama more easily than other types of museums, they are now at the forefront of the "performing museum" paradigm'.[12] Theatrical tropes in museums include stage-set-like reconstructions of historical scenes, as well as the dramatisation of the act of testimony: in live performances or video recordings, real or fictional people that were directly involved in significant events of the past tell their personal stories, accompanying and guiding visitors through the exhibition. Staged historical events, audio-visuals, multi-media technologies, and the planning of immersive and interactive environments turn the museum into a theatrical space, inviting the visitor to take part in a performance. He or she is fully immersed in a context that solicits emotional participation, appealing to senses and bodily experience.

The main aim of many contemporary history museum is, rather than to inform about past events, to actively involve visitors and to solicit their feelings, creating for them a memorable 'experience'.

MUSEUMS AND THE 'EXPERIENCE ECONOMY'

The reference to the theatre underpins Joseph Pine and James H. Gilmore's well-known book *The Experience Economy*, published in 1999. According to the model proposed by the authors, rather than simply selling a product, companies stage a series of events and activities for the consumers, who pay in exchange for being involved emotionally, physically, intellectually, and/or spiritually. Customer attraction does not rely so much on the intrinsic value of the product as on the intensity of the consumer experience. Such an experience is strictly personal, insofar as it stems from the tastes and inclinations of each individual, and is designed to be memorable. In other words, companies sell memories rather than material products. With explicit reference to Pine and Gilmore's proposal, marketing experts Neil and Philip Kotler divide museum experiences into four categories, arranged along a continuum, spanning intellectual, emotional, and visceral characteristics: learning, contemplation, amusement, and excitement.[13] The last element, which corresponds to the extreme 'visceral' plan, is associated with 'Thrill, Adventure, Fantasy, Immersive experience'.[14]

Such interpretations assume that museums are in competition with other actors of the leisure and entertainment industry, also through a variety of activities (conferences, commercial and catering premises, pedagogical activities, and libraries), which complement and accompany the exhibitions as such.[15] According to Andreas Huyssen, the museum has become 'a site of spectacular *mise en scène* and operatic exuberance',[16] marked by consumerist tendencies that debase or cancel the experience of alterity. The total immersion experience proposed by museums is increasingly similar to that of other entertainment venues such as theme parks, as well as media such as video games.

In this scenario, the convergence between museums and other sites of cultural consumerism affects the very definition of their own identity, to the point that a museum exhibition and the experiential dimension that is typical of a theme park are now rarely considered as mutually exclusive, either by the public or by some museum professionals.

Quite to the contrary, the borders between the two are rather permeable. A case in point is the Abraham Lincoln Presidential Library and Museum, opened in 2005 in Springfield, IL. The museum retraces the history of the sixteenth president of the United States through the most salient episodes of his education, civic struggles, and government activities. The display makes ample use of mannequins placed in spectacularly illuminated historical dioramas and is accompanied by a soundtrack of environmental sounds, music, and voices. Even though the distinction between original artefacts and replicas is not always explicit,[17] the reconstruction of the environments is so detailed that it verges on hyperrealism, and the dramatic poses seem to suggest that characters were caught in the very instant they performed those actions. This kind of installation revitalises a number of popular display strategies from the nineteenth and twentieth centuries, such as the wax cabinet, but also uses multi-media and interactive devices, drawing on a twenty-first century imagery. A convergence strikingly illustrated by the exhibit 'The Civil War in Four Minutes', where various TV monitors show the presidential campaign of 1860 using the textual structure of news bulletins and TV ads.[18] Moreover, many of the devices used in museums are reminiscent of theme parks,[19] like the Whispering Gallery, a winding hall with the walls covered with offensive political cartoons and quotes from newspapers of the period, illustrating the great deal of criticism raised against Lincoln and his wife. The asymmetrical picture frames create an unsettling environment, and, when visitors walk through the hall, they hear whispering voices murmuring the cruel things that were said about the president. This produces a disturbing effect, which led visitors to empathise with the discomfort felt by Lincoln.

Daniel Spock notes that even the public circulation plan of the museum, with all the rooms converging around a central courtyard, is quite similar to that of Disneyland.[20] Unsurprisingly, the Abraham Lincoln Presidential Library and Museum was designed by BRC Imagination Arts, the same company that is also responsible for the Disney MGM Studios Theme Park and the Universal Studios Japan.[21]

BRC describes the museum as 'the first truly experiential museum in the world'.[22] A claim driven by promotional rhetoric, which, however, touches a crucial point: the centrality of the notion of 'experience' in contemporary museology. It is very difficult to identify in curatorial discourses a univocal definition of the concept, or of what an 'experiential museum' should be. For sure, 'experience' is not intended in the general meaning of 'museum visit', but entails an intense, multi-sensory, affective, and often interactive involvement. As Patrizia Violi states, the *'experientialist visitor'* is 'a visitor that will, first and foremost, "have an experience" during his [*sic*] visit, rather than being informed, by acquiring more knowledge of past events, which was the principal underlying idea behind traditional museums'.[23]

A number of recurring discursive claims and display practices help to outline the main attributes of contemporary 'experiential museums': the privileging of multi-sensory and emotional engagement over cognitive involvement; the design of immersive and spectacular environments; the emphasis on interactivity and visitors' participation; the central role of storytelling and personal stories; and the extensive use of multi-media technologies.

Many contemporary museums aim to offer to their public a total sensory experience, which gives them the impression of emotionally re-experiencing past events. I agree with Violi when she argues that we should not underestimate the influence of the broader 'spectatorship culture' in which museums are immersed, which renders them 'spectacular media showplaces'.[24] For this reason, 'the main emotion they aim to provoke ... is often one of *wonder*: visitors are to be surprised and captured by spectacular innovations and new presentation forms'.[25]

Museum scholars propose contrasting readings of the notion of 'experience', oscillating between enthusiasm for the new possibilities of audience involvement, and concerns about the anesthetisation of critical reasoning. One tendency in museological discourse is to consider emotional involvement as an opportunity for visitors to become directly and critically involved. The emphasis is on the role of the public, who is called to actively participate in order to achieve a deeper understanding of a given issue. Museum scholars such as Sheila Watson,[26] Kate Gregory and Andrea Witcomb,[27] focusing on historical museums and heritage sites, have highlighted the potential of emotional rather than strictly cognitive aspects in creating a more powerful and meaningful visitor experience. In a similar vein, Alison Landsberg argues for an 'experiential' relationship with mass media products, including museums, and for an acquisition of knowledge based on sensitivity and empathy rather than rational cognition.[28] According to Landsberg, developing such a relationship with past narratives enables the acquisition of a 'prosthetic memory'. The term designates memories with no direct connection with the first-hand experience of an individual, but that are nonetheless essential for the development of his or her subjectivity. 'Prosthetic memory', whose emergence is driven by the forces of capitalism and mass culture, can be transposed to a variety of social and cultural contexts. In Landsberg's view, despite involving some risks, the same process also brings a positive impulse to the construction of individuals and society.

A different interpretation stresses the risks of privileging the affective and emotive experience over the rational dimension. Hooper-Greenhill claims that the numerous 'newly pleasurable technologies of discipline and control' in museums 'have evolved to soften the contradictions and to disguise the inequalities':[29] 'the total experience (in living history or interactive exhibits), the total immersion (in gallery workshops and events), can have the function, in the apparently democratised environment of the museum marketplace, of soothing, of silencing, of quieting questions, of closing minds'.[30] To Hooper-Greenhill, an excessive emphasis on 'experience' radically limits the opportunities for personal interpretation and restores the museum's authoritarian voice. More radically, Hilde Hein strongly criticises the museum's shift of interest from the authenticity of the objects to the emotional and subjective experience. In the author's view,

> the museum's capacity to fabricate experiences (rather than to confirm reality) is celebrated as its raison d'être. The measure of the museum is taken by the intensity of the experience it commands and the degree to which that experience 'feels real'.[31]

Such a 'representation of the museum experience', Hein states, 'purports to highlight the visitor's individual creative freedom of interpretation; but actually, it underlines the manipulative interventions of the museum designer'.[32] The emphasis on experience replaces old monolithic values with a new one.[33]

MOVING IMAGES AND THE MUSEUM EXPERIENCE

How can screens, projections, sounds, and images become instrumental in ensuring the intensity of the viewer's involvement? When it comes to the museum's exhibition strategies, multi-media devices usually have a number of functions. First, they are valued for their capacity to convey directly, rapidly, and synthetically a large amount of information that would otherwise be quite difficult to provide.[34] Films and documentaries can deliver a wealth of information on the historical framework of the exhibit; for instance, historical reconstructions of life scenes from the past have now become commonplace in archaeological museums.[35] Moreover, moving images can illustrate complex scientific concepts or aspects that would be difficult to represent statically, such as the functioning of a piece of machinery (as with the Mutoscopes at the Imperial War Museum). Finally, thanks to video testimonies, personal accounts have found their way into museums, offering a wealth of stories and viewpoints on past events. Besides the function of conveying information, however, audio-visuals may serve a different yet somewhat complementary purpose: when displayed alongside exhibits and artefacts, films and moving images seem to almost 'animate' the display by introducing movement and 'life' in a space that is traditionally conceived as static and lifeless.[36]

Over the last decades, screens, projections, and audio-visual displays have become widely accepted museographic tools. Therefore, they are now not only expected, but even almost mandatory in order to make exhibitions more attractive. Their increased popularity has originated a double trend. On the one hand, screens and projections have become fully integrated with the other elements of the display, such as objects, artworks, display cases, and panels displaying texts, photographs, or diagrams. Ross Parry describes the gradual assimilation of digital media in exhibition strategies in terms of 'naturalisation': 'digital ICT [information and communications technology] is less an afterthought, or something adjunct to the exhibition, but is instead conceived as another quality of the gallery ... it becomes an integral and ambient component of the exhibition'.[37]

In this scenario, moving images are in no way 'privileged' in terms of either content or visibility, but rather constitute one of the many tiles composing the mosaic of an exhibition. However, if screens and projections are now common in museums, designers often employ a series of display strategies that aim to restore what we might call the 'attractional' component of audio-visual media. As is well known, Tom Gunning and André Gaudreault developed the notion of 'attraction' in film studies, building upon Sergei Eisenstein's early theories from the 1920s.[38] Gunning defines the cinema of attractions as 'a cinema that displays its visibility'.[39] As the scholar explains, 'the cinema of attractions directly solicits spectator attention, inciting visual curiosity and supplying pleasure through an exciting spectacle'.[40]

The notion of 'attraction' was applied not only to a specific phase of early cinema, replaced in about 1906 by the cinema of narrative integration, but also in a wider sense to other periods in cinema history:[41] according to Gunning, the cinema's 'exhibitionist' tendencies[42] persisted throughout the decades, emerging in specific practices such as those of the avant-gardes, or as components of narrative films – in some genres (such as musicals) more evidently than in others.[43]

The notion of attraction was also fruitfully applied to other contexts: Viva Paci uses it to analyse how the cinema 'migrated' into museums and was thereby revived as a 'new invention', leading to a new archaeology of the cinematic *dispositif*.[44] Along the same line, I believe that the notion of attraction could prove highly useful in investigating the role of moving images in museum exhibitions. When embedded in displays, films and moving images often produce spectacular mises en scène with a number of immersive effects: by providing a form of pleasure based on shock and 'strong sensations', they engage visitors on an emotional and embodied level, stimulating visceral and sensory reactions.

Notes

1. See Schubert, *The Curator's Egg*.
2. See at least Black, *The Engaging Museum*; Witcomb, *Re-Imagining the Museum*.
3. See Anderson, *Reinventing the Museum*.
4. Hooper-Greenhill, *Museums and the Interpretation of Visual Culture*.
5. Hooper-Greenhill, *Museums and the Shaping of Knowledge*, p. 211.
6. See Crew and Sims, 'Locating Authenticity: Fragments of a Dialogue'.
7. See Cati, *Immagini della memoria*, pp. 111–13.
8. See Charlton, et al. (eds), *History of Oral History*.
9. See UNESCO, Convention for the Safeguarding of the Intangible Cultural Heritage 2003, available at <http://portal.unesco.org/en/ev.php-URL_ID=17716&URL_DO=DO_TOPIC&URL_SECTION=201.html/> (last accessed 30 September 2018).
10. Available at <http://icom.museum/the-vision/museum-definition/> (last accessed 30 September 2018).
11. Kirshenblatt-Gimblett, *Destination Culture*, pp. 3–4.
12. Williams, 'Memorial Museums and the Objectification of Suffering', p. 223. Paul Williams uses the term 'memorial museums' to designate a specific kind of museum devoted to preserving the memory of collective suffering. See Williams, *Memorial Museums: The Global Rush to Commemorate Atrocities*. We prefer here the notion of 'memory museum' proposed by Arnold-de Simine: 'these museums define themselves not just as sites of academic and institutional history but as spaces of memory, exemplifying the shift from a perceived authoritative master discourse on the past to the paradigm of memory which supposedly allows for a wider range of stories about the past'. *Mediating Memory in the Museum*, pp. 10–12.
13. Kotler and Kotler, *Museum Strategy and Marketing*, p. 136.
14. Ibid.
15. See Biel-Missal and vom Lehn, 'Aesthetics and Atmosphere in Museums'.
16. Huyssen, *Twilight Memories*, p. 14.
17. Pine and Gilmore, 'Museums & Authenticity', p. 80.
18. See Serrell, 'The Abraham Lincoln Presidential Library and Museum'.
19. See Englem, 'History with Special Effects'.
20. Spock, 'Lincolns in Latex', p. 95.
21. See the company website at <https://www.brcweb.com> (last accessed 30 September 2018).
22. Ibid.

23. Violi, 'Spectacularizing Trauma', p. 53; emphasis in the original.
24. Ibid. p. 55.
25. Ibid.; emphasis in the original.
26. Watson, 'Emotions in the History Museum'.
27. Gregory and Witcomb, 'Beyond Nostalgia'.
28. Landsberg, *Prosthetic Memory*.
29. Hooper-Greenhill, *Museums and the Shaping of Knowledge*, p. 214.
30. Ibid. p. 214.
31. Hein, *The Museum in Transition*, p. xi.
32. Ibid. p. 147.
33. Ibid. p. xii.
34. See, for instance, Cristiá, 'El puente entre el visitante y el objeto'.
35. See Stogner, 'The Media-Enhanced Museum Experience'.
36. See Martin, 'Making Movies'.
37. Parry and Sawyer, 'Space and the Machine', p. 46.
38. Gunning, 'Attractions: How They Came into the World'; Gunning, 'The Cinema of Attractions'; Gaudreault and Gunning, 'Early Cinema as a Challenge to Film History'.
39. Gunning, 'The Cinema of Attractions', p. 382.
40. Ibid. p. 384.
41. See the essays collected in Strauven (ed.), *The Cinema of Attractions Reloaded*.
42. Gunning, 'The Cinema of Attractions', p. 382.
43. Ibid. p. 382.
44. Paci, *La Machine à voir*, p. 228.

CHAPTER SIX

Audio-visuals in Exhibitions

This chapter presents an overview of the various typologies of audio-visual texts used in museum exhibitions, preliminary to the analysis developed in the following chapters. I will focus on four main categories: archival footage (both 'raw' and manipulated), educational documentaries and specially designed montages, historical reconstructions ('docufictions'), and video testimonies.

ARCHIVAL FOOTAGE

In the first part of this book, we have seen how the footage of the Imperial War Museum had to be transferred from film to cards in order to be shown in the Mutoscopes. In a way, contemporary museums go through a similar process: archival photo and video footage, mostly preserved on fragile film reels, are being digitised in order to be included in exhibitions. This covert operation has a number of implications in terms of how images can be used, shown, manipulated, and received.[1]

One of the first consequences of the greater flexibility of digital photo and video footage is the wider visibility of archives *inside* the museum space: visitors enjoy direct access to a large quantity of images that document historical events and that are seamlessly placed alongside objects or artworks. Moving images and photographs are showcased as if they were concrete exhibits, as witnesses to the past: they seem able to preserve, despite the change of format, their 'ontological' capacity to carry the trace of reality and offer direct access to past events. According to a belief rooted in the origins of the medium, the photographic image creates a univocal relation between the sign and its referent: images are perceived as objective representations of the real world, and hence as an ideal tool of historical preservation. Exhibitions, however, are never neutral: to the contrary, they constitutively imply a selection of the exhibits (be they objects or archival footage), based on their consistency with the museum's wider narrative.

In some cases, the exhibition is designed to problematise the items on display, revealing how images can convey a meaning that is different from what they apparently show. At the In Flanders Fields Museum in Ieper

(Belgium), devoted to the First World War on the Flanders Western Front, the visit begins with the projection of archival footage on irregular, large curved panels. The archival footage shows the euphoric atmosphere and imagery of the Belle Époque. And yet, the exhibition layout seems precisely to question the capacity of these images to actually capture the deep tensions that marked the period just before the start of the war: the surface on which they are projected is shattered, broken, as if to evoke the undercurrent angst and unease of the souls. The conflict, while still latent, is already present as a power that can cause deep cracks in the structure of reality. Rather than stopping at the immediate evidence, the display highlights what is concealed under the appearance of the images. In order to visit the rest of the exhibition, the viewer must go through, both literally and metaphorically, the surface of what is being shown. The archival footage of the Belle Époque is therefore treated as a mediated account of the past that tells us about the modes of self-representation of a given time rather than providing a supposedly objective description.

The second implication of the digitisation of archival footage concerns the possibilities of manipulation. While analogue photography and (later) video (but also Mutoscope cards) were not impossible to modify as such, their digital counterparts are so easily manipulated that they encourage a variety of options and combinations, often – and here is the most problematic point – in a covert way. This problematises the relationship between the archival images and the historical content they convey, emphasising the fact that they are never an objective and unmediated representation of the past.

The display of archival film footage can introduce a great degree of ambiguity between the (supposed) transparency of images and a high level of mediation in the construction of the museum discourse. A particularly representative case in this regard is the Churchill War Rooms in London, which uses a large amount of audio-visual footage and a large number of interactive devices. In this museum, films, photographs, text, graphics, and audio recordings have the same value as objects in the transmission of historical knowledge, and are combined to create a coherent narrative about Churchill's life. The exhibition is largely based on 4:3-ratio, black-and-white silent film footage, which has been digitised and is projected on screens and monitors of different sizes. As stressed by John Pickford, one of the exhibition's designers, this footage has undergone processes such as re-shaping, colorisation, and cropping. What is at stake here is thus not limited to the possible changes constitutively imposed by digitisation; designers moreover deliberately edited film footage to give it a new appearance and a new meaning. Furthermore, throughout the whole exhibition, a visual language was developed that is recognisably mid-20th century in character, consciously evoking the period in which Churchill was alive ... all screens were coordinated to have a mid-20th century, paper-heavy feel; a virtual analogue recalling a pre-digital age dominated by paperwork, filing cabinets, folders, maps, telephones and busy working desks – the stuff of Churchill's life. Content on the screen was treated as real; papers, photos held the attributes of the real thing.[2]

The 'visual style' applied to the whole display contributes to the distancing of the archival images from our time to underline the fact that they were filmed in the past. The exhibition exploits a vast range of digital and up-to-date technologies, but at the same time its visual style is arranged to seem as dated as possible, to fulfil visitors' expectations about the atmosphere of Churchill's age.

At the Historial Charles de Gaulle in Paris, based on multi-media and interactive devices, the archival footage composing the documentary on de Gaulle presented in the first exhibition room[3] was reframed and retouched to emphasise the grain of the image in order to 'convey a certain emotion' and to 'sublimate' the effects of black-and-white pictures.[4] Despite the digitisation of analogue images, the curators tried not to lose the characteristic patina of the pictures, but rather to emphasise it. Defining the patina, with the words of French semiologist Jacques Fontanille, as any time-induced and regular alteration of the surface of an object,[5] it follows that the patina plays a dual role: it constitutes a manifestation of how 'transient time' and usage are inscribed on the external surface of the object, and it is also an expression of 'endurance through time', as testified by the solidity and durability of the object's material.[6] The operation conducted on the archival footage at the Historial Charles de Gaulle therefore goes beyond a simple transposition from analogue to digital: it has a direct impact on the visibility of the traces of the past, through the double operation of cancelling the original patina and simulating a new one. The difference between past and present is blurred, if not cancelled, and their relationship becomes more ambiguous. In other words, what matters here is not the integrity and 'authenticity' of the images as much as the 'aged effect' that the images can produce, as well as their capacity to conjure up, in the words of Fredric Jameson, the 'pastness of the past'[7] from a combination of expectations, beliefs, and tastes that are actually typically contemporary.

Both at the Churchill War Rooms and at the Historial Charles de Gaulle, the recreation of the tone and style of a historical period (revisited to make it more comprehensible to present visitors) proves to be as important as the information provided itself. To make this point is not to question the accuracy, richness, and completeness of the historical sources used by the museums; rather, I am claiming that the emphasis here is more on an overall 'experience' of the atmosphere of Churchill's or de Gaulle's era, as well as on the emotions engendered by objects and videos.

These examples suggest that the use of archival materials is not always a neutral process that presents history in its own integrity, but must be considered in relation to the museums' more general exhibition strategies, and to the type of spectatorial response they aim to solicit.

DOCUMENTARIES

Documentaries are among the most widespread audio-visual documents shown in exhibitions.[8] While museums may use existing documentaries, in many cases they commission or produce them specifically for the display.

One of the most common documentary formats used in museums involves a montage of archival footage accompanied by a voice-over providing textual historical narrative. The narrative often aims to provide a historical context in such a way as to be synthetic, effective, and 'engaging' – hence the use of audio-visuals, supposedly less demanding on the viewer's attention span than lengthy introductory panels. Depending on their length and complexity, but also on the museum's specific choices, documentaries can be shown directly in the museum's galleries or in dedicated viewing spaces equipped with screens and seats.

The films often provide an important part of the information that the museum wishes to convey. For instance, the documentary *Timescapes* at the Museum of the City of New York shows in less than thirty minutes the history of the city from the first settlements to contemporary New York, with the help of archival documents and present-day video footage. The film is presented on three screens in a room on the second floor, minimally furnished with a few rows of seats placed in front of the projection surface. The focus is entirely on the film and there is nothing in the room to distract the viewer from the unfolding narrative. The montage exploits the three-screen structure of the projection surface by alternatively composing a single image or by juxtaposing different materials, such as maps, graphics, archival photographs, and videos that illustrate the story of the city. The large dimensions of the screens ensure the immersive character of the installation, so as to visually convey the metropolis' gigantism. The voice-off narrative provides not only a wealth of information on the history of New York, but also a carefully designed interpretation that emphasises its exceptional growth since its beginnings as a small settlement. It also describes it as a modern, welcoming, and dynamic city, always ready to reinvent itself and to face new challenges.

In other cases, the montage can be more evocative. A case in point are the so-called 'reflection spaces' in the First World War Galleries of the Imperial

War Museum: branching from the main exhibition itinerary, these rooms allow the viewers to pause and collect their thoughts for a few minutes. Alongside a few objects, these reflection spaces showcase films where the montage of still and moving images is accompanied by extracts from the letters and personal diaries of soldiers, read aloud by a voice-off. Rather than providing a historical context, these spaces offer the opportunity to develop a personal reflection on war-related themes, as emerges from titles such as *Should Wars Have Rules?* or *Kill Or Be Killed?*

RECONSTRUCTIONS AND FICTIONAL FILMS

On-screen historical reconstructions are a typical feature of archaeology and history museums, especially if dedicated to historical periods that preceded the possibility of photographic or cinematic documentation. In these museums, the function of films is mostly educational, as they aim to 'bring back' the past in a fictional but scientifically accurate form. For instance, the Virtual Archaeological Museum Herculaneum (Museo archeologico virtuale di Ercolano) near the famous Italian archaeological site, features about seventy multi-media reconstructions of the everyday life of Herculaneum before the city was destroyed by the eruption of Mount Vesuvius in AD 79. Reconstructions, however, are also used to present more recent events and aspects of collective or individual history, either because they were not directly captured by the camera, or because they need to be presented in a more engaging form.

Immersive and realistic on-screen reconstructions are reminiscent of other means of communication used by museums, such as theatre performances,[9] or dioramas and life groups. The last form of display is a three-dimensional reconstruction of animal habitats or human scenes, often used in natural history or ethnographic museums.[10] These illusionistic displays emerged in the nineteenth century as a result of the evolution of museums towards more educational purposes. On the one hand, they conveyed scientific information about the characteristics and living conditions of animals or human groups; on the other, they were highly spectacular and enticing to visitors. In a sense, moving images inherited that power: although dioramas were never completely dropped, Karen Wonders notes that they were frequently replaced by IMAX and OMNIMAX movie theatres or, more recently, by virtual reality (VR) experiments that take up and enhance the illusionistic experience.[11]

Audio-visuals do not necessarily need to be realistic to deal with problematic events. The installation *Shock* in the First World War Galleries of the Imperial War Museum illustrates the devastating impact of the 75 mm cannons that were used at the time. This computer animation shows a body of German and French soldiers advancing towards the weapon and falling under a shower of shrapnel balls before they are able to reach it. The violence of the scene, already stylised despite the realism of the movements shown in motion capture, is toned down even further by the irregular projection surface that follows the outlines of the soldiers, fragmenting the images. However, the sound of gunfire and the groans of wounded soldiers carry a strong emotional impact, emphasised by, and reflected in, the weapon's tangible presence.

The installation aims to communicate to visitors, less than the technical characteristics of the weapon, the effect of its use on human lives. The goal is first and foremost to provoke an unsettling emotional response, even if the content is made less direct and violent by the use of animations rather than realistic images.

VIDEO TESTIMONIES

As mentioned above, museum narratives often include video testimonies. This term was originally coined in order to define the audio-visual recordings collected from 1979 onwards by the Fortunoff Video Archive for Holocaust Testimonies. The collection aimed to give Holocaust survivors the opportunity to tell their own version of the events, and to use these stories in educational products. This pioneering initiative was followed in 1994 by Steven Spielberg's decision to found the USC Shoah Foundation Institute for Visual History and Education, whose wide-scale collection programme has produced an archive containing more than 52,000 audio-visual testimonies.[12]

Thanks to these and other similar initiatives, video testimonies have gradually become institutionalised and are no longer limited to the theme of the Holocaust. Indeed, the collection of video interviews has now become a common means of recording, preserving, and transmitting the memory of (often traumatic) events from our recent past.[13]

Besides the impressive effort of collecting and archiving these video testimonies, such initiatives must also ensure their visibility. Some are available online,[14] used in documentaries or TV programmes, or in the educational programmes of schools and museums.

In the last case, the sense of the videos on display is mediated through a series of choices. First, the narrator tries to organise his or her experiences into a coherent structure. The account also depends on the interviewer's methods as well as on specifically cinematic parameters, such as framing, photography, sound, montage, and mise en scène.[15] For instance, the witness interviews carried out by the USC Shoah Foundation Institute for Visual

History and Education follow a series of rigorous guidelines regarding the articulation of the narrative and even the direction in which the participants are supposed to look.[16] Moreover, the presentation of video testimonies implies that a curator has selected the materials according to the museum's wider agenda and to other, strictly museographic criteria, such as the spatial arrangement and duration of the extracts: audience reception studies show that exhibition visitors tend to pause in front of videos only for a short time, and the materials must be selected accordingly.[17]

Another crucial aspect, when presenting video testimonies, is the kind of relationship that they are meant to establish with the visitor. The interviewer (or diegetic listener) tends to conceal his or her presence, remaining off-screen. The focus is on the relationship between the interviewee and the audience, who becomes the recipient of the narrative and of the commitment to remember it, with all the responsibilities implied by this position. The Los Angeles Museum of the Holocaust insists on the centrality of the public in the installation *Tree of Testimony*, which gives visitors access to the video testimonies of the USC Shoah Foundation Institute. On a wall, about seventy screens of various sizes compose a kind of tree-like structure inspired from the work of video-artist Nam June Paik and from Ben Rubin's data visualisation sculpture in the hall of The New York Times Building.[18] Each screen shows a different video testimony that the viewer can select on an audio-guide.

The co-presence of multiple voices weaves a complex relationship between witnesses and viewers. Thanks to the headphones, viewers are isolated and can enjoy a direct, almost intimate relationship with the witness. However, the proliferation of screens on the wall prevents one from isolating a single face: this strategy contributes to giving a sense of the extent of the tragedy and of the dramatically high number of people involved, while also implicitly hinting at all those who were unable to bear witness.[19]

Paul Ricœur defines the witness as a subject whose authority is ensured by its first-hand experience of the events that he or she is publicly relating.[20] Bearing witness is therefore a performative speech act that both asserts the reality of the narrated event and identifies a recipient.[21] According to Ricœur, the receiver 'gets inscribed in an exchange that sets up a dialogical situation. It is before someone that the witness testifies to the reality of the scene of which he [*sic*] was part of the audience, perhaps as actor or victim.'[22] Thus, the witness 'asks to be believed. He does not limit himself to say "I was there", he adds "believe me"'.[23] The aim is to establish a contract of trust that regulates the interaction between the witness and the audience. Moreover, the *Tree of Testimony*'s many screens seem to enable a mosaic of narratives that implicitly validate one another. The subjectivity of every witness is inscribed in a wider community united by a shared experiential horizon: subjective memory may be patchy and inaccurate, but the emphasis is on a collective narrative that transcends it.

However, there is a downside to this strategy. Alice Cati notes that personal memories preserved in the USC Shoah Foundation are all 'merged into the same story, the same macro-narrative through which the group that founded the project legitimizes itself'.[24] When audio-visual devices become the mediators of cultural memory[25] and determine the creation of a canon, the risk pointed out by Cati is that memories become homologated.[26] This mechanism is particularly evident in the installation at the Los Angeles Museum of the Holocaust: the emphasis on the unique character of each individual story is counterbalanced by the invitation, inherent in the very format of the installation, to consider them in their totality.

The visitor can play a crucial role in this dialectic. The contract of trust highlighted by Paul Ricœur implies the acceptance of reciprocity. In *Tree of Testimony*, the task of selecting the testimony to which they will listen appeals to the visitors' sense of responsibility and forces them to acknowledge their role of recipients. Their choices may be guided by keywords, by the empathy they may feel towards some of the faces, or by chance. On the one hand, the range of possibilities creates a more conscious involvement with the images and the testimony, and highlights the role of the recipient; on the other, the whole operation risks being reduced to something akin to channel surfing. Moreover, it raises the problem of managing the often exorbitant amount of (video) testimonies that saturate contemporary culture and introduces the need of creating meaningful ways to explore them.

Notes

1. On how the digitization of heritage objects alter our relationship with the past, see Treleani, *Qu'est-ce que le patrimoine numérique?*
2. Pickford, 'Making the Churchill Museum', http://www.cassonmann.co.uk/publications/making- the-churchill-museum, last visit 7 march 2015.
3. See Chapter 9.
4. As stated by Christian Puren, curator of the Historial, in a promotional text about Panasonic projectors used in the exhibition, 'Musée des invalides. Projecteurs sur l'Histoire' (our translation).
5. Fontanille, *Soma et Séma*.
6. Ibid.
7. Jameson, *Postmodernism*, p. 19.
8. As it would be impossible to mention the entire literature on documentary cinema, see at least Nichols, *Introduction to Documentary*; Chapman, *Issues in Contemporary Documentary*; Balsom and Peleg (eds), *Documentary Across Disciplines*.

9. On museum theatre, see Bridal, *Exploring Museum Theatre*; Hughes, *Museum Theatre*.
10. See Griffiths, *Wondrous Difference*; Wonders, *Habitat Dioramas*.
11. Wonders, *Habitat Dioramas*, p. 222.
12. On these archives, see Wieviorka, *The Era of the Witness*; Shandler, *Holocaust Memory in the Digital Age*.
13. See Sarkar and Walker (eds), *Documentary Testimonies*.
14. Available at <http://web.library.yale.edu/testimonies/singlewitness>; <https://sfi.usc.edu/watch> (last accessed 30 September 2018).
15. See Shenker, *Reframing Holocaust Testimony*; Stier, *Committed to Memory*.
16. See Shenker, *Reframing Holocaust Testimony*.
17. See de Jong, 'Mediatized Memory'.
18. Lewis, 'L.A. Museum of the Holocaust's Tree of Testimony'.
19. Ibid.
20. Ricœur, *Memory, History, Forgetting*.
21. See Guerin and Hallas, 'Introduction', p. 10. On 'speech acts' see Searle, *Speech Acts*.
22. Ricœur, *Memory, History, Forgetting*, p. 164.
23. Ibid.
24. Cati, *Immagini della memoria*, p. 251 (our translation).
25. On the notions of cultural memory and communicative memory, see Assman, 'Communicative and Cultural Memory'.
26. Cati, *Immagini della memoria*, pp. 251–5.

CHAPTER SEVEN

The Museum and its Spectres

Cinema has always had a spectral dimension. Thanks to moving images, the figures on the screen could be brought back to life – an ambiguous and evanescent one that vanished with the fading out of the light cone.[1] This spectral quality permeated not only the medium itself,[2] but also its subjects: many films of the early cinema are about ghosts, from George Méliès' *Le manoir du diable* (The House of the Devil) (1896) to George Albert Smith's *Photographing a Ghost* (1898). Although it does not directly feature ghosts, Émile Cohl's *Fantasmagorie* (1908), the first animated cartoon according to film historians,[3] evokes in its title the late eighteenth- and nineteenth-century spectacular form known as Phantasmagoria.[4] This connection suggests that, as Murray Leeder stated, 'cinema's supernatural affinities stemmed as much from its continuities with previous media as its newness'.[5]

Lynda Nead describes the unsettling power of early cinema through the metaphor of the 'haunted gallery', which she associates with other forms of expression such as painting and photography, all of which share the aim of animating motionless images.[6] Cinematic images are thus inscribed in a tradition that runs from the myth of Pygmalion to Wilhelm Jensen's *Gradiva* (1903),[7] and it is therefore no coincidence if early films often featured paintings coming to life.[8]

As we have seen in Part I, one of the first functions of moving images in museums was precisely to animate – and therefore to bring back in motion – the items presented in a static form, much to the amazement of the viewers. Also, by virtue of their spectral (that is, evanescent yet 'persistent') nature, moving images in museums bring up forgotten or repressed episodes from the past, as well as painful or socially unacceptable traumas and experiences. Thus, the fascination of contemporary museums for ghost-like figures, often shown by means of moving images, has at least two facets. On the one hand, it is part of the generalised fascination for spectacular forms that characterises contemporary culture. On the other, the spectres haunting the museum rooms point to the institution's concerns about its own identity, social function, and way of connecting the past, present, and future.

The 1990s 'spectral turn' in social sciences has shown that the figure of the spectre can also become a tool of critical enquiry.[9] As stressed by Federico Boni, the ghost is 'an apt conceptual metaphor for the observation, analysis and understanding (or, no less importantly, the recognition) of forgotten or repressed social phenomena'.[10] Individuals, populations, ethnic and social groups who were or still are invisible and marginalised by power, take up a number of spectral attributes, and appear as suspended between life and death, materiality and immateriality, reality and imagination, presence and absence.[11] These qualities have become in turn 'conceptual (theoretical and ... methodological) tools that cultural studies started using in order to analyse an impressive range of social, ethical, political, and cultural questions'.[12] The stake of these 'politics *of* or *for* spectres'[13] is to challenge the established systems of knowledge and power and to propose a new reading of the relationship between past and present, in order to identify what has been repressed or deliberately concealed.[14] This approach invites us to acknowledge the power of action of ghosts, which are no longer seen as passive victims but as agents that can actively influence what is going on in the world of the living.[15]

The next pages will be devoted to the analysis of 'spectral apparitions' in exhibitions. More generally, the tendency towards 'spectralisation' is widespread in contemporary history and memory museums.[16] Therefore, the ghostly nature of moving images becomes a privileged point of observation for examining the politics of memory inside museums.

THE MIRROR AND THE PORTRAIT: THE WIDESPREAD MUSEUM OF THE RESISTANCE IN TURIN

The Widespread Museum of Resistance, Deportation, War, Rights and Freedom (Museo Diffuso della Resistenza, della deportazione, della guerra, dei diritti e della libertà) in Turin preserves the memory of the Second World War in Italy through the testimonies of people who experienced it. The permanent display, *Turin 1938–1948. From the Racial Laws to the Constitution*, illustrates everyday life during the war, the German occupation, the Italian Resistance, and the return of democracy, entirely through a combination of audio-visual, multi-media and interactive devices. Large-scale projections on the building's walls show historical archival footage, while smaller screens, placed behind semi-transparent mirrors, feature frontal head shots of witnesses narrating their first-hand experience of the events. Their voices can be heard through the headphones provided at the beginning of the visit, fostering a more intimate relationship with the listener.

One of the most typical stylistic features of video testimonies is the so-called 'talking head', where the focus is on the face of the subject talking

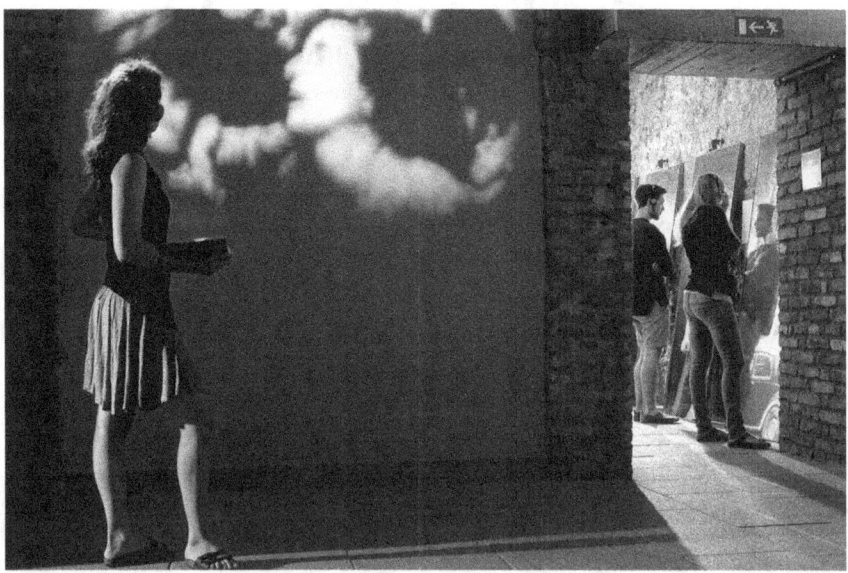

Figure 7.1 Widespread Museum of Resistance: projections on the walls of the building (photo Fabrizio Esposito, courtesy of Museo Diffuso della Resistenza, Turin).

straight to the camera. Literally on display on the museum's walls, video testimonies can be considered as the audio-visual equivalent of the pictorial portraits traditionally conserved in museums and picture-galleries. In his study on the Italian Renaissance, John Shearman shows how some paintings and sculptures explicitly assumed the presence of a viewer, whose function was not only to decipher their meaning, but also to complete their narrative structure and composition, creating an ideal continuity between the pictorial space and reality.[17] The portrait, according to Shearman, was a privileged genre through which painters attempted to establish a contact with the viewer. Its status, however, was ambiguous: on the one hand, it was granted the power to preserve the memory and to ensure the immortality of the deceased; on the other, a poetic motif dating back to the Antiquity, and that had returned into fashion during the Renaissance, insisted on the fatal impossibility to actually 'breathe life' into the represented subjects.

This ambivalence was at the core of a dispute between painters and poets. The former defended the first hypothesis, namely the vitality of the portrait, which was epitomised, according to Shearman, by Leonardo's *Mona Lisa*. Indeed, what generated an impression of life in the portrait was 'the transitive relationship between sitter and spectator, and the fiction of the reaction of the one to the presence (perhaps the entrance) of the other'.[18] In other words, through means such as the individualisation of the subject's facial expressions, as well as a perspective suggesting the presence of the viewer, painters established a direct and mutual relationship between observer and the observed subject. This relationship implied 'the awareness on the part of the sitter of the spectator in front of the picture, the illusion at least of potential communication',[19] and intensified the involvement of the recipient.

Shearman's observations can also be applied to the witnesses presented in the Widespread Museum of Resistance. I could argue that what makes them 'alive' is their capacity to face the viewers and address them directly. The visages of the witnesses are both a sign of their irreducible singularity and an interface with the other. And this 'transitivity'[20], to use Shearman's words, is precisely what enables the dialogical relationship that Paul Ricœur considers as the defining characteristic of the transmission of testimony.[21]

The relationship between the two subjects involved in the testimony is based on trust. As stressed by Jacques Derrida, following Ricœur, testimony differs from proof in that the latter requires a demonstration, whereas with the former we have no other choice but to believe:[22] the witness

> pledges to tell the truth, give his word, and asks to be taken at his word in a situation where nothing has been proven – where nothing will ever be proven, for structural reasons, for reasons that are essential and not contingent.[23]

In the museum, the authenticity of the testimony does not derive from evidence, but from 'a series of negotiations between the witness . . ., the audience, but also the testimony's institutional and social context'.[24] In this light, truthfulness is ensured by at least two means. On the one hand, the museum's institutional framework ratifies the contents with its own authority. Also, the ways in which images are displayed affect their meaning and the relationship that the visitor establishes with the witness who tells his or her story.

At the Widespread Museum of the Resistance, the display establishes a reciprocity between the subjects involved in the transmission of testimony. First, the narrative is initiated by the spectator: the headphones are equipped with sensors that activate the devices, so that the witnesses remain silent and motionless until the visitor approaches. Only when the two subjects are face to face, and the visitor is in a listening position, does the witness start talking.

Moreover, the visages of witnesses appear on reflecting screens that create a double mirroring game. As the screens reflect the projections on the museum walls, historical images are superimposed over the images of the witness and their words, as if to make them visible. Also, the face of the viewer is mirrored in those of the witnesses: the reflection recreates the reverse shot that was excluded from the actual image, and the viewer is explicitly designated as the recipient of the testimony. This is the heart of Shearman's considerations about the ambiguity between the portrait's vitality and its inability to

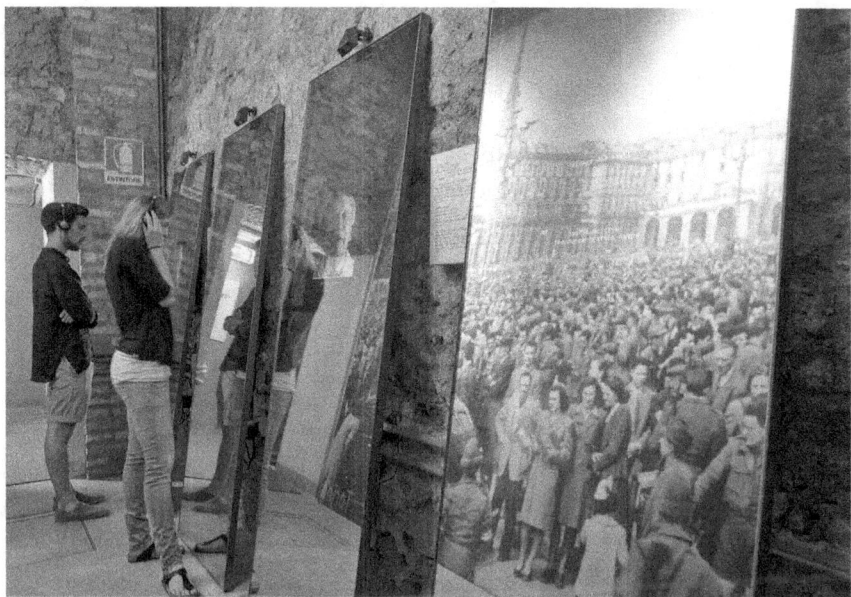

Figure 7.2 Widespread Museum of Resistance: the witnesses (photo Fabrizio Esposito, courtesy of Museo Diffuso della Resistenza, Turin).

convey the 'breath of life'. This ambivalence perfectly fits the situation of the witnesses presented at the Widespread Museum of Resistance, whose figures come to life in front of a visitor, and then return to silence until the next visitor comes near: their task of bearing witness is possible only in the presence of someone who is willing to listen to them.

As a counterpoint to the solutions emphasising the reciprocity of the communication, the witnesses in the videos are not looking directly into the camera but slightly to the side, thereby creating a barely perceptible discordance with the perspective and position of the spectator. Derrida underscores the spectral dimension of the gaze looking off-screen. According to him, the gaze of the witness is that of a ghost looking at us 'without any possible symmetry, without reciprocity, insofar as the other is watching only us, concerns only us, we who are observing it . . . without even been able to meet its gaze'.[25]

Collecting video testimonies is a way of preserving, for future generations, the appearance and the voices of people who are inevitably destined to die,[26] and who in a sense become spectres as soon as their image is captured by the camera. What emerges is the crucial theme of the legacy and of individual responsibility: to Derrida, the gaze of the witness both looks at and watches over us as it hands down its memory to us.[27]

Dominick LaCapra identifies two ways in which the account of traumatic events may have an impact on the recipients, whom he calls 'secondary witnesses'.[28] The first involves an identification so strong as to change them into 'surrogate victims'. The second determines 'a kind of virtual experience through which one puts oneself in the other's position while recognizing the difference of that position and hence not taking the other's place'.[29] This experience generates an 'empathic unsettlement', triggering a transmission of memory in which the subject positively acknowledges his or her irreducible distance from the witness. At the Widespread Museum of Resistance, the relationship between the witness and the viewer is not a given, but is translated into the viewer's constant drive to establish a contact with those men and women on-screen. Since they never really meet the eyes of the spectators, what is emphasised here is the impossibility for the latter to fully identify with the witnesses. The display solutions contribute to delineating a relationship with the past that is not simply an emotional immersion, but generates an appropriation and re-elaboration of the past, with the aim to solicit the building of active citizenship in the present.

The 'Ghosts' of the Witnesses: The In Flanders Fields Museum

The pervasive presence of the video testimony and its centrality in the strategies of museum narrative are exemplified by the format's cross-pollination with another kind of audio-visual text listed above, namely historical reconstructions. The In Flanders Fields Museum in Ieper is a case in point. The museum's narrative focuses on the personal histories of individuals who were involved in the First World War. The exhibition emphasises human experience, conveying a pacifist message with a strong educational purpose: the museological approach aims to arouse empathy as a means to generate in the visitors an ethical response leading them to refuse the war.[30]

Besides original items, maps, and paper documents from the wartime years, a considerable part of the exhibition features audio-visuals and interactive installations. Almost life-size projections of historical characters, interpreted by actors in costume, are placed at various points of the exhibition. They are soldiers, civilians, and also a priest, who narrate their war experiences.

This solution threads a thin line between adherence to reality and historical reconstruction, supported by material evidence and the institution's scientific authority. The witnesses are clearly fictional: they are actors playing the roles of men and women who did exist and experience the events. The actors wear period costumes and uniforms, but artificially reconstructed backgrounds are avoided, and the monologues are based on sources (such as letters or written testimonies), preserved in the museum's archive.

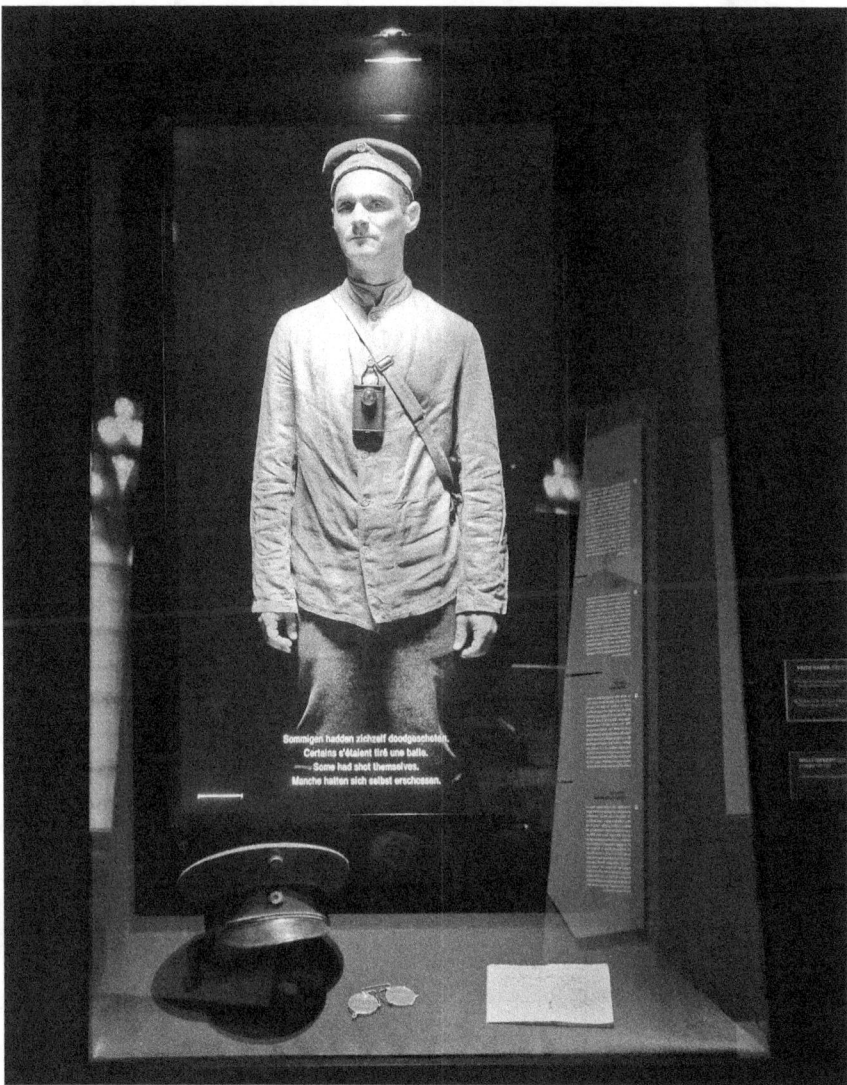

Figure 7.3 In Flanders Fields Museum: the witnesses' display cases (courtesy of In Flanders Fields Museum).

The projected figures are always placed in correspondence with display cases containing authentic historical evidence – mostly personal items of the character: uniform accessories, weapons, diaries, and so on. This combination of filmed narrative and material evidence is a recurring device in contemporary museums, where objects and video witnesses are often placed side by side, as if to mutually authenticate one another.[31] However, the relationship between objects and projections can be ambiguous. It is as if what needed validation was not so much the credibility of the video testimonies as the credibility of the objects and documents on display. An educational text provided by the museum underlines that

> it is important to remember that a picture, a drawing, a letter, a diary, a book or an object are also witnesses to the war and they are just as important as the stylised recordings you watch and hear in helping you to understand the various histories of the war.[32]

This remark clearly shows the level of integration of audio-visual documents in contemporary museums, particularly when addressing younger audiences. The historical discourse conveyed by images is often considered no less legitimate than the one conveyed by objects. This shift is all the more remarkable when the images in question are not drawn from archival footage, but from artificial reconstructions.

The issue is not so much whether the video is intrinsically authentic, but how it is authenticated as truthful.[33] The witnesses on the screens of the In Flanders Fields Museum are explicitly fictional, but the museum institution guarantees the historical accuracy of their accounts, just as it ensures the authenticity of the objects.

Authentication strategies are also played on another level: they concern the capacity of the video testimonies to arouse a feeling of 'experiential authenticity'. The actors' interpretation emphasises the emotional dimension of the events: their bodies and faces communicate the emotions that the events have elicited in them. This effect is the fruit of a carefully designed discursive strategy: not only do the witnesses speak in the first person, but they also look straight in the eyes of the visitors, as if to call them into question, inviting them to acknowledge their role as direct interlocutors.[34] The face-to-face encounter is inescapable, and the presence and attention of the viewer become instrumental to the transmission of the testimonial account. The first person, direct address and deictics clearly designate the 'me' and 'you' positions as well as the 'here' and 'now' that are shared by the speaker and the listener. This is a peculiar characteristic of the historical reconstructions proposed by the In Flanders Fields Museum: whereas witness accounts are typically conjugated in the past tense and establish a chronological and spatial 'there' that is set against our own 'here',[35] the characters of the In Flanders Fields Museum speak in the present tense. This strategy is close to the historical on-stage dramatisations that are also frequently used by museums to re-enact past events.

The viewer and the witness establish a communicative pact that works on an emotional level: the former does not need to believe in the actual existence of the represented figure, but in the authenticity of the narrated experience. In other words, testimonial reconstructions aim to convey the 'emotional reality' of a given event through first-hand (albeit simulated) accounts. The idea is reminiscent of Ien Ang's concept of 'emotional realism', although Ang applied it to a different context, namely an analysis of the reception of the soap opera *Dallas*. Ang proposes to use the notion of 'emotional realism' to underscore that spectators do not perceive a 'denotative' realism (realism of the characters and situations), but the authenticity of the emotions at play and their resonance with the everyday experience of the viewers.[36] The witness accounts presented at the In Flanders Fields Museum play on the same register: past events are filtered through the emotions they elicit, and their impact depends on their capacity to be meaningful for contemporary visitors.

The figures of the witnesses are almost life-size. Their faces are pale, the colours of their clothes desaturated, and their bodies seem aerial as they emerge from the shadow. Their transparency and immateriality are further emphasised by the play of light, as the building's gothic glass windows are reflected on the figures. The projected image is inscribed on display cases, which are classical exhibition devices. On the one hand, the vitrines attract the visitor's gaze; on the other, they inevitably keep his or her body separated from what they show. The visitor's own physicality is called into question as soon as it is denied the possibility to touch, conveying almost immediately a sense of evanescence. According to Derrida, this ambivalence is characteristic not only of the spectre, but also of the cinematic image as such: '*The desire to touch, the tactile* effect or affect, is violently summoned by its very frustration, summoned to come back, like a ghost, in the places haunted by its absence.'[37]

The ghostly quality of the witnesses suggests the idea of an emergence from the past, threading the line between presence and absence. The characters have the appearance of ghosts or, in the words of Arnold-de Simine, of the 'dead speaking from "beyond the grave"'.[38] Suspended between two worlds, they simultaneously offer and deny their presence: 'the figures come forward out of the dark and walk back into it, thereby creating the effect of returning temporarily from the dead to deliver their haunting stories as a warning to the listeners'.[39] They are shown as they emerge back from history:

> [T]hey deliver their messages as though they could only find rest and stop haunting the living once the latter acknowledge their experiences. Even though their messages are not comforting, their very presence on the screen seems to suggest that they are not gone without a trace but can still reach (out to) us.[40]

Painful memories and images of death run through their narratives, made even more unsettling by the blunt evocation of the traumas of a devastating war. The entire museum display is characterised by a sombre, occasionally distressing atmosphere. The pervasive soundtrack is modulated into different variations along the exhibition itinerary. Moreover, the exhibition space is interspersed with monitors and projections of various sizes and formats that function as sources of light in an otherwise dark environment. This is a recurring feature of contemporary museums: if dramatic lighting is a historically consolidated museographic device,[41] the introduction of moving images created a convergence between the white and brightly illuminated space of modernist museums and the projection room plunged into darkness. It has now become fairly common to visit weakly illuminated museums, ambiguously suspended between light and shadow. Discussing art installations, Boris Groys remarks that 'the museum as a museum of media art is no longer the space of absolute visibility. In this museum the invisible, the darkness, the uncertainty of the space at night is also displayed.'[42] Groys observes that the illumination that comes from monitors and projections implies, on a more or less conscious level, a sense of instability, of fear that the lights may go out for good, plunging the entire space into darkness. This certainly appears to be the case at the In Flanders Fields Museum, where the lighting dramatises the feeling of menace and angst that marked the experience of the war, and contributes to depicting it in a negative light, consistent with the museum's pacifist stance.

Phantasmagoria

Silke Arnold-de Simine compares the video testimonies of the In Flanders Fields Museum to the first magic lantern performances or to the séances through which, after the First World War, people tried to contact their loved ones who had not returned from the front.[43] With their eerie and spectral appearance, the figures of the witnesses are also reminiscent of popular entertainments dating back to the late eighteenth century such as Phantasmagoria, which involved ghostly apparitions that both terrified and amused an audience in search of thrills.

The fact that the spectacular tendencies of contemporary exhibitions draw on the forms of entertainment of past centuries is now widely recognised among curators. In an article published in *Museum Practice*, Scott Billing mentions, for instance, the modern reinterpretation of the device known as Pepper's Ghost. Named after John Henry Pepper, the lanternist to whom it owes its popularity, the Pepper's Ghost played with mirrors to project the image of a person (situated outside the audience's field of vision) on a transparent glass screen placed on a stage. Today, similar solutions are used in an increasing number of museum exhibitions, where the hidden actor is replaced by still or moving images, so that switching on or off the lights triggers the appearance or disappearance of the reflected image.[44]

More broadly, according to Arnold-de Simine, the 'combination of education and entertainment in a dramatic, performance-based use of new technologies'[45] of contemporary museums is part of the same tradition as these spectacular forms from past centuries, with which it shares an uncanny dimension that contributes to perturbing the museum narrative.[46]

The reference to Phantasmagoria is a much wider phenomenon that also extends to contemporary art. Thomas Elsaesser notes, for instance, that Phantasmagoria is the closest ancestor of today's moving-image installations, both for its 'environmental' (or shall I say 'immersive') nature, which blurs the spatial separation between inside and outside, and for being based on the aesthetics of 'appearance as presence'.[47] In her study on artists' cinema, Maeve Connolly suggests that since the 1990s, multi-screen installations have been placing the emphasis on an otherworldly dimension[48] through the recourse to ghostly figures and the uncanny disintegration of the spatial and chronological order.[49] About the rejection of rationality that seems to characterise numerous contemporary artworks that explore the history of a place or community, Connolly notes that it could be read as a means to uncover what has been hidden or repressed. If many of the artworks mentioned by Connolly are somehow connected to urban regeneration processes, their ghostly quality seems to activate a kind of 'resistance' and open a 'further' dimension associated with the fear of memory loss.[50] The evanescent yet persistent and pervasive nature of the 'spectre', in its connection with memory and with the uncanny dimension of its reappearance, interestingly points to an intimate connection between museology and the artistic practice.

History museum exhibitions are increasingly populated by shadows. This is the case, for instance, of the Martinitt and Stelline Museum (Museo Martinitt e Stelline) in Milan, which narrates the lives of orphans in two institutes in the nineteenth century. The outlines of children are projected as if they were walking up and down the staircase just in front of the entrance, and the noise of their footsteps, whisperings, and laughter can be heard in the background. The shadow of the visitor overlaps with that of the orphans, so that the former is called to identify with the latter and to share their experience, unsettling as it may be. Similarly, in the First World War Galleries at the Imperial War Museum, the silhouettes of soldiers are projected on the trenches, as if they had returned to haunt the places where hardships and suffering had turned them into shadows.

Ghostly figures are also used to bring historical characters to life, as with the Phantasmagoria that lanternist Robertson used to evoke the assassinated or guillotined protagonists of the French Revolution. At the Palazzo Ducale in Gubbio (Italy), for example, a shadowy projection of an actor playing Duke Federico da Montefeltro converses with an angel (not by chance a creature from an otherworldly dimension) recalling the salient episodes of his life. The technological innovations adopted by contemporary museography act as catalysts of deeper tendencies that re-emerge and re-present themselves in a complex dialectic between continuity and ruptures, identity and innovation.

Audio-visual installations are today a common feature of museum displays, where they integrate more and more homogeneously, losing in many ways the novelty character that captures the visitor's curiosity and interest. More generally, we are accustomed to the diffusion of screens and moving images in a variety of everyday spaces, competing for our attention. In many exhibitions that revive ghostly figures from the past who address the audience, emerges the attempt to restore the image's ability to capture the spectators' gaze and to create an attraction, in Gunning's and Gaudreault's sense.[51] The ghostly nature of the figures, the possibility of modulating the alternation between their presence and absence, but also the wonder created by the technological device itself, become expedients designed to give to the display a power that attracts the emotional and visceral involvement of the visitors.

Notes

1. See Nead, *The Haunted Gallery*, p. 52.
2. See Leeder, 'Introduction', p. 6; Löffer, 'Ghosts of the City'. Friedrich Kittler has stressed the double meaning of the term 'medium', arguing that 'there is no difference between occult and technological media'. Kittler, *Discourse Networks 1800/1900*, p. 229.
3. Crafton, *Emile Cohl*.
4. See Carels, 'From the Ossuary', p. 39. Phantasmagoria became popular thanks to the performances of Etienne-Gaspard Robert, better known as Robertson, at the Cour des Capucines in Paris. Through a combination of rear-projected lanterns and glass slides, Robertson projected figures such as ghosts, skeletons, and demons upon walls, sheets or clouds of smoke. See Mannoni, *The Great Art of Light and Shadow*, pp. 136–75.
5. Leeder, 'Introduction', p. 6.
6. Nead, *The Haunted Gallery*, p. 82.
7. See Stoichita, *The Pygmalion Effect*.
8. See Nead, 'The Artist's Studio', pp. 23–7.
9. Among the extensive literature on the topic, see at least Sconce, *Haunted Media*; Luckhurst, 'The Contemporary London Gothic and the Limits of the "Spectral Turn"'; Gordon, *Ghostly Matters*; Blanco and Peeren (eds), *Popular Ghosts*.
10. Boni, 'La svolta spettrale', p. 196 (our translation).
11. See Blanco and Peeren (eds), *The Spectralities Reader*, p. 2.

12. Boni, 'La svolta spettrale', p. 196.
13. Blanco and Peeren (eds), *The Spectralities Reader*, p. 19; emphasis in the original.
14. Boni, 'La svolta spettrale', p. 197.
15. Ibid. p. 202.
16. See Arnold-de Simine, *Mediating Memory in the Museum*.
17. Shearman, *Only Connect*. See in particular Chapter 3, 'Portraits and Poets', pp. 108–48.
18. Ibid. p. 124.
19. Ibid. p. 143.
20. Ibid. p. 33.
21. Ricœur, *Memory, History, Forgetting*, p. 164
22. Derrida and Stiegler, *Echographies of Television*, pp. 92–4.
23. Ibid. pp. 93–4.
24. Cati, *Immagini della memoria*, p. 109 (our translation).
25. Derrida and Stiegler, *Echographies of Television*, p. 120.
26. See de Jong, 'Mediatized Memory', p. 75.
27. Derrida and Stiegler, *Echographies of Television*, p. 122.
28. LaCapra, *Writing History*, passim.
29. Ibid. p. 78.
30. See Arnold-de Simine, *Mediating Memory in the Museum*, pp. 45–6.
31. See de Jong, 'Mediatized Memory', pp. 80–4; de Jong, 'Who is History?'.
32. In Flanders Fields Museum, *Educational Package*, p. 20.
33. On the authentication of video testimonies in history museums, see de Jong, *The Witness as Object*.
34. Francesco Casetti has defined this direct address to the spectator as an 'interpellation'. See *Inside the Gaze*, p. 16.
35. See Ricœur, *Memory, History, Forgetting*; Cati, *Immagini della memoria*, p. 100.
36. See Ang, *Watching* Dallas.
37. Derrida and Stiegler, *Echographies of Television*, p. 115; emphasis in the original.
38. Arnold-de Simine, *Mediating Memory in the Museum*, pp. 73–4.
39. Ibid. p. 74.
40. Ibid. p. 193.
41. See Barnaby, 'Lighting Practices in Art Galleries and Exhibition Spaces, 1750–1850'.
42. Groys, 'Media Art in the Museum'.
43. Arnold-de Simine, *Mediating Memory in the Museum*, pp. 192–3.
44. Billing, 'Smoke and Mirrors'.
45. Arnold-de Simine, *Mediating Memory in the Museum*, p. 191. On the persistence of Phantasmagoria through the centuries and in contemporary culture, see Warner, *Phantasmagoria*.
46. Arnold-de Simine, *Mediating Memory in the Museum*, pp. 187–200.
47. Elsaesser, 'Entre savoir et croire', p. 71 (our translation).
48. Connolly, *The Place of Artists' Cinema*, p. 86
49. Ibid. p. 107.

50. On this subject, see at least Gibbons, *Contemporary Art and Memory*.
51. Gunning, 'Attractions: How They Came into the World'; Gunning, 'The Cinema of Attractions'; Gaudreault and Gunning, 'Early Cinema as a Challenge to Film History'.

CHAPTER EIGHT

A Walk through Images

The concern for the visitors' itinerary inside the museum emerged during the nineteenth and twentieth centuries. Back then, according to Tony Bennett, museum institutions (as well as fairs and universal expositions) became places for 'organised walking' where the visitors' behaviour and the transmission of knowledge were regulated by more or less pre-determined itineraries, as was the (more or less implicit) imposition of a certain ideology and power relationships.[1] In contemporary museography, where the connection between objects and narrative has become more fluid and open to different interpretations,[2] the movements of the visitors remain nonetheless central for their capacity to activate, follow, and re-design meaningful itineraries.

The link between the museum path and the cinematic *dispositif* could be addressed in light of the broader question of the relationship between moving images and architecture. It was during the 1920s and 1930s that a strong connection between film and architectonic space came into place, both in theory and practice. Sergei Eisenstein's well-known essay 'Montage and Architecture' constitutes a pivotal attempt to ground theoretically the intersections between cinema and architecture.[3] Starting from Auguste Choisy's description of the positioning of buildings on the Acropolis of Athens, as related to the variable point of view of a walking observer, Eisenstein postulates a link between montage and the composition of an architectural ensemble, from the perspective of a moving spectator. Eisenstein considered sequentiality and montage as the two essential conditions of film as a medium and used them as a grid for the appreciation of other arts. His notion of 'cinematism', a series of structural proprieties that are independent from any medium,[4] allowed him to underline the temporal dimension inscribed in architecture as well as in painting.

Moreover, during the 1920s, as Olivier Lugon has explained, exponents of the avant-garde also established a strong link between the cinematic *dispositif* and the exhibition.[5] By experimenting with innovative ways of arranging objects, they conceived a series of displays that were deeply influenced by the dynamism and mobility of cinema. As Lugon writes, what designers envied most about film was the possibility of controlling a sequence of images, of imposing on the visitor a planned progression of pictures, impressions and information. Hence the following challenge: how to extend this principle of unfolding to a three-dimensional space . . . ?[6]

In 1942, the previously mentioned exhibition designer Herbert Bayer described the MoMA exhibition *Road to Victory*[7] with a cinematic metaphor: 'to tell the story dramatically, I wanted to reverse the procedure of looking at the film were the public is still and the film moves. Therefore, in this case, I had the public move through the exhibition.'[8] As Olivier Lugon reminds us, Edward Steichen, the author of the exhibited photographs, reaffirmed the concept more incisively: 'the show is a moving picture . . . where you do the moving and the pictures stand still'.[9]

In the wake of this suggestion,[10] it is possible to imagine a reversal, between the scrolling of the film strip and that of the viewer: in cinema, the images move on the screen and the viewer remains still; in an exhibition, it is the viewer who moves and creates connections between the images. The components of the exhibition as well as the arrangement and lighting of the objects can mimic the cinematic language and its expressive components, such as shots, frames, montage, and camera movements.[11]

Moving images are characterised by a temporality that is intrinsic to their own unfolding, a fixed duration that is independent from the viewer's intervention. However, when featured in museums, they seem to produce an 'interference' with the layout. Indeed, in an exhibition, it is the visitors who determine the viewing time by means of their own movements. This opposition can introduce a conflicting dimension in contemporary museums: a 'shock of temporalities',[12] in the words of Dominique Païni, which requires a constant re-negotiation between the rhythm of the visitor and that of the display. The exhibition becomes a place where 'antagonist speeds'[13] intersect: moving images are usually repeated in loops that the visitor is free to abandon and return to.[14]

The exhibition of moving images thus emerges as the result of a mutual re-definition between spatial, chronological, and dynamic regimes that only appear to be mutually incompatible. This is the dialectics underlying numerous contemporary exhibitions, where linear itineraries are shattered into multiple temporalities by the encounter between the visitor and the moving images.

GALLERIES, PROJECTIONS AND CINEMATIC EFFECTS: THE TRENTO TUNNELS

The Galleries of Piedicastello, also known as the Trento Tunnels, are two former road tunnels that were converted into exhibition spaces during 2007 and 2008 and included into the Historical Museum of Trentino. Mostly devoted to regional history, they hosted a number of temporary exhibitions on various aspects of local history and populations. The first, presented in 2008 and titled *The Trentino and the Great War. The Disappeared People/The Found History*, described the First World War through the experience of ordinary people. As the exhibition epitomised a number of defining features of contemporary museology, it is worth analysing it, despite its temporary nature.

The first operation made by the curator Jeffery Schnapp was to differentiate the two galleries in terms of appearance and function: the first was painted entirely in black, the second in white, as if to mimic the black-and-white colours of the documents, letters, photographs, and film reels dating from the First World War.[15] In other words, the memory of the conflict was first and foremost perceived as a *mediated* if not *media-based* memory, and this defining characteristic determined the appearance of the entire exhibition space. Moreover, the two galleries were distinguished not only in terms of colour, but also in terms of atmosphere, display, and audience interaction: as Schnapp stated, the black gallery, 'emotive in emphasis, would provide an immersive experience of the war',[16] appealing to visitors' emotions and soliciting their bodily involvement. The white gallery had a more analytical nature, and illustrated through objects and labels 'how the memory of the war was constructed and translated into institutions during the post-war era'.[17]

The itinerary started with the black gallery. Divided into five chapters – one for each year of the war – the exhibition presented a series of projections on the walls, on the floor and ceiling, as well as on hanging tulle screens. Curators selected from historical archive materials such as photographic portraits of soldiers and civilians, fragments of letters written by fighters in the army, and extracts from documentary films, including the one that the Italian film pioneer Luca Comerio had shot in the Dolomites during the war. Visitors moved from south to north on a linear path that was slightly bent by the tunnel's curvature, across a space drowned in obscurity except for the light of the projections.

War scenes, family portraits, figures of soldiers, landscapes, and written texts, in black and white or tinted in purple, green, or blue, followed one another on the walls and on the floor, punctuating the visitors' stride. Different speeds were alternated and combined in the gallery: the unfolding of film loops, the alternation between moving and still images, the movement of the public through the tunnel. It was the visitors who, moving forward in the space, created a montage between the various projected images, creating their unique 'cinematic grammar': close-ups and details, full shots and overall views, and different angles (frontal, oblique, from above) followed one another in a dramatic alternation of climaxes and pauses. The visitors walked

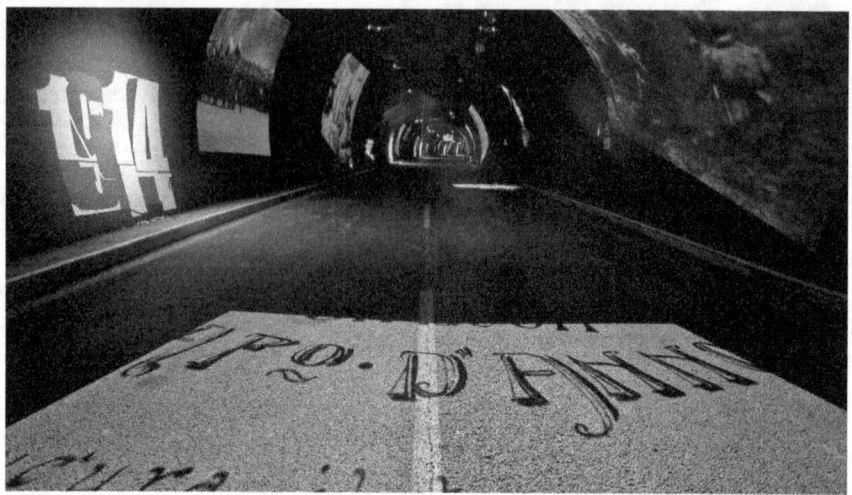

Figure 8.1 Trento Tunnels: the black gallery (photo Pier Luigi Faggion, courtesy of the photographer).

through figures of military and family groups; faces of children and elder people seemed to materialise and stare at them from the darkness; and marching soldiers seemed to emerge from the walls and move towards the visitors. The cinematic nature of the space was evident in the dynamic transitions from one image to another, which stressed the key role of the montage. The cinematic dimension also emphasised the temporal and spatial progression of the visit: the spectators' movement through the tunnel was characterised by changing rhythms and paces. It was therefore the displacement of the visitors' bodies that 'set in motion' the museum narrative.

The emotional impact of these images was enhanced by a variety of dramatic devices: for instance, figures of soldiers projected on tulle screens looked like actual ghosts conjured up in front the observers. The return from the past was assimilated to a kind of 'afterlife',[18] offering a fragmentary and enigmatic historical narrative.

The audience was involved not only as a looking subject, but also as a physical body. The projections covering the entire surface of the galleries literally surrounded visitors: the natural curvature of the walls distorted and almost deformed the images, creating an immersive and enveloping environment. Occasionally, visitors were turned into a projection surface as evanescent images overlapped with their moving bodies.

All the projections were mute, but the sound had a fundamental importance in the tunnel. Extracts of popular writings read aloud by the local elderly were diffused in the space: cardboard cylinders hanging from the

A Walk through Images   109

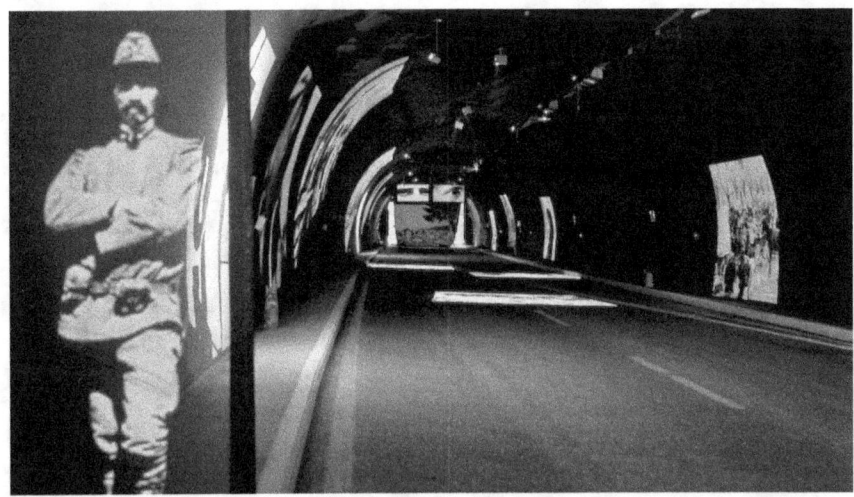

Figure 8.2 Trento Tunnels: figures of soldiers projected on tulle screens (photo Pier Luigi Faggion, courtesy of the photographer).

ceiling oriented the direction of the audio so that the visitors passing under one of them could distinctly hear the voice reading aloud.

As a result, the words written during the wartime merged with the ghostly images of people from the same period, and also with the voices of living persons and the visitors' bodies, thus connecting past and present and dramatising the resurgence of memory and its transmission to future generations.

As Jeffrey Schnapp states, 'the black tunnel resuscitated ... the phantasmagoria'.[19] As we have seen, the reappearance of this spectacular form in contemporary exhibition design is a kind of leitmotiv, especially when considering the role of moving images in displays.

Although the black tunnel show could not be literally considered a Phantasmagoria, it did revisit some of its peculiar features. Phantasmagoria is characterised by the presence of an invisible lantern placed behind a screen and by the movements of the figures, who seem to advance towards the motionless viewer. While the projectors in the tunnels were not entirely invisible, they remained nonetheless concealed by obscurity, and the images seemed to appear from the darkness. Also, unlike the motionless public of Phantasmagoria,[20] the visitors moved inside the gallery: however, they had to follow a pre-determined and linear itinerary, and were free to wander around only to a limited extent.

The black tunnel also created a Phantasmagoria-like effect in the spectator. As pointed out by Tom Gunning, the novelty of this nineteenth-century spectacular form resided in its capacity to manipulate the audience's perception, and to generate a fascination for uncertain and uncanny phenomena.[21] In other words, viewers were divided between the disquieting impact of what they perceived by the senses and their rational awareness that what they saw and heard was nothing but an illusion – an ambivalence that lays at the source of their pleasure.

Similarly, the black tunnel aimed to conjure up a range of uncanny effects to disturb the audience, such as the re-emergence of the dramatic history of the war, the portraits of wartime men and women that seem to stare at the public, the ghostly voices that recited words from the past. At the same time visitors rationally knew that these were merely illusions and theatrical tricks. However, the emotional impact was so strong that some of the visitors, especially among the elderly, were too disturbed to continue the visit.

A FILM IN SPACE: *PEOPLING THE PALACES* AT VENARIA REALE

Peopling the Palaces is an installation created in 2007 by the artist and filmmaker Peter Greenaway for the interiors of the Venaria Reale (Turin), a palace built in the second half of the seventeenth century as a hunting base for the aristocracy. As the title suggests, Greenaway's installation aims to bring back 'life' in the deserted rooms of the palace and to offer a slice of life at the royal court.[22]

Greenaway's original itinerary unfolded through eleven rooms, of which five have become permanent,[23] featuring 100 'archetypal' figures of life at the palace, interpreted by actors and represented as they carried on their daily activities: the servants bustling about in the kitchens, the hunting parties, the court balls, and the final procession. These period characters are treated as ideal and exemplary figures rather than as real people: alongside the duchess, the architect, and the doctor, there is the idiot and the devotee, forming an ensemble of professions, social roles, and moral traits.

The idea of cataloguing, the process of enumeration, and the symbolic choice of the number 100 are a recurring motif in Greenaway's work. In the exhibition *100 Objects to Represent the World*,[24] the filmmaker acted as curator and created a list, halfway between the serious and the ironic, of objects that could represent every aspect of human culture. In the urban installation *Stairs Geneva*[25] he identified 100 locations, and in *Stairs Munich*[26] he illustrated the history of cinema in 100 screens.

If some of the motives present in *Peopling the Palaces* are in continuity with Greenaway's other work as an artist and filmmaker,[27] the fictional representation through audio-visual technologies of real or imaginary characters who 'return' from the past to show historical events is a recurring interpretive strategy of contemporary museums. Exhibition design and art installation converge in a project that epitomises the close and multi-faceted connections between art and historical/educational displays, not only in terms of tools and solutions, but also in terms of communication strategies.

The original installation started with the presentation of the court in the first room of the palace and included the two rooms of the kitchens, the four rooms of the private lodging of the duke, the haunting scene, and the two rooms of the procession of the court.[28] Greenaway's audio-visual narrative is composed of fragments of varying length, whose spatial distribution and presentation change from room to room. In the kitchens, for instance, we find a large central screen flanked by twenty smaller transparent ones, symmetrically arranged to the sides. During the dialogues, the images of the head chef and his assistants are scattered and multiplied across the different projections, whose reflections on the ceiling create a highly evocative spectacle. The spectral effect is emphasised by the interplay of transparencies and overlays: the images' evanescent quality is used as a means to create the characters' spectral appearance: they seem to return from past centuries to haunt the palace and share its spaces with the visitors.

The presentation of the moving images underscores their insubstantial quality, almost in counterpoint to the solidity of the objects and artefacts

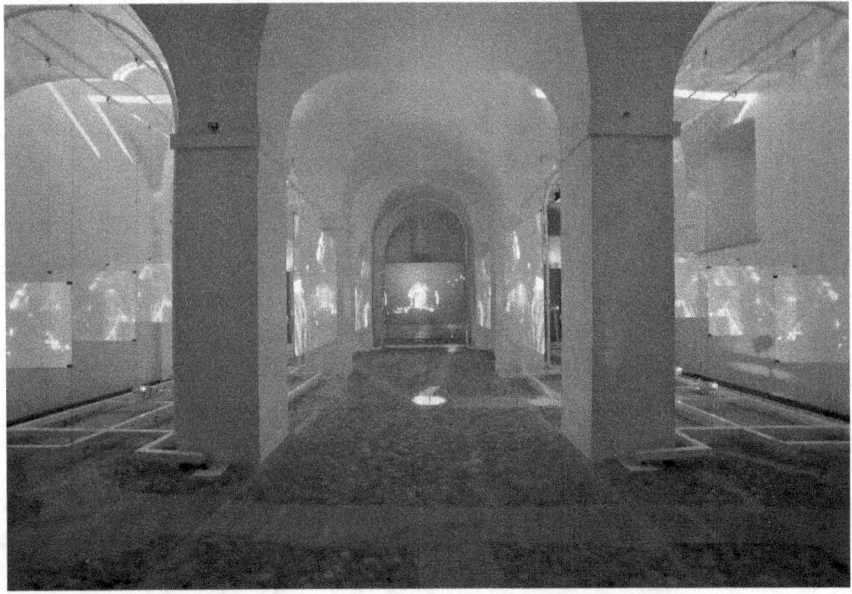

Figure 8.3 Installation *Peopling the Palaces*: the kitchens (courtesy of La Venaria Reale, Turin).

that usually constitute a museum display. The very architecture of the venue seems to lose its solidity and acquires an ambiguous status. The projected figures blend with and overcome the tangible architectural surface: the walls no longer delimitate the room, but give access to a further space, both evanescent and teeming with life.

In its combination of reconstruction and invention, this audio-visual narrative can in a sense be considered to be the heir of an older narrative form, the historical novel, which for Frederic Jameson is actually the other side of the ghost story:

> [W]hat is the [historical novel], indeed, if not an attempt to raise the dead, to stage a hallucinatory fantasmagoria [*sic*] in which the ghosts of a vanished past once again meet in a costumed revel, surprised by the mortal eye of the contemporary spectator-voyeur?[29]

For Jameson, the ghost story is always rooted in a physical space, primarily a home, 'a building of some antiquity, of which it is the bad dream'.[30] If the Venaria Reale Palace appears to the visitors as a haunted building, the initially uncanny experience of encountering these characters from the past soon turns into a curious cohabitation, in which the visitors can peek at the ghosts' lives, intrigues, and secrets. And the latter are precisely the aspects to which Greenaway chose to draw attention, so that the spectator is occasionally made to feel like a voyeur spying on the fragments of someone's private life: for instance, in the initial version of the installation, the figures of sleeping dukes were projected on the bed, at a short distance from the public.

The moving images and the space of the Venaria Palace in which they are projected are inextricably entwined. Greenaway developed the installation by bearing in mind the original function of the different rooms, and the spaces themselves – from the kitchens to the private lodgings – determined the action that was to be staged inside of them.

The full integration of moving images in the palace's itinerary can be seen as soon as in the first room, where the presentation of the court takes place: where ten characters, projected on six large screens disposed in a circle, introduce themselves to the visitors and chat with them. These eighteenth-century characters move around freely, sometimes disappearing, but re-emerging again at some point along the itinerary. Thus, from the very beginning, the visitor of this historical site also becomes the spectator[31] of a 'film in space' whose plot – which narrates the life at the court – unfolds even when the characters are not directly present, by virtue of the very possibility of their reappearance.

Although the various scenes could easily be brought together and composed into an actual film, their significance is precisely due to their being scattered across various and not necessarily contiguous rooms. The visitors/spectators connect the presence and absence of the moving images, in a montage that does not only concern the chronological order, but rather the spatial continuities and discontinuities of the projections, whether presented in adjoining rooms (as for the duke's lodgings in the original installation), or interrupted by rooms that contain 'only' furniture and artworks.

One of the narrative's dramatic devices consists in the transition from rooms devoid of projections, ideally silent, to crowded choral scenes of court life, creating a contrast between the quiet composure of the palace as a contemporary historical site and its past hustle and bustle. In other cases, the moving images create connections between spaces. During the court procession, the characters move between two rooms, disappearing from one only to reappear, shortly after, in the next. Their movement underscores the continuity between the two contiguous rooms, in a mise en abyme of the visitor's own movements. Also, the projections communicate with one another as well as with the objects and artworks on display. In the original installation, small portraits of ladies-in-waiting, interpreted by actresses, were projected on the walls of the private lodgings. The ladies dialogued with the 'real' portraits hanging from the walls, either by copying their iconography or by literally addressing them.

Visitors are free to design their own itinerary inside the palace, reconstructing the life of the time by intertwining the narrative of the moving images with the stories suggested by the motionless furniture and artworks.[32] The cinematic nature of the installation is at play not only through the presence of an actual audio-visual narrative, but also through its dynamic arrangement from one room to the next. As stated by Giuliana Bruno about Greenaway's installations – and *Peopling the Palaces* is no exception – the sequential organisation of cinema becomes the principle though which to read the exhibition.[33] Thus, the 'museographic walk'[34] and the flow of cinematic images are connected by a double thread, in a spatial montage in which the viewer acts as the element of junction.

NOTES

1. Bennett, *The Birth of the Museum*, p. 6.
2. See Hooper-Greenhill, *Museums and the Interpretation of Visual Culture*.
3. Eisenstein, 'Montage and Architecture'.
4. See Albera, 'Introduction', p. 12.
5. See Lugon, 'Dynamic Paths of Thought'.
6. Ibid. p. 131.
7. The exhibition was curated by Herbert Bayer, with photographs by Edward

Steichen. It was held from 21 May to 4 October 1942 at the MoMA in New York. See 'Road to Victory: A Procession of Photographs of the Nation at War'.
8. Cited in Lugon, 'Dynamic Paths of Thought', p. 135.
9. Ibid.
10. On the relationships between cinema, architecture, and exhibition, see also Bruno, *Atlas of Emotion*.
11. See also Bal, 'Exhibition as Film'.
12. Païni, *Le temps exposé*, p. 17.
13. Dubois, 'A "Cinema Effect" in Contemporary Art', p. 17.
14. Ibid.
15. Schnapp, 'Unlevel Crossings', p. 26.
16. Ibid.
17. Ibid.
18. The term is resumed by Aby Warburg's *Nachleben*, which indicates the survival, or the re-emerging of images from the past, with their nature of revenants. An idea that breaks with linear transmission patterns and suggests a different temporality in the history of images, made of breaks and returns, of repetitions and differences. See Warburg, *Der Bilderatlas: Mnemosyne* and Johnson, *Memory, Metaphor, and Aby Warburg's Atlas of Images*.
19. Schnapp, 'Unlevel Crossings', p. 27.
20. See Mannoni, *The Great Art of Light and Shadow*, pp. 136–75.
21. Gunning, 'Fantasmagorie et fabrication de l'illusion'.
22. See the catalogue of the exhibition: Greenaway, *Ripopolare la Reggia/Peopling the Palaces*.
23. Namely the presentation of the Court (room 1), the kitchens (rooms 9 and 10), and the procession (rooms 28 and 29).
24. See the catalogue of the exhibition: Greenaway, *100 Objects to Represent the World*.
25. See Greenaway, *The Stairs 1: Geneva, the Location*, catalogue of the exhibition.
26. See Greenaway and Schweeger (eds), *The Stairs 2: Munich, Projection*, catalogue of the exhibition.
27. On Greenaway's installations, see Pascoe, *Peter Greenaway: Museums and Moving Images*.
28. Only the presentation of the court, the kitchens, and the procession are included in the permanent exhibition.
29. Jameson, *Signatures of the Visible*, p. 124.
30. Ibid. p. 123.
31. See Chittenden, 'The Cook, the Marquis, his Wife, and her Maids', p. 268.
32. On the interpretation of the meanings of objects in museums, see Pearce, *Interpreting Objects and Collections*.
33. Bruno, *Atlas of Emotion*, p. 316.
34. Ibid. p. 154.

CHAPTER NINE

New Interpretations of the Movie Theatre

Maeve Connolly has noted a widespread tendency among artists to produce, inside art venues such as exhibition galleries or pavilions, what she calls 'cine-material installations', that is, works that recreate the architecture of cinema. These artworks do not limit to create 'black-boxes' inside the gallery space, but explore and elaborate more radically on the structure of movie theatres.[1] According to Connolly, the reference to the cinema as a venue for collective viewing enables an investigation of the reception of contemporary art. She stresses that, by evoking a different viewing context, art rethinks and reconfigures its relationship with its own viewers or public:

> [I]t is . . . possible to identify a greater emphasis on the collective and social dimensions of reception, to the extent that cinema may even be understood specifically for its historical associations with an ideal public sphere. In other words, cinema history (rather than film theory) seems to hold an appeal for some practitioners because it may offer models or prototypes for the community.[2]

Designing their works on the model of the architectures of movie theatres, artists explore the possibility of restoring a social space within the gallery, in a context where also film consumption has become more and more an individual and solitary practice. Erika Balsom argues that moving-image installations (part of what she calls 'othered cinema')[3] draw the attention back to the social and shared dimension of reception:

> [T]he othered cinema evinces a distinct emphasis on cinema as a public institution throughout its many facets. The museum and gallery emerge as public sites of spectatorship in an era marked by individual, domestic viewing, while many artists take up questions of collectivity, sociality, and publicity in their work.[4]

In particular, in Balsom's view, installations of this kind are charged with a sense of nostalgia for the cinema not only in terms of its material support, the film reel, but also as a public space, a site of relationality now gradually replaced by forms of individual viewing.[5] The reference to forms of fruition historically associated with the cinema is therefore associated with the role of public sphere that the latter has assumed since its origins.[6]

Very similar phenomena can be observed in contemporary museums, many of which started, from the beginning of the nineteenth century, including auditoriums for film screenings or actual movie theatres[7] (as for IMAX theatres, which have now become commonplace, especially in science museums). However, I am especially interested in exhibitions that 'incorporate' the movie theatre – or, conversely, in movie theatres that 'colonise' the exhibition space.[8] I will investigate exhibitions that blur the distinction between cinematic and museum reception, and where the display itself takes on the form of a 'movie theatre'. The introduction inside the museum of a space that follows the rules (or at least some of the rules) of a movie theatre implies a very specific management of time, especially when the projection has a clear beginning and end, and introduces the possibility of regulating, more or less strictly, the visitor's itineraries.

These practices imply also a problematic issue. As Balsom stresses, the tendency of museums of seeking spectacular effects in order to attract a wider public: 'cinema's entry in the museums is ... a matter of that institution's desire to (post)modernize by proving an experience of technological seduction that would guarantee box office revenues'.[9] Today, spectacular presentation forms and a bold use of technology are used by museums as a mean to surprise and captivate visitors. The case studies examined in the following pages epitomise how the cross-pollination between the viewing experiences of the museum and the cinema may involve a spectacular dimension, positioning museums among the other sites of entertainment and problematising their very identity.

'A BIT LIKE A LARGE CINEMA': THE BIG PICTURE SHOW AT THE IMPERIAL WAR MUSEUM NORTH

'A globe shattered into fragments', whose ruins are recomposed into a combination of inclined planes, curves, and edges, interlocked and divided into three sections representing the elements of earth, air, and water:[10] here is, in a few words, Daniel Libeskind's project for the Imperial War Museum North, in Manchester. Aiming to give an architectural form to the devastations of war, Libeskind designed a dramatic and fragmented structure that could not fail to affect the museum's interior spatial configuration. The floor of the central exhibition space, on the first level, is slightly curved, and all the columns are slanted with respect to the perpendicular plane, conveying a sense of unease and of altered balance. The continuity of this space is in turn broken by the so-called 'silos' – six exhibition areas, enclosed by walls more than 10 m high, each focusing on a specific aspect of the conflict, such as the experience of soldiers and the life of civilians during wartime, and contributing to the configuration of an irregular space that is devoid of reference points. Several large exhibits stand in the centre of the space: a tank, a jet, a few military vehicles, and some pieces of artillery. What prevails is a complex spatial fragmentation that imposes on the visitor a likewise fragmented and non-linear space filled with deviations and asperities. Audio stations, screens with audio-visual material and interactive devices are distributed so as to seamlessly integrate the lettering on the walls and display cases. Architectural critic Giles Worsley comments that the resulting effect is 'surprisingly low-tech but impressively effective'.[11]

At regular intervals, the main room is plunged into darkness, and a recorded voice reminds us that 'every image, every document, every voice is part of someone's story'. This announcement marks the beginning of the Big Picture Show, an hourly multi-media performance that literally invades the entire exhibition space: a system of projections accompanied by an audio commentary covers in images not only the blank spaces on the walls but also the display cases, the artefacts, and even the visitors. The integration between the images of the Big Picture Show and the rest of the exhibition creates a complex and stratified spatial configuration. The room itself becomes a screening surface, although the exhibits are never entirely concealed: the floor lighting outlines the objects placed at the centre of the space, while the display cases on the walls remain visible under the projections that enfold them.

'When the Big Picture Show is on, the Main Exhibition Space is a bit like a large cinema', we can read on the museum guide.[12] What are then the forms of negotiation between the two *dispositifs*? When the walls are turned at regular intervals into projection surfaces, the dynamic at play is at least two-fold: spatial and temporal. Spatially, we have an extension (or, to quote from the title of Gene Youngblood's well-known study, an *expansion*[13]) of the projection area to the entire exhibition room, exhibits and visitors included. In other words, what we have here is not a screen inscribed in an environment, but an environment that becomes a screen. Visitors must face a series of montage strategies that involve both the sequence of images and the individual projections that compose the overall show.

A further level of montage is provided, at least potentially, by the visitor's movements: unlike in a movie theatre, he or she is free to move around, to explore the environment following independent, individual or collective paths, and to carve out a personal and meaningful itinerary. However, in practice, visitors do not usually behave this way: from what I could observe, they rather tend to stand still, sit down, or quickly move towards a position that offers good visibility, joining their former group or creating new ones before scattering again at the end of the show. This behaviour, besides, is already foreseen in the museum's design, which may explain the benches placed against the walls or the following note in the brochure: 'we advise you to remain still while the show is on'.[14] Another guide, addressed to schools, does indicate that 'ideally the Big Picture Show should be experienced by walking around the Main Exhibition Space'.[15] However, this advice is immediately followed by a list and map of best positions from which one can watch the show as a group without having to move around, a suggestion most likely prompted also by security reasons. These more or less explicit (and more or less contradictory) directions orient the traditional forms of museum reception towards more cinematic forms, somewhat inhibiting more complex modes of negotiation between the two *dispositifs*, such as the visitor's mobility during the show.[16]

Moreover, the fact that the Big Picture Show is presented at regular intervals somehow mimics a typical movie schedule. The Imperial War Museum North offers a programme of audio-visual performances, approximately fifteen minutes long, presented throughout the day according to a predetermined programme that is communicated to visitors beforehand. Each show is identified by a title and a synopsis, so that the public could potentially choose the time of their visit according to the schedule. This is quite a radical change: as opposed to the traditional 'open' mode of museum reception, these schedules determine a temporality that is imposed from the outside, as in a movie theatre – to the point that the institution needs to remind the visitors that they are free to choose what (not) to watch, and when: 'if you don't want to see the Big Picture Show you can leave at any time'.[17]

Though visitors tend to behave as if they were attending a film projection, it does not mean that the museum is altogether turned into a movie theatre. Cinema viewing does not mechanically overlap with museum viewing, cancelling its specific features, but rather the two *dispositifs* intertwine, generating original configurations. During the Big Picture Show, visitors are fully immersed[18] in the environment as their body is turned into a projection surface. They are therefore physically implicated, and their own corporality is both confirmed (as they are actual projection surfaces) and diluted in the wider environment that 'incorporates' them.

The consequences become all the more evident when considering the specific contents of the different shows. They combine heterogeneous elements, such as archival footage, animations, written documents, interviews, and specially shot films. The soundtrack makes use of the oral testimonies preserved in the Imperial War Museum audio archives: original audio recordings (such as radio broadcasts), excerpts from autobiographies read by actors, or dramatic sounds related to war. For instance, the show *The War at Home* uses original materials to reconstruct the experience of families who stayed at home during the Second World War, and *Weapons of War* focuses on the experience of producing, using, or falling victim to weapons throughout the last centuries. The latter mixes photographs from the Imperial War Museum archives with evocative images and graphic art, accompanied by a soundtrack of audio recordings and 'original war sounds', as announced on the brochure: air-raid sirens, explosions, and gunshots. The seamless flow of images and sounds from different historical contexts and times makes it quite difficult to identify the sources.[19] For instance, the section on rifles and bayonets skips from First World War trenches to contemporary armies, while the one about tanks uses footage from both world wars. More than the recognition of the individual sources or historical events, what counts here is the overall discourse on war for which the museum is responsible.

The contents of the Big Picture Show are not centred on the objective unfolding of the events or on the desire to investigate their causes, but on how these events were perceived by and affected the lives of the individuals involved.[20] An emblematic case in point is *Service and Separation: A Volunteer Nurse in Afghanistan*, which juxtaposes images of military camps and domestic scenes shot by the nurse herself or by her family, with a soundtrack underscoring the emotional impact. In *Remembrance*, the focus is on the personal story of the family and friends of a British soldier who died in Iraq. What is emphasised here is the image's capacity to illustrate individual stories, to evoke dramatic events, and to elicit an emotional involvement, making history and memory 'alive'. This aim is made quite explicit in the presentation of the Big Picture Show: 'it immerses you in the heart of the action, creating a complete sensory experience which is totally involving, and often very moving'.[21] The emotional impact of this experience is further asserted by the warning broadcast at the beginning of each screening, which invites children and faint-hearted viewers to leave the room. As advertised on the museum brochure addressed to schools, 'none of the images or sounds are in themselves unsuitable for children, but the accumulation of them, and the overall experience of being in the space may be difficult for some'.[22] What is crucial in the reception of the various audio-visual texts proposed by the Big Picture Show is not so much the analytical insights provided by each individual segment as the potentially overwhelming emotional impact of the whole.[23]

A MOVIE THEATRE INSIDE THE MUSEUM: THE HISTORIAL CHARLES DE GAULLE

The Historial Charles de Gaulle in Paris is presented on its own website as 'an audio-visual monument'.[24] And indeed there is something monumental to this elliptical space at the heart of the museum, shaped like a reversed dome and hosting a movie theatre with five screens collectively measuring 20 m x 2 m and accommodating more than 200 people. The movie theatre is not meant to be an external addition to the museum visit, but an integral component of it, a focal point to which the visitors are directed immediately after the introductory room of the exhibition.

The screening provides some basic information that helps the public understand the rest of the exhibition, in the form of a biographic documentary (an 'emotional documentary', as it is called in the presentation text), simply titled *Charles de Gaulle* (Olivier L. Brunet, 2005–8). It proposes a thirty-minute long portrait of de Gaulle, based on archival photographs and footage. The multi-projection display exploits virtually every possible combination of images, making an explicit reference to Abel Gance's 'Polyvision', a three-screen projection device designed by the French director to show his film *Napoléon* (1927) – linking de Gaulle to Napoleon.[25] Gance's system involved the simultaneous projection of three different images, playing with symmetries or contrasts to stress the pathos of several crucial episodes. Through the reference to Polyvision, the screen of the movie theatre of the Historial therefore becomes implicitly inscribed in a tradition of experimentation with multi-screen projections (from László Moholy-Nagy's 'polycinema'[26] to Gene Youngblood's theories on 'expanded cinema'[27]), but also evokes the large-scale projections set up by the Lumière brothers at the Exposition Universelle of 1900, as well as the Cinerama and the IMAX screens.[28]

In the movie theatre of the Historial Charles de Gaulle, the film requires the audience to sit still and silent from the beginning to the end while it receives the necessary information to continue the visit. Moreover, the movie theatre constitutes the architectural core of the entire museum. Inserted in an architectural context with a circular plan specially conceived by the architects Alain Moatti and Henri Rivière, the Historial is divided into three main areas that differ in terms of spatial collocation, themes, and modes of display. The immersive cinema hall is surrounded by the so-called 'ring of history': a circular corridor one hundred metres long, with striped glass walls that surround and envelop the visitor, on which audio-visual materials narrating the main events of de Gaulle's epoch are projected. In the third space, the 'alcoves', various types of interactive devices allow for exploration of de Gaulle's figure and political activity. The cinematic experience is therefore physically and cognitively at the heart of the museum experience: on the one hand, this choice is perfectly in line with the concept of the museum, which gives prominence to audio-visual elements; on the other, it carries a number of implications on the kind of message that is being conveyed and on the way it is meant to be received, as I will explain in the following paragraph.

An 'Emotional Biography'

The shape of the movie theatre at the Historial Charles de Gaulle is designed to plunge the viewer into an immersive and comfortable environment – a quiet space, as it is described in the presentation brochure.[29] This perception is enhanced by the alveolar wooden structure, inset with more than 2,000 light bulbs, and in which the seats appear to be floating in space. The elliptically shaped screen stretches out up to the sitting area, suggesting a kind of continuum between the two. As in many contemporary museums, the structure draws attention to its own configuration before its content, and becomes itself an object of attraction and fascination.[30]

The documentary presents in chronological order the main episodes of de Gaulle's life and political career. A voice-over alternates with original recordings of the General's speeches, and the solemn music soundtrack is interspersed with 'spectacular' examples of wartime cacophony, like bombs or sirens. The film makes use of all the possible combinations allowed by multi-projection systems. A variety of montage effects are adopted in the documentary, with a marked preference for symmetrical composition and for the repetition of frames from one screen to the next.

The most recurring framings and camera movements are tracking shots running across ecstatic crowds or following marching troops, high-angle shots on crowded squares, and head shots and low-angle bust shots of de Gaulle. The language of the documentaries and media images of the time is reinterpreted in a spectacular form, composing an epic and celebratory portrait with an explicit celebratory intent and the aim to inform by playing on the public's emotions.

The configuration of the movie theatre on the one hand and of the contents and communication strategies on the other jointly contribute to defining the position of the viewer: sitting in an architectural structure that is both solemn and reassuring, almost surrounded by the screens conveying the epic history of de Gaulle and of France, the viewer becomes almost literally part of what is being shown, and is encouraged to identify with the crowd that celebrates the General. The powerful sense of wonder that the device aims to create in the viewer, along with the awe-inspiring treatment of the figure to which the memorial is devoted, produces a deep emotional impact on the entire museum experience, even though the continuation of the visit occasionally shifts from collective viewing modes to more individual and interactive ones.

Notes

1. Connolly, *The Place of Artists' Cinema*, Chapter 5, 'Cine-material Structures and Screens', pp. 165–212. On this subject, see also Balsom, *Exhibiting Cinema in Contemporary Art*; Bishop, *Installation Art*.
2. Connolly, *The Place of Artists' Cinema*, p. 10.
3. Balsom draws from Bellour's 'other cinema', and defines with the term of 'othered cinema' the gallery-based practices that 'represent a site at which the cinema has become other to itself. They differ from it and yet share elements in common as well.' Balsom's aim is to 'interrogate the ways in which the boundaries between media are both articulated and blurred, to see the pair convergence/specificity as existing in a dialectical tension with one another that allows for a new thinking of historicized ontologies rather than a dissolution, or even disappearance, of a given medium'. See *Exhibiting Cinema in Contemporary Art*, pp. 16–17.
4. Ibid. p. 187.
5. Balsom, 'Screening Rooms', pp. 26–7.
6. See Hansen, *Babel and Babylon*.
7. See part I of this volume.
8. We refer here to the concept of 'relocation', proposed by Francesco Casetti to refer to 'the process in which a media experience is reactivated and re-purposed elsewhere in respect to the place it was formed, with alternate devices and in new environments' ('The Relocation of Cinema'). See also Casetti, 'Cinema Lost and Found: Trajectories of Relocation'.
9. Balsom, 'Screening Rooms', p. 35.
10. See the museum presentation on Studio Libeskind's website: <http://daniel-libeskind.com/projects/imperial-war-museum-north> (last accessed 30 September 2018).
11. Worsley, 'A Globe Ripped to Pieces'. On the design of spaces at the Imperial War Museum North, see MacLeod, et al., 'New Museum Design Cultures'.
12. Imperial War Museum North (IWM North), *Accessible and Easy to Read Guide*.
13. Youngblood, *Expanded Cinema*.
14. IWM North, *Accessible and Easy to Read Guide*.
15. IWM North, *Your Visit Learning Resources*.
16. See MacLeod, et al., 'New Museum Design Cultures'. On the Big Picture Show, see also Hoskins and Holdsworth, 'Media Archaeology in/of the Museum', pp. 31–7.
17. IWM North, *Accessible and Easy to Read Guide*.
18. On the concept of 'immersion', see Grau, *Virtual Art: From Illusion to Immersion*.
19. See Arnold-de Simine, *Mediating Memory in the Museum*, p. 115.
20. See Ibid. p. 114.
21. Former presentation of the show on the IWM North's website, cited in Arnold-de Simine, *Mediating Memory in the Museum*, p. 74.
22. IWM North, *Your Visit Learning Resources*.

23. See Arnold-de Simine, *Mediating Memory in the Museum*, p. 116.
24. Available at <http://www.musee-armee.fr/collections/base-de-donnees-des-collections/objet/salle-multi-ecrans-de-lhistorial-charles-de-gaulle.html> (last accessed 30 September 2018).
25. On *Napoléon* see Brownlow, *Napoleon, Abel Gance's Classic Film*.
26. Moholy-Nagy proposed to explore the possibilities of projection on multiple screens, even of different sizes and shapes, assuming the creation of a device called 'polycinema' or 'simultaneous cinema', where projection surfaces were arranged on multiple levels, or semispherical screens, on which to project several films simultaneously. See Moholy-Nagy, *Painting, Photography, Film*.
27. Youngblood, *Expanded Cinema*.
28. On Cinerama, see Belton, *Widescreen Cinema*; on IMAX screens, see Acland, 'IMAX Technology and the Tourist Gaze'.
29. Historial Charles de Gaulle, *Dossier de presse*, p. 11.
30. On contemporary museum buildings, see Greub and Greub (eds), *Museums in the Twenty-First Century*.

CHAPTER TEN

Touching Images

Audience interaction is today considered an essential feature of museums that aspire to be cutting-edge and attractive.[1] In particular, in recent exhibitions, screens can often be touched and serve as an interface between viewers and contents. Interactive kiosks, which remain to this day an occasionally encumbering presence among the artefacts and artworks, are being replaced by devices that tend to hide their technological component in favour of forms of interaction that aim to be as spontaneous as possible.

The impact of interactive devices on the configuration of contemporary exhibitions is at least two-fold. First, it underscores the tactile dimension of reception, whose influence on museum history has been more pervasive than is usually recognised. The interdiction of touch in the museum context is a relatively recent phenomenon, which intervened progressively after the eighteenth century. In previous centuries, touching the objects was common practice for the visitors of both public and private collections: merely looking at the exhibits was considered superficial, and it was believed that only through physical contact could one fully experience them.[2] However, the museum perception was later identified tout court with the sense of sight, to the point that, as noted by Susan Stewart, museums are conceived in such a natural way as 'empires of sight' that rarely happens to imagine that their fruition can take place through other senses.[3] However, considered in relation to the display of moving images, this supremacy of the sight reveals to be less pervasive than one might imagine. From the Mutoscopes of the Imperial War Museum, activated by turning a handle, to the interactive tables we will discuss in this chapter, which function thanks to the touch, moving images in museums often solicit the tactile involvement of the visitors.

Wanda Strauven identifies the origins of the 'tactile' tradition in the practice of touching the exhibits of private collections back in the second half of the seventeenth century, before their gradual institutionalisation. According to Strauven, after the practice of touching museum items started being prohibited at the end of the eighteenth century and start of the nineteenth, it found a new expression in optical games and educational devices, where the screen becomes a surface to touch: 'one could . . . claim that early-nineteenth-century optical toys ensured, within the private sphere of home entertainment, a continuation of the hands-on practice that for more than a century invaded the semi-private/semi-public sphere of early museums'.[4] In other words, if according to Strauven the cultural practice of touching spread even to traditionally distant fields, following its many occurrences allows for the weaving of a further connection between museum and the cinema.

Second, contemporary exhibition strategies tend to use the entire extension of still or moving images as touch-sensitive surfaces: the screen is seamlessly integrated in the museum space, and both jointly create a concrete yet elusive field of encounter between the visitor and the contents proposed by the institution. Images can therefore be seen as material surfaces that articulate a contact, a significant and transformative relationship.

TOUCHING, BROWSING: INTERACTIVE TABLES

One of the devices most commonly found in contemporary museums is the so-called 'interactive table', which is a kind of horizontal touch screen. For instance, at the Audiovisual Museum of the Resistance (Museo Audiovisivo della Resistenza) in Fosdinovo (Italy), a large 'memory table' is installed in the middle of the exhibition space. On the black surface, whose exact shape fades into the semi-darkness of the room, the luminous reliefs of books and posters draw the viewer's attention. When touched, the images come to life thanks to archival films and photographs, through which the viewer can browse as if they were the pages of a book.

The book metaphor is often extended to the very organisation of the contents, which can be arranged as if on the pages of a volume whose images come to life under the eyes of the visitor. The reference object can also be a photo album, on which fragments of films and photographs compose a mosaic of places and faces through which the visitor can browse by the simple touch of the hand.

The Audiovisual Museum of the Resistance collects testimonies and documents related to the Second World War in Italy, when a number of people, the partisans, fought against the Fascist regime and its allies. The screens along the walls of the museum space show, in the form of video testimonies, the faces and voices of eighteen partisans who recount their experience of the war. There is a thematic consonance between the documents on display on the interactive table and the corresponding video fragments, so that the memories of the witnesses are directly related to each visitor's individual itinerary through the traces of the past disseminated on the table, 'as if they were asking the question and therefore taking responsibility for the answer'.[5] One can say that the museum literally stages the process of transmission of memory, inviting the visitor to a performance that is both physical (through the touch that initiates and mediates the exploration of contents) and imaginative: only the viewer's participation can enable the exchange that constitutes the underlying principle of the museum installation.

In the Widespread Museum of Resistance in Turin, one of the last rooms of the exhibition itinerary presents an interactive table. War, racial discrimination, occupation, the Italian resistance movement, and the liberation are narrated through historical footage, written documents, and original photographs. Recovered from archives and digitised, these documents come back to life on the table only when the visitors activate them by touch: they must touch the interactive table to select the themes and chronological landmarks that interest them.

The interactive tables of contemporary exhibitions use the flexibility of digital archives to present an eclectic ensemble of written documents, footage, and photographs, whose significance is mostly determined by interconnections that are spatially translated into montage effects. Touch activates the table's memory and arranges it into a mosaic of which the film image is only one component, while also constituting the dynamic principle that animates all the others.

Even if moving images are only one of the features of interactive tables (together with photographs, sounds, and written texts), these displays are intrinsically cinematic. For instance, in the installation *World That Was* at the

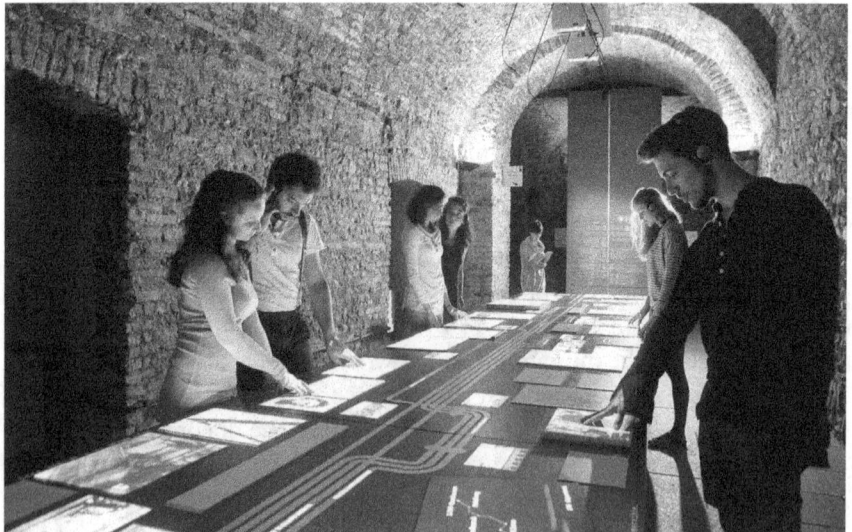

Figure 10.1 Widespread Museum of Resistance: the interactive table (photo Fabrizio Esposito, courtesy of Museo Diffuso della Resistenza, Turin).

Los Angeles Museum of the Holocaust, several old photographs – mostly individual, family, and group portraits – can be observed from three luminous openings corresponding to the three interaction stations on the table. The images appear to be floating on the surface and to be shuffled and reshuffled in front of the viewer's eyes before fading back into darkness.

The visitor can select one of these images with a simple touch, and drag it to the lower edge of the table, where it will reveal the name and story of the subjects. In some cases, the still images turn into short video fragments, whose audio is broadcast through the earphones of the audio-guide. The viewer's simple and immediate gesture reactivates the memory of otherwise silent archives, creating original and personal connections between the documents. At the same time, the slow and constant shuffling of the images recombines the images in a montage that plays with the different depths of field, changes of scale, zooms, and juxtapositions. The result is an exploration of the multiple possible combinations of images not only through the movements on the table's surface, but also through the viewer's intervention. If the interactive table only occasionally shows actual moving images, its dynamic approach to images is based on the intrinsically cinematic principle of montage. The latter is a constitutive element of its significance and creates a deep connection between the archive and the viewer. The movement of the images thus become the factor that 'brings back to life' archival images, also thanks to the active intervention of the visitors who explore the archive documents.

Rewriting Space: The Museum Laboratory of the Mind

Set up by Studio Azzurro in the former psychiatric hospital of Santa Maria della Pietà in Rome, the Museum Laboratory of the Mind (Museo Laboratorio della Mente) addresses issues of mental distress and the de-humanisation of patients that characterised psychiatric institutions until the psychiatrist Franco Basaglia enforced their abolition with the eponymous Basaglia Law (Italian Mental Health Act) in 1978. The Museum Laboratory of the Mind is emblematic of the 'spectral turn' that marked the humanities and social sciences in the past decades, and its aim is to address the concealed, repressed, or forgotten elements of society, as well as the acting power of the revenant.[6]

The entire museum display solicits the active participation of the audience in order to fully understand the message. The itinerary begins with a large video projection where the eyes of patients stare at the visitor. Placed almost at the height of the visitor's face, the patients' eyes follow the visitors as they enter a world where the markers of so-called normality are reversed: the patients become the observer, and the supposedly 'healthy' visitors become the observed.[7] The exhibition itinerary follows the original layout of the former psychiatric hospital: the accepted points of reference are overturned since visitors are placed in the uncomfortable position of those who were forced to live in those premises.

In the second installation, at a short distance in front of the visitor, an invisible wall can be perceived through the dull thuds of bodies desperately and violently smashing against it, unable to come through. This inescapable physical presence is contrasted with blurred images bathed in a supernatural blue hue – spectral images from a time and space other than those of the world outside the museum.

The visit path brings the viewer to 'gradually adopt a subjective position with respect to mental illness'.[8] The presence of the patients is never fully concrete and tangible but is suggested by glances, voices, and faces that are revealed only through the eyes of someone else (for instance, through the portraits made by a doctor/painter, or trough file photos) and through semi-transparent moving images.

The section of the display titled *The Closed Institution* presents, with only a few modifications, the deposit where the inmates' belongings were kept, the doctor's office, and the room of seclusion. All the spaces are empty of human figures: the first two can be seen from behind a glass window, while the third is shown through a peephole. Here the patients are suggested by their own

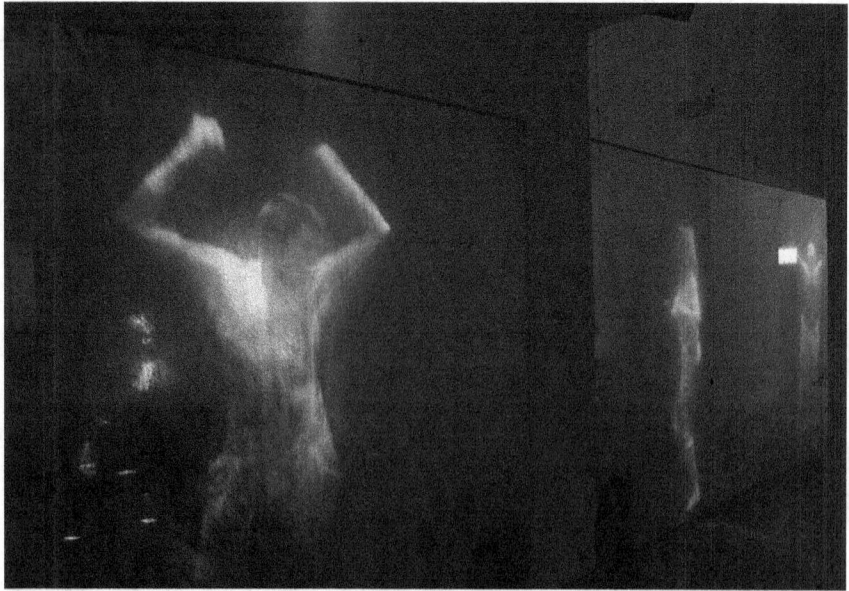

Figure 10.2 Museum Laboratory of the Mind: the invisible wall (courtesy Museo Laboratorio della Mente, ASL Roma 1, Rome).

absence: their figures are not shown but nonetheless visitors can imagine they were formerly there. The display itself becomes a disciplinary device that implies the virtual and spectral presence of inmates whose existence it organises.

From the very entrance, the display revolutionises our temporal and spatial coordinates (through magnified objects or invisible but impassable walls) as well as the relationship between the observer and the observed – and, as a consequence, between interior and exterior (the first section of the museum is aptly titled 'Enter outside and exit inside'). The visitors thereby realise the impossibility of true understanding, and especially the impossibility of understanding the alterity that separates them from those figures with whom they try to establish a contact throughout the exhibition itinerary.

The exhibit demonstrates how the metaphor of the ghost can be used. The spectral figures that haunt the museum epitomise what has been marginalised on a social – even more than on an individual – level: the mentally disturbed patient, confined in a mental institution, is excluded from society under the pretence of delimiting what is 'normal' and acceptable.

The pavilion of the former Psychiatric Hospital contains an actual set of instructions that places the visitor at the heart of a tension between the space and the 'presences' that inhabit it. In the middle of the room *Talking*, a microphone invites the visitors to say something, to 'talk aloud to themselves',[9] as the designers write, just as a typical stereotype portrays mentally ill persons. In front of the microphone, a projection shows the framed image of a huge disembodied mouth in all its spectral and even monstrous force, evoking the freakish and menacing figure of mental illness. The projection contradicts the microphone's invitation: if the visitor tries to speak, the mouth starts moving too, covering the visitor's words with its own. It therefore becomes impossible to say anything that makes sense while simultaneously listening to the other voice. The moving image of the mouth acts on the visitors, disturbing their rational speech. The never-ending and never-satisfied interpretive effort – the attempt to listen while speaking – puts them in the position of patients by forcing them to repeat the latter's behaviours and to share their inability to achieve a full understanding.

As visitors proceed through the exhibition, their 'condition slowly and unwittingly turns into an interpretation of the various stages of madness, of its postures and obsessive behaviours'.[10] After being photographed and registered, just as the patients were upon entering the institution, the visitors proceed towards a table where, by placing their elbows in two hollows and their hands over their ears, they can listen to fragments of stories about people who hear voices in their heads.[11]

In the next installation, visitors should oscillate their bodies back and forth in front of a board. This movement activates the display of images on the board surface, showing photographs not only of patients, but also of previous visitors who let themselves be photographed in a previous installation. By physically moving back and forth from the table, the visitor adjusts the focus on the portraits and can listen to extracts from patient stories. Also, considered from the perspective of an external observer, he or she replicates the gestures commonly associated with mentally ill persons.

The former inmates haunt the museum space like ghosts, inviting the visitors to repeat their gestures – the only way to fully understand life in a mental institution. In an almost paradoxical twist, soliciting visitors to engage actively with the exhibition, the patients-ghosts regain the agency of which they had been deprived by the institution.

In the dining room, two interactive tables allow visitors to touch a series of everyday objects used in the psychiatric hospital, activating the projection of short clips where patients and nurses recount how they spent their everyday life when the mental institution was open. Among the testimonies, a nurse emphasises that patients were completely deprived of the possibility to act:

> [A]nd what did the patients do? Nothing! Nothing whatsoever! We woke them up at 6 am and sent them naked and barefoot to the surveillance room, because the nurses had to change the beds and clean up everything before the next shift. The patients would spend all day in the surveillance room: they did nothing, they could do nothing because everything was forbidden![12]

The patients were left in a limbo where time went by indistinctly, one hour identical to the next except for mealtimes and other primary necessities. However, the former inmates who inhabit the spaces of the museum like ghosts regain their capacity of action in the very process of soliciting visitors to repeat their gestures.

Thus, on the one hand, the conceptual metaphor of the spectre becomes an analytical and interpretive tool that enables, to use Federico Boni's words, the 'return of the repressed that had been concealed or made invisible by discursive practices and "regimes of truth"',[13] while also 'retracing the action of the subject marginalised in the world'[14]. On the other hand, by recovering their agency as revenants, the figures of the Museum Laboratory of the Mind also recover their capacity to act by enabling others to evoke and mirror their own gestures. They can finally be understood as subjects – which does not mean, however, that they are integrated back into a supposed 'normality'.

INTERACTIONS/INTERRELATIONS

> When, a little over two centuries ago, Art was consigned to the Museum, its banishment was sealed with a prohibition: 'Do not touch!' This was no

> doubt a way of hindering any attempts to transgress the visual experience – considered the only legitimate way in which to approach a work – and it was also an injunction destined to invalidate any effort to connect Art and Life by any means other than pure contemplation. The plea 'Do not touch!' was (and still is) the consequence of the triumph, in the work of art, of the *image* over the *thing*, the continuation of a consecration of its unreal side. Images, as we know, are different from the rest of the world: *they do not exist*. 'To touch the work' is to demote it to the status of an object and, in a very fundamental way, to offend its essence, which belongs to the imagination.[15]

This is how Victor Stoichita commentates on the prohibition to touch in museums. According to Stoichita, the fascination for touching the image, perceived as an actually existing entity, runs through Western culture and aesthetics but has long been marginalised due to its transgressive and threatening character. The interdiction 'do not touch' that accompanies the works of art in the museum contributes to deaden the menace represented by the sense of touch. What happens when the prohibition is turned on its head, that is: 'forbidden *not* to touch'?[16] As noted by Studio Azzurro, 'going into a museum and being able to touch and feel immediately changes the attitude of the visitor toward the museum and consequently her or his relationship with the institution'.[17] Similar dynamics are at play at the Museum Laboratory of the Mind, where the term 'institution' can refer to either the museum or the psychiatric hospital, or more generally to any entity that aims to regulate what does not conform to normality. The viewers' active participation on a physical, emotional, but especially cognitive level, led them to understand the current processes of marginalisation and social exclusion and to rethink one's daily approach to diversity.[18]

The same goes for the section of the Museum called *Bearers of stories – no one is normal from up close* (*Portatori di storie – Da vicino nessuno è normale*), added at a later stage in the nearby scientific library 'Alberto Cencelli'.[19] In a room dedicated to ancient volumes, an entire wall is covered with a screen on which life-scale figures are projected. They are today patients, their families, psychologists, nurses, and other healthcare workers: a cohesive community that finds in the spaces of the former asylum, where mental health services are now located, a place of aggregation.

The figures on the screen walk back and forth, occasionally pausing to stare at the visitor. A brief touch triggers them to say a few words, while by maintaining the contact and moving in the space the visitors can make the figures follow him or her and move to another screen, which is placed into a smaller room. Here the figures recount their experience. The room is equipped with a seat and is organised in such a way as to enable a more intimate encounter. The various figures tell of their experience with mental illness, delivering their stories to the listener. The physical proximity becomes a human and ethical proximity: 'ultimately it is difficult to tell for sure whether we just listened to a patient, a nurse, or a doctor... Their human, daily stories are so "close" that they defy any form of labelling.'[20] The meditative mood of the second room, however, could not happen without the preliminary touch and contact that take place in the first room. Through that initial gesture, a human and emotional proximity is established between the visitors and the represented figures that last until the end of the itinerary.

In this installation, visitors are asked to play simple gestures as the act of touching. The gesture is not only a component, but also a condition of the communication, and is enabled by a subdued rather than flaunted use of technology, aimed at 'increasing the sensitivity of the environment'.[21] This is the idea underlying the so-called 'natural interfaces' used by Studio Azzurro in most of its exhibitions: these are 'interactive systems which react without the use of technological intermediaries (mouse, keyboard etc.), but through traditional methods of communication, using touch, voice, gestures, breathing... so as to create a more natural situation which is not frustrated by unfamiliar procedures'.[22] This principle is at the basis of the entire cycle 'Bearers of Stories', which also includes 'No One is Normal From Up Close': launched by Studio Azzurro in 2008 and still in progress, the cycle consists of

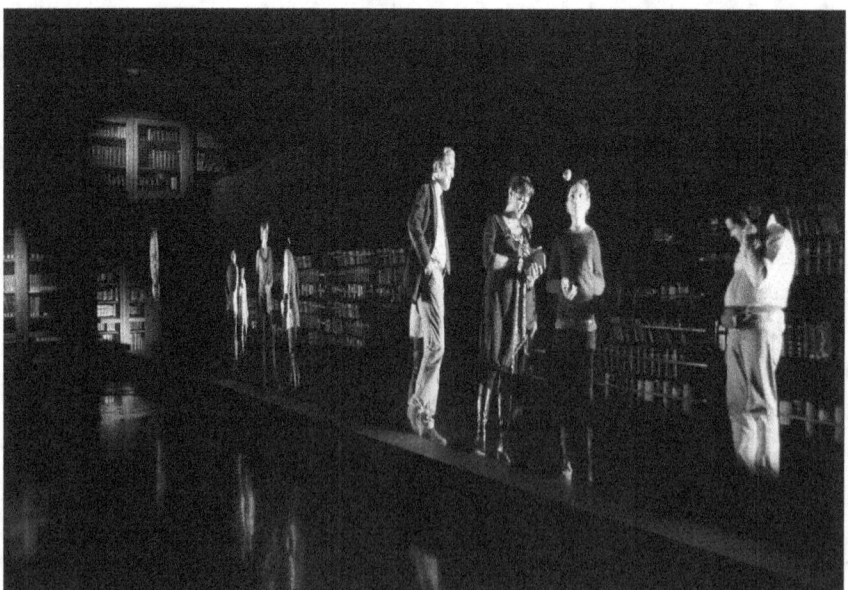

Figure 10.3 Museum Laboratory of the Mind: installation *Bearers of Stories* (courtesy Museo Laboratorio della Mente, ASL Roma 1, Rome).

a series of installations destined to exhibitions and art fairs, including *Sensitive City*, presented at the Italian pavilion of the 2010 Expo in Shanghai.[23]

The cycle's installations are all based on three fundamental principles: the principle of being rooted in a geographically defined territory, and the identification of the latter as a 'container of the stories' of its inhabitants, a space where they are generated and circulate. The figures of Studio Azzurro are conveyors of *stories*, as if to claim that listening to multiple life experiences is conducive to a shared dimension of mutual exchange and discovery. Building upon the intrinsic connection to a place, the memories of the individual or collective past are intertwined with the narrative of contemporary experiences. Both narratives are conveyed through a device whose articulations of meaning are determined by the interaction with the viewer.

Interaction is the third fundamental principle underlying the functioning of such 'bearers of stories'. In her analysis of *Sensitive City*, Miriam De Rosa argues that the encounter, touch, and contact allow us to interpret the installation and its spatial articulation. De Rosa's observations can be also applied to 'No One is Normal From Up Close':

> [T]he environment created by the installation is composed of images that are used and spatially arranged in function of the interaction. They are not only designed for a visitor-viewer, but also require a contact: presence is not sufficient but must lead to the action, however elementary, of moving a hand.[24]

When they enter the room where the installation is placed, visitors see human figures moving on the screen. The projection is the only source of brightness in a dark space, and immediately catches the eyes and catalyses the attention of the viewers. But the sense of vision offers only a partial installation experience. Visitors are confronted with people who move back and forth in the space without paying too much attention to them. Some are pensive, others are engaged in simple actions, like writing on a notebook. It is only when a visitor decides to touch the screen that they look at him or her and begin to speak. It is only the physical contact that allows the establishment of a relationship.

These dynamics bring attention to the surface of the screen as a place of contact. The screen is not intended as a 'window' through which one must look, but as a surface that must be touched. The screen is not transparent, but draws attention to itself and its materiality. The concepts of surface and screen as elaborasted by Giuliana Bruno are particularly fitting to understand how the relationship between the viewer, the images, the screen, and the surrounding space articulates in Studio Azzurro's installation. According to Bruno, the surface should be considered as a privileged place for expression and communication in the era of dematerialisation. The scholar reconsiders the concept of materiality in relation to the many different screens that surround us and saturate the spaces we inhabit. Materiality is not conceived as 'a question of materials', but as 'the substance of material relations'.[25] Through an interdisciplinary approach that ranges from architecture to cinema, from visual arts to fashion and contemporary installation art, Bruno investigates 'the space of those relations, questioning how they manifest themselves on the surface of different media'.[26] She identifies the surface as the actual core of many contemporary artworks and architectures. It is conceived as a place where a process of convergence between canvas, wall, and screen takes place, generating 'renewed forms of projection'.[27] The tangibility of the surface is where the reciprocal contact between us and objects or environments occurs.[28]

Bruno connects the haptic mode of reception implied by the touching of the surface, the reciprocity of the relationship it establishes between subjects and objects, and the affective reaction it entails. When we touch something, we cannot avoid being touched in return:

> When we touch a surface, we experience immersion and inversion fully, and reciprocity is a quality of this touch . . . When we look we are not necessarily being looked at, but when we touch, by the very nature of pressing our hand or any part of our body on a subject or object, we cannot escape the contact. Touch is never unidirectional, a one-way street. It always enables an affective return.[29]

Since it inevitably implies a reciprocity, touch is to Bruno inextricably related not only to the senses, but also to sentiments. 'Touching' is also 'being touched'. It is exactly what happens in Studio Azzurro's installation: touch generates the emotional contact of visitors with patients and health operators who talk on the screen. The few words they say introduce listeners to their story, stimulating their curiosity to know more about it. Visitors are invited to go further to establish a relationship with the represented people. A decision that passes primarily through the corporality of the gesture: to listen to the full story of figures on the screen, visitors must not interrupt the physical contact. Moving the hand on the surface, they can move the figures towards the adjacent room, where they narrate their experience with mental health issues. Touch engenders an emotional contact, which in turn generates another action, that of moving in space.

The movement of the visitor implies at the same time the movement of the projected figures. To create a stronger sense of connection, the virtual space on the screen replicates exactly the physical space of the library in which the installation is located: behind the figures' backs, like behind those of the visitors, there are shelves full of ancient volumes. Therefore, the installation implies different levels of involvement: with the surface of the screen and with the figure represented, as well as with the space in which the installation is located. Visitors must become aware of their relationship with the space: they should observe it in its entirety to understand how it is organised, and then walk through it without losing the contact with the surface. The installation is a site of multiple relations,[30] between the visitors and the people represented on the screen, as well as between both of them and the space in which they are situated.

When the figure passes into the little projection room, the physical contact with the visitor is interrupted, but the emotional closeness remains strong. The snug space fosters the creation of a sense of personal, intimate communication. However, in the room the visitor is not alone, but there is space for a small group of spectators. If in the first room the touch created a relationship between one of the visitors and one of the figures on the screen, in the second room the communication extends to other visitors. Each visitor can listen to the story of the person he or she brought to the projection room as well as the stories of the people brought by other visitors. The one-to-one relationship established through the touch becomes public, shared.

The choice to keep the contact with a figure rather than another, made by the public in the first part of the installation, determines what testimonies will be heard in the adjacent projection room. So, the overall narrative, made by multiple voices, is the result of the intervention of many different visitors. The action made by of each of them does not therefore concern them as individuals, but influences the sense that will be transmitted to all the spectators.

After being actively involved through the gesture of touch, visitors should adopt a receptive position, accepting to listen also to the stories suggested by other people. So, they become fully aware of being part of a wider group, aggregated around the theme of mental disease. Interacting with the installation, visitors also connect with one another: in 'No One is Normal From Up Close' interactivity is not an end in itself, but rather the starting point to construct and experiment with meaningful relations.

Notes

1. On interactivity in museums, see Witcomb, 'Interactivity: Thinking Beyond'.
2. See Classen and Howes, 'The Museum as Sensescape', pp. 201–2. On the tactile dimension in museums, see also Classen, 'Touch in the Museum'.
3. Cf. Stewart, 'Prologue: From the Museum of Touch', p. 28.
4. Strauven, 'Early Cinema's Touch(able) Screens'.
5. Studio Azzurro, 'Museo audiovisivo della Resistenza', p. 56.
6. Boni, 'La svolta spettrale'; Peeren, *The Spectral Metaphor*.
7. Studio Azzurro, *Progettare musei, liberare menti*, p. 22.

8. Ibid. p. 30.
9. UOS Centro Studi e Ricerche ASL Roma and Studio Azzurro (eds), *Museo Laboratorio della Mente*, p. 24 (our translation).
10. Ibid. p. 19 (our translation).
11. Ibid. p. 30.
12. Vincenzo Boatta, cited in Claudia Demichelis, 'I regolamenti, le voci e i vissuti dell'istituzione chiusa', p. 97 (our translation).
13. Boni, 'La svolta spettrale', p. 197 (our translation).
14. Ibid. p. 201 (our translation).
15. Stoichita, *The Pygmalion Effect*, pp. 1–2; emphasis in the original.
16. Studio Azzurro, 'From Museums as Collections to Museums as Narration', p. 31; emphasis in the original.
17. Ibid. p. 31.
18. UOS Centro Studi e Ricerche ASL Roma and Studio Azzurro (eds), *Museo Laboratorio della Mente*, p. 15.
19. UOS Centro Studi e Ricerche ASL Roma and Studio Azzurro, *Museo laboratorio della mente – Portatori di storie*.
20. Studio Azzurro (ed.), *Studio Azzurro. Immagini sensibili*, p. 105 (our translation).
21. Studio Azzurro, 'From Museums as Collections to Museums as Narration', p. 27.
22. Ibid.
23. The cycle includes: *Sensible Map* (Espace d'Art Actua, Casablanca, 2008), *La quarta scala* (Santa Fe, Biennale Internazionale, Lucky Number Seven, 2008), *Fanoi* (Potenza, 2009), *Sensitive City* (Padiglione Italia, Expo, Shanghai, 2010) *Estrella del deserto* (Antofagasta, Cile, 2011), *In principio (e poi)*, Padiglione Santa sede, 55° Esposizione d'Arte Biennale di Venezia, 2013), *Miracolo a Milano* (Palazzo Reale, Milano, 2016).
24. De Rosa, *Cinema e postmedia*, p. 140.
25. Bruno, *Surface*, p. 2.
26. Ibid.
27. Ibid. p. 101.
28. Ibid. p. 3.
29. Ibid. p. 19.
30. Studio Azzurro's idea of 'aesthetic of relations' is certainly aware of Nicholas Bourriad's well-known concept of 'relational aesthetics' (see *Relational Aesthetics*), but also of the criticism it has received by scholars like Claire Bishop (see 'Antagonism and Relational Aesthetics'). Studio Azzurro refuses Bourriaud's assumption that participation is inherently positive, insisting on the need to consider the *quality* of the relationships established by the work of art (see Balzola and Rosa, *L'arte fuori di sé*).

Conclusions

In the first part of the book, the in-depth study of the Mutoscopes at the Imperial War Museum proved to be strategic in many ways. On the one hand, it brought to light a lesser-known form of film exhibition for an institution renowned for its role as a film archive. On the other hand, the close investigation of the use of cinematographic devices in the halls of this museum provided a wealth of details about a practice that was at the time uncommon but not unique.

The study of exhibitions designed by twentieth-century avant-garde artists allowed me to show not only how moving images were progressively incorporated in museums' galleries, but also how the design of the exhibition spaces was shaped according to the cinematic model, deploying in space the principles of unfolding, montage, and movement, and applying these principles to both images and audiences.

In the 1960s and 1970s, with the advent of video technology, moving images spread in the exhibition spaces of museums, with a number of pioneering experimentations. Videos were not accessory tools, but played an increasingly essential role in the configuration of the whole space, in the transmission of contents, and in the establishment of a stronger relationship with the public. The analysis of museum professionals' discourses about the use of moving images in exhibitions outlined the opportunities and problems arising at that time, as well as the roots of present-day curatorial discussions.

The investigation of the contemporary landscape allowed me to map out the various uses of moving images in contemporary museum installations. My aim was to identify how moving images permeate and deeply transform the museum's space, and how the latter could be shaped by intertwining with components of the cinematic *dispositif*.

Some of the exhibitions I described evoke features typical of the cinematic experience inside the movie theatre, as it is deep-rooted in the collective imagination (what Bellour defines as 'le vrai cinéma' – the 'true cinema')[1]: the images projected on a screen, the dark room, the immobility of the spectator. However, most of the displays analysed in this book distance themselves more dramatically from this model. The Mutoscopes installed since 1924 in the galleries of the Imperial War Museum proposed a form of individual vision that was at the time more and more marginalised by the forms of collective spectatorship. This case reveals how different forms of circulation of moving images could coexist in the same period in different contexts, and at the same time raises problems like that of technological obsolescence.

Likewise, the scientific films of the Museum of Science and Industry could be related less to the narrative feature films shown in movie theatres than to the educational films that circulated in schools and other educational contexts.[2] The same can be said for the testimonial films that are presented in contemporary museums like the Widespread Museum of Resistance, which are part of a constellation of audio-visual forms that, deposited in the archives, find their ideal place in contexts such as museums, classrooms, and on the Web.[3]

The ghostly images that populate the In Flanders Fields Museum, or the Museum Laboratory of the Mind, restore the spectral and disquieting component that characterised cinema at its origins, but also re-emerges in the contemporary forms of the artists' cinema. Even though the Big Picture Show and the screening room of the Historial Charles de Gaulle seem to encourage a vision that recalls the dark hall of the cinema theatre, they push it beyond its limits, towards an immersive presentation that characterises so many contemporary spectacular forms.

In this context, conceiving the museum as 'cinematic space' means to ask questions, rather than proposing definitions: which components of the cinematic *dispositif* migrate to the museum? How do they influence the museographic layout? And how do they rewrite the forms of communication and transmission of knowledge, as well as the relationship with the visitor?

This does not imply that all the exhibitions I described could be considered forms of cinema. Rather, I claim that they are 'inhabited' by cinema, which intersects with the exhibition, and changes the very configuration of the museum space. The museum display cross-talks with cinema, calls it into question, and appropriates it, not as a fixed and immutable spectacular form, but as a multifaceted *dispositif*, capable of constantly remodelling itself as well as the contexts it intertwines with.

Notes

1. Bellour, *La Querelle des dispositifs*, p. 13.
2. Orgeron, et al. (eds), *Learning with the Lights Off*.
3. See <https://sfi.usc.edu/watch> (last accessed 30 September 2018).

Bibliography

'A Chat with Uncle Sam's Trusted Mail Service Men', *The Washington Herald*, 15 January 1911.
Acland, Charles R., 'Imax Technology and the Tourist Gaze', *Cultural Studies*, 12, 3, 1998, pp. 429–45.
Acland, Charles R. and Haidee Wasson, 'Introduction: Utility and Cinema', in Charles R. Acland and Haidee Wasson (eds), *Useful Cinema* (Durham, NC and London: Duke University Press, 2011), pp. 1–14.
Acland, Charles R. and Haidee Wasson (eds), *Useful Cinema* (Durham, NC and London: Duke University Press, 2011).
'A Commercial Museum', *Museums Journal*, 26, 7, 1927, pp. 166–9.
Albera, François, 'Exposé, le cinéma s'expose', in Olivier Lugon (ed.), *Exposition et médias: photographie, cinéma, télévision* (Lausanne: L'Age d'Homme, 2012), pp. 179–208.
Albera, François, 'Introduction', in Sergei M. Eisenstein, *Cinématisme: peinture et cinéma* (1980) (Bruxelles: Editions Complexe, 2009), pp. 7–19.
Albera, François, 'Les Passages entre les arts. Cinéma, architecture, peinture, sculpture', in Jean-Christophe Royoux (ed.), *Qu'est-ce que l'art au 20e siècle?* (Jouy-en-Josas: Fondation Cartier and Paris: Ensba, 1992), pp. 17–35.
Albera, François and Maria Tortajada, 'Introduction to an Epistemology of Viewing and Listening Dispositives', in François Albera and Maria Tortajada (eds), *Cinema Beyond Film: Media Epistemology in the Modern Era* (Amsterdam: Amsterdam University Press, 2010), pp. 9–22.
Albera, François and Maria Tortajada, 'Le Dispositif n'existe pas', in François Albera and Maria Tortajada (eds), *Ciné-dispositif* (Lausanne: L'Age d'Homme, 2011), pp. 60–3.
Albera, François and Maria Tortajada, 'The 1900 Episteme', in François Albera and Maria Tortajada (eds), *Cinema Beyond Film: Media Epistemology in the Modern Era* (Amsterdam: Amsterdam University Press, 2010), pp. 25–44.
Albrecht, Donald, *The Work of Charles and Ray Eames: A Legacy of Invention* (New York: Harry N. Abrams, 1997).
Anderson, Gail, *Reinventing the Museum: Historical and Contemporary Perspectives on the Paradigm Shift* (Walnut Creek: AltaMira Press, 2004).
Ang, Ien, *Watching Dallas: Soap Opera and the Melodramatic Imagination* (New York: Methuen, [1982] 1985).
Arnold-de Simine, Silke, *Mediating Memory in the Museum: Trauma, Empathy, Nostalgia*, (Basingstoke: Palgrave Macmillan, 2013).
Arnold-de Simine, Silke, 'Memory Museum and Museum Text: Intermediality in Daniel Libeskind's Jewish Museum and W.G. Sebald's Austerlitz', *Theory, Culture & Society*, 29, 1, 2012, pp. 14–35.
Assman, Jan, 'Communicative and Cultural Memory', in Peter Meusburger, Michael Heffernan

and Edgar Wunder (eds), *Cultural Memories: The Geographical Point of View* (Heidelberg: Springer, 2011), pp. 15–27.

Aubert, Michelle, Laurent Mannoni and David Robinson (eds), 'The Will Day Historical Collection of Cinematograph & Moving Picture Equipment', *1895: bulletin de l'Association française de recherche sur l'histoire du cinéma*, special issue, 1997.

Aumont, Jacques, *Que reste-t-il du cinéma?* (Paris: Vrin, 2013).

Autelitano, Alice (ed.), *The Cinematic Experience* (Udine: Campanotto, 2010).

Azuar, Rafael, 'Del museo de nuevas tecnologías al sostenible. Del MARQ al ARQUA', in Comité Español de ICOM (ed.), 'Recursos audiovisuales en museos, pros y contras', *Digital. Revista Digital del Comite Español de ICOM*, 7, 2013, pp. 74–87.

Bal, Mieke, 'Exhibition as Film', in Sharon Macdonald and Paul Basu (eds), *Exhibition Experiments* (London: Blackwell Publishing, 2007), pp. 71–93.

Balsom, Erika, *Exhibiting Cinema in Contemporary Art* (Amsterdam: Amsterdam University Press, 2013).

Balsom, Erika, 'Screening Rooms. The Movie Theatre in/and the Gallery', *Public: Art/Culture/Ideas*, 40, 2009, pp. 24–39.

Balsom, Erika and Hila Peleg (eds), *Documentary Across Disciplines* (Cambridge, MA: MIT Press, 2016).

Balzola, Andrea and Paolo Rosa, *L'arte fuori di sé. Un manifesto per l'età post-tecnologica* (Milano: Feltrinelli, 2011).

Barnaby, Alice, 'Lighting Practices in Art Galleries and Exhibition Spaces, 1750–1850', in Michelle Henning (ed.), *Museum Media* (New York: Wiley Blackwell, 2015), pp. 191–213.

Baudry, Jean-Louis, 'Ideological Effects of the Basic Cinematographic Apparatus', *Film Quarterly*, 28, 2, [1970] 1974/5, pp. 39–47.

Baudry, Jean-Louis, 'The Apparatus: Metapsychological Approaches to the Impression of Reality in Cinema', in Leo Baudry and Marshall Cohen (eds), *Film Theory and Criticism. Introductory Readings* (New York and Oxford: Oxford University Press, [1975] 2009), pp. 171–188.

Bayer, Herbert, 'Aspects of Design of Exhibitions and Museums', *Curator*, 4, 3, 1961, pp. 257–88.

Bayer, Herbert, *Exposition de la société des artistes décorateurs: Section allemande* (Berlin: Verlag H. Reckendorf, 1930).

Bellour, Raymond, *La Querelle des dispositifs* (Paris: P.O.L, 2012).

Bellour, Raymond, 'Of Another Cinema', in Tanya Leighton (ed.), *Art and the Moving Image. A Critical Reader* (London: Tate/Afterall, [2000] 2008), pp. 406–22.

Belton, John, *Widescreen Cinema* (Cambridge, MA: Harvard University Press, 1992).

Beneš, Josef, 'Audiovisual Media in Museums', *Museum*, XXVIII, 2, 1976, pp. 121–4.

Bennett, Tony, *The Birth of the Museum* (London and New York: Routledge, 1995).

Biel-Missal, Brigitte and Dirk vom Lehn, 'Aesthethics and Atmosphere in Museums', in Michelle Henning (ed.), *Museum Media – The International Handbooks of Museum Studies* (New York: Wiley Blackwell, 2015), pp. 235–58.

Billing, Scott, 'Smoke and Mirrors', *Museum Practice,* summer 2008, pp. 36–40.

Bishop, Claire, 'Antagonism and Relational Aesthetics', October, fall 2004, pp. 51–79.

Bishop, Claire, *Installation Art: A Critical History* (London: Tate Publishing, 2005).

Black, Graham, *The Engaging Museum: Developing Museums for Visitor Involvement* (London and New York: Routledge, 2005).

Blanco, María del Pilar and Esther Peeren (eds), *Popular Ghosts: The Haunted Spaces of Everyday Culture* (New York and London: Continuum, 2010).

Blanco, María del Pilar and Esther Peeren (eds), *The Spectralities Reader. Ghosts and Haunting in Contemporary Cultural Theory* (New York and London: Bloomsbury, 2013).

Bois, Yve-Alain, 'El Lissitzky: Reading Lessons', *October*, 11, 1979, pp. 113–28.

Boni, Federico, 'La svolta spettrale. Case possedute e immaginazione sociologica', *Studi culturali*, 2, 2014, pp. 195–218.

Borde, Raymond and Charles Perrin, *Les Offices du cinéma éducateur et la survivance du muet (1925–1940)* (Lyon: PUL, 1992).

Bordina, Alessandro, Vincenzo Estremo, and Francesco Federici (eds), *Extended Temporalities* (Milano-Udine: Mimesis, 2016).

Bottomore, Stephen, '"The Collection of Rubbish". Animatographs, Archives and Arguments: London, 1896–97', *Film History*, 7, 3, 1995, pp. 291–7.

Bottomore, Stephen, 'The Panicking Audience?: Early Cinema and the "Train Effect"', *Historical Journal of Film, Radio and Television*, 19, 2, 1999, pp. 177–216.

Bottomore, Stephen, '"The Sparkling Surface of the Sea of History". Notes on the Origins of Film Preservation', in Roger Smither and Catherine A. Surowiec (eds), *This Film is Dangerous: A Celebration of Nitrate Film* (Bruxelles: FIAF, 2002), pp. 86–97.

Bourriaud, Nicolas, *Relational Aesthetics* (Dijon: Presses du réel, 2002).

Bridal, Tessa, *Exploring Museum Theatre* (Walnut Creek: AltaMira, 2004).

Brown, Richard and Barry Anthony, *A Victorian Film Enterprise: The History of the British Mutoscope and Biograph Company, 1897–1915* (Trowbridge: Flicks Books, 1999), pp. 188–214.

Brownlow, Kevin, *Napoleon, Abel Gance's Classic Film* (New York: Knopf, 1983).

Bruno, Giuliana, *Atlas of Emotion: Journeys in Art, Architecture, and Film* (New York: Verso, 2002).

Bruno, Giuliana, *Public Intimacy: Architecture and the Visual Arts* (Cambridge, MA: MIT Press, 2007).

Bruno, Giuliana, *Surface: Matters of Aesthetics, Materiality, and Media* (Chicago: University of Chicago Press, 2014).

Bryman, Alan, *The Disneyization of Society* (London: Sage, 2004).

Buchloh, Benjamin H. D., 'From Faktura to Factography', *October*, 30, 1984, pp. 82–119.

Burnette Stogner, Maggie, 'The Media-Enhanced Museum Experience. Debating the use of Media Technology in Cultural Exhibitions', *Curator*, 52, 4, 2009, pp. 385–97.

Burns, William A., 'Museum Exhibition: Do-It-Yourself or Commercial?', *Curator*, 12, 3, 1969, pp. 160–7.

Burns, William A., 'Should Museums Try TV?', *Curator*, 1, 4, 1958, pp. 63–8.

Bussolini, Jeffrey, 'What Is a Dispositive?', *Foucault Studies*, 10, 2010, pp. 85–107.

Cameron, Fiona and Sarah Kenderdine (eds), *Theorizing Digital Cultural Heritage. A Critical Discourse* (Cambridge, MA: MIT Press, 2007).

Carels, Edwin, 'From the Ossuary: Animation and the Danse Macabre', *TMG – Tijdschrift voor mediageschiedenis*, 15, 1, 2012, <http://www.tmgonline.nl/index.php/tmg/article/view/2/5> (last accessed 30 September 2018).

Casetti, Francesco, 'Cinema Lost and Found: Trajectories of Relocation', *Screening the Past*, 32, 2011, <http://www.screeningthepast.com/2011/11/cinema-lost-and-found-trajectories-of-relocation/> (last accessed 30 September 2018).

Casetti, Francesco, *Inside the Gaze: The Fiction Film and Its Spectator* (Bloomington: Indiana University Press, [1986] 1998).

Casetti, Francesco, *The Lumière Galaxy. Seven Key Words for the Cinema to Come* (New York: Columbia University Press, 2015).

Casetti, Francesco, 'The Relocation of Cinema', *NECSUS: European Journal of Media Studies*, 2, 2012, <http://www.necsus-ejms.org/the-relocation-of-cinema/> (last accessed 30 September 2018).

Cataldo, Lucia, *Dal museum theatre al digital storytelling: nuove forme della comunicazione museale fra teatro, multimedialità e narrazione* (Milano: Franco Angeli, 2011).

Cati, Alice, 'Displaying Memories. Studio Azzurro and the Turn to Audiovisual Museum', in Philippe Dubois, Frédéric Monvoisin and Elena Biserna (eds), *Extended cinema. Le cinéma gagne du terrain* (Udine: Campanotto, 2010), pp. 76–81.

Cati, Alice, *Immagini della memoria. Teorie e pratiche del ricordo tra testimonianza, genealogia, documentari* (Milano-Udine: Mimesis, 2013).

Cauman, Samuel, *The Living Museum. Experiences of an Art Historian and Museum Director: Alexander Dorner* (New York: New York University Press, 1958).

Chapman, Jane, *Issues in Contemporary Documentary* (Cambridge: Polity, 2009).

Charlton, Thomas L., Lois E. Myers and Rebecca Sharpless (eds), *History of Oral History: Foundations and Methodology* (Lanham: Rowman & Littlefield, 2007).

Chittenden, Tara, 'The Cook, the Marquis, his Wife, and her Maids: The Use of Dramatic Characters in Peter Greenaway's *Peopling the Palaces* as a Way of Interpreting Historic Buildings', *Curator*, 54, 3, 2011, pp. 261–78.

Christie, Ian, 'A Disturbing Presence? Scenes from the History of Film in the Museum', in Angela Dalle Vacche (ed.), *Film, Art, New Media. Museum without Walls?* (Basingstoke: Palgrave Macmillan, 2012), pp. 241–55.

'Cinematograph Films in Museums', *Museums Journal*, 23, 6, 1923, pp. 114–15.

City Museum Leicester and Art Gallery, *Twenty-seventh Report of the Committee 1930–1931* (Leicester: City Museum Leicester and Art Gallery, 1931).

City Museum Leicester and Art Gallery, *Twenty-sixth Report of the Committee 1929–1930* (Leicester: City Museum Leicester and Art Gallery, 1930).

Classen, Constance, 'Touch in the Museum', in Constance Classen (ed.), *The Book of Touch* (Oxford: Berg, 2005), pp. 275–86.

Classen, Constance and David Howes, 'The Museum as Sensescape: Western Sensibilities and Indigenous Artifacts', in Elizabeth Edwards, Chris Gosden and Ruth Phillips (eds), *Sensible Objects: Colonialism, Museums and Material Culture* (Oxford and New York: Berg, 2006), pp. 199–222.

Cohen, Arthur A., *Herbert Bayer: The Complete Work* (Cambridge, MA: MIT Press, 1984).

Colomina, Beatriz, 'Enclosed by Images: The Eameses' Multiscreen Architecture', in Christopher Eamon and Stan Douglas (eds), *Art of Projection* (Ostfildern: Hatje Cantz, 2009), pp. 35–56.

Commission on Educational and Cultural Films, *The Film in National Life: Being the Report of an Enquiry Conducted by the Commission on Educational and Cultural Films into the Service which the Cinematograph May Render to Education and Social Progress* (London: Allen and Unwin, 1932).

'Conference on Museum, Film and Television Experts at Brussels', in UNESCO, *Film and Television in the Service of Opera and Ballet and of Museums* (Paris: UNESCO, 1961), pp. 32–55.

Connolly, Maeve, *The Place of Artists' Cinema: Space, Site and Screen* (Chicago: Intellect, 2009).

Cooke, Lynne and Peter Wollen (eds), *Visual Display: Culture Beyond Appearances* (Seattle: Bay Press, 1995).

Coombes, Annie E. and Ruth B. Phillips (eds), *Museum Transformations* (New York: Wiley Blackwell, 2015).

Crafton, Donald, *Emile Cohl, Caricature, and Film* (Princeton: Princeton University Press, 1990).

Crew, Spencer R. and James Sims, 'Locating Authenticity: Fragments of a Dialogue', in Ivan Karp and Steven D. Lavine (eds), *Exhibiting Cultures: The Poetics and Politics of Museum Display* (Washington, DC: Smithsonian Institution Press, 1991), pp. 159–75.

Cristiá, Ignasi, 'El puente entre el visitante y el objeto', *Digital. Revista Digital del Comite Español de ICOM*, 7, 2013, pp. 12–19.

Crough, Olivia, 'El Lissitzy's Screening Rooms', in Dominique Chateau and José Moure (eds), *Screens. From Materiality to Spectatorship: A Historical and Theoretical Reassessment* (Amsterdam: Amsterdam University Press, 2016), pp. 223–35.

Crow, Reginald V., 'The Film in the Museum: An Inquiry', *Museums Journal*, 34, 8, 1934, p. 336.

Cummings, Carlos E., *East is East and West is West* (Buffalo: Buffalo Museum of Science, 1940).

Dandridge, Frank, 'The Value of Design in Visual Communication', *Curator*, 9, 4, 1966, pp. 331–6.

de Jong, Steffi, 'Mediatized Memory. Video Testimonies in Museums', in Michelle Henning (ed.), *Museum Media* (New York: Wiley Blackwell, 2015), pp. 69–93.

de Jong, Steffi, *The Witness as Object. Video Testimony in Memorial Museums* (New York and Oxford: Berghahn Books, 2018).

de Jong, Steffi, 'Who is History? The Use of Autobiographical Accounts in History Museums', in Kate Hill (ed.), *Museums and Biographies: Stories, Objects, Identities* (London: Boydell & Brewer, 2012), pp. 295–308.

De Lauretis, Teresa and Stephen Heath (eds), *The Cinematic Apparatus* (London: Macmillan, 1980).

Deleuze, Gilles, 'What is a Dispositif?', in Gilles Deleuze, *Two Regimes of Madness. Texts and Interviews 1975–1995* (Los Angeles: Semiotext(e) and Cambridge, MA: MIT Press, [1989] 2006), pp. 338–48.

Deleuze, Gilles and Félix Guattari, *A Thousand Plateaus: Capitalism and Schizophrenia* (Minneapolis: University of Minnesota Press, [1980] 1987).

Demichelis, Claudia, 'I regolamenti, le voci e i vissuti dell'istituzione chiusa', in UOS Centro Studi e Ricerche ASL Roma and Studio Azzurro (eds), *Museo Laboratorio della Mente* (Cinisello Balsamo: Silvana Editoriale, 2010), pp. 93–104.

De Pastre, Béatrice, 'Créer des archives cinématographiques à Paris. L'oubli du pre ou les héritiers parisiens de Boleslas', in Magdalena Mazaraki (ed.), *Boleslas Matuszewski/Écrits cinématographiques* (Paris: Cinémathque française/AFRHC, 2006), pp. 67–85.

De Rosa, Miriam, *Cinema e postmedia. I territori del filmico nel contemporaneo* (Milano: postmedia books, 2013).

De Rosa, Miriam and Vinzenz Hediger, 'Post-what? Post-when? A Conversation on the "Posts" of Post-media and Post-cinema', *Cinéma & Cie. International Film Studies Journal*, 26–7, 2016, pp. 9–18.

Derrida, Jacques, *Archive Fever: A Freudian Impression* (Chicago and London: University of Chicago Press, [1995] 1996).

Derrida, Jacques, *Specters of Marx. The State of the Debt, the Work of Mourning and the New International* (London and New York: Routledge, [1993] 2006).

Derrida, Jacques and Bernard Stiegler, *Echographies of Television: Filmed Interviews* (Cambridge: Polity, 2002).

Dierbeck, Robert E., 'Television and the Museum', *Curator*, 1, 2, 1958, pp. 34–44.

Eamon, Christopher and Stan Douglas (eds), *Art of Projection* (Ostfildern: Hatje Cantz, 2009).

Dubois, Philippe, 'A "Cinema Effect" in Contemporary Art', in Julia Noordegraaf, Cosetta G. Saba, Barbara Le Maître and Vinzenz Hediger (eds), *Preserving and Exhibiting Media Art: Challenges and Perspectives* (Amsterdam: Amsterdam University Press, 2013), pp. 311–25.

Dubois, Philippe, 'Cinéma et art contemporain: Vers un cinéma d'exposition? De la migration d'un dispositif', unpublished paper.

Dubois, Philippe, 'Présentation', in Phlippe Dubois, Frédéric Monvoison, and Elena Biserna (eds), *Extended cinema: Le cinéma gagne du terrain* (Pasian di Prato: Campanotto, 2010), pp. 13–14.

Dubois, Philippe, Frédéric Monvoisin, and Elena Biserna (eds), *Extended cinema. Le cinéma gagne du terrain* (Udine: Campanotto, 2010).

Dubois, Philippe, Lúcia Ramos Monteiro, and Alessandro Bordina (eds), *Oui, c'est du cinéma/ Yes, It's Cinema. Formes et espaces de l'image en mouvement/Forms and Spaces of the Moving Images* (Udine: Campanotto, 2009).

Dulac, Nicolas and André Gaudreault, 'Dispositfs optiques et attraction', *Cahier Louis-Lumire*, 4, 2007, pp. 91–108.

Durand, Jacques, 'The Use of Cultural and Scientific Films in the Museums of the World. Statistical and Qualitative Report on a Joint UNESCO/ICOM Survey', *Museum*, XVI, 2, 1963, pp. 82–114.

Eisenstein, Sergei M., 'Montage and Architecture', introduction by Yves-Alain Bois, *Assemblage*, 10, 1989, pp. 110–31.

Elcott, Noam M., 'Rooms of Our Time: Laszlo Moholy-Nagy and the Stillbirth of Multi-Media Museums', in Tamara Trodd (ed.), *Screen/Space. The Projected Image in Contemporary Art* (Manchester: Manchester University Press, 2011), pp. 25–52.

Elder, Bruce, *Harmony and Dissent: Film and Avant-Garde Art Movements in the Early Twentieth Century* (Waterloo: Wilfrid Laurier University Press, 2008).

Elsaesser, Thomas, 'Archives and Archaeologies. The Place of Non-Fiction Film in Contemporary Media', in Vinzenz Hediger and Patrick Vonderau (eds), *Films that Work: Industrial Film and the Productivity of Media* (Amsterdam: Amsterdam University Press, 2009), pp. 19–34.

Elsaesser, Thomas, 'Early Film History and Multi-Media. An Archaeology of Possible Futures?', in Wendy Hui Kyong Chun and Thomas Keenan (eds), *New Media, Old Media: A History and Theory Reader* (London and New York: Routledge, 2006), pp. 13–25.

Elsaesser, Thomas, 'Entre savoir et croire: le dispositif cinématographique après le cinéma', in François Albera and Maria Tortajada (eds), *Ciné-dispositifs* (Lausanne: L'Age d'Homme, 2011), pp. 39–74.

Elsaesser, Thomas, *Film History as Media Archaeology. Tracking Digital Cinema* (Amsterdam: Amsterdam University Press, 2016).

Elsaesser, Thomas, 'The New Film History as Media Archaeology', *Cinémas*, 14, 2–3, 2004, pp. 75–117.

Elwes, Catherine, *Installation and the Moving Image* (New York: Columbia University Press, 2015).

Englem, Jane, 'History with Special Effects: Is It Museum or Haunted Mansion?', *Los Angeles Times*, 19 March 2006, <http://articles.latimes.com/2006/mar/19/travel/tr-insider19> (last accessed 30 September 2018).

Eskildsen, Ute and Jan-Christopher Horak (eds), *Film und Foto der zwanziger Jahre: Eine Betrachtung der Internationalen Werkbundausstellung 'Film und Foto' 1929* (Stuttgart: Gerd Hatje, 1979).

Exhibition of Mechanical Aids to Learning (London: The British Institute of Adult Education, 1930).

'Exhibition of Mechanical Aids to Learning', *Museums Journal*, 30, 5, 1930, p. 206.

'Exhibition of Visual and Aural Aid to Education', *Museums Journal*, 30, 2, 1930, p. 65.

Fagalay, William, Gilbert Wright and Frederick Dockstader, 'Thoughts on the Audio-Visual Revolution', *Museum News*, 51, 5, 1973, pp. 13–14.

Federici, Francesco, *Cinema esposto. Arte contemporanea e immagini in movimento* (Udine: Forum, 2017).

Fine, Paul A., 'The Role of Design in Educational Exhibits', *Curator*, 6, 1, 1963, pp. 37–44.
Flacke-Knoch, Monika, *Museumskonzeptionen in der Weimarer Republik: Die Tätigkeit Alexander Dorners im Provinzialmuseum Hannover* (Marburg, Jonas Verlag, 1985).
Fontanille, Jacques, *Soma et Séma: Figures du corps* (Paris: Maisonneuve et Larose, 2004).
Foster, H., 'The Imperial War Museum: Its New Home at Southwark', *Museums Journal*, 36, 5, 1936, pp. 215–22.
Foucault, Michel, *Discipline and Punish: The Birth of the Prison* (New York: Random House, 1975).
Foucault, Michel, 'The Confession of the Flesh', in Michel Foucault, *Power/Knowledge. Selected Interviews and Other Writings 1972–1977*, edited by Colin Gordon (New York: Pantheon Books, [1977] 1980), pp. 194–228.
Friedberg, Anne, *The Virtual Window. From Alberti to Microsoft* (Cambridge, MA and London: The MIT Press, 2006).
Friedberg, Anne, 'Trottoir roulant: The Cinema and New Mobilities of Spectatorship', in John Fullerton and Jan Olsson (eds), *Allegories of Communication: Intermedial Concerns from Cinema to the Digital* (Rome: John Libbey Publishing, 2004), pp. 263–76.
Friedberg, Anne, *Window Shopping. Cinema and the Postmodern* (Berkeley and Oxford: University of California Press, 1993).
Furse, William, 'The Panorama and the Cinema at the Imperial Institute', *Museums Journal*, 29, 10, 1930, pp. 336–42.
Gagnon, Monika Kin and Janine Marchessault, 'Introduction', in Monika Kin Gagnon and Janine Marchessault (eds), *Reimagining Cinema. Film at Expo 67* (Montreal and Kingston: McGill-Queen's University Press, 2014), pp. 3–14.
Gagnon, Monika Kin and Janine Marchessault (eds), *Reimagining Cinema. Film at Expo 67* (Montreal and Kingston: McGill-Queen's University Press, 2014).
Gardner, George S., 'The Shape of Things to Come', *Curator*, 22, 1, 1979, pp. 5–20.
Gaudreault, André and Tom Gunning, 'Early Cinema as a Challenge to Film History', in Wanda Strauven (ed.), *The Cinema of Attractions Reloaded* (Amsterdam: Amsterdam University Press, [1989] 2006), pp. 365–80.
Gaudreault, André, Catherine Russell and Pierre Véronneau (eds), *Le Cinématographe, nouvelle technologie du XXe siècle/The Cinema, A New Technology for the 20th Century* (Lausanne: Payot, 2004).
Gauthier, Christophe, *La Passion du cinéma. Cinéphiles, ciné-clubs et salles spécialisées à Paris de 1920 à 1929* (Paris: AFRHC/École des chartes, 1999).
Gebert, Jakob and Kai-Uwe Hemken, 'Raum der Gegenwart: Die Ordnung von Apparaten und Exponaten', in Ulrike Gärtner, Kai-Uwe Hemken, and Kai Uwe Schierz (eds), *KunstLichtSpiele: Lichtästhetik der klassischen Avantgarde* (Biefeld: Kerber Verlag, 2009), pp. 138–55.
Gibbons, Joan, *Contemporary Art and Memory. Images of Recollection and Remembrance* (London and New York: I. B. Tauris, 2007).
Gordon, Avery F., *Ghostly Matters: Haunting and the Sociological Imagination* (Minneapolis and London: University of Minnesota Press, [1997] 2008).
Gough, Maria, 'Constructivism Disoriented: El Lissitzky's Dresden and Hannover Demonstrationsräume', in Nancy Perloff and Brian Reed (eds), *Situating El Lissitzky: Vitebsk, Berlin, Moscow* (Los Angeles: The Getty Research Institute, 2003), pp. 77–125.
Grau, Oliver, *Virtual Art: From Illusion to Immersion* (Berlin: Reimer, 2001).
Greenaway, Peter, *Ripopolare la Reggia/Peopling the Palaces. 100 Archetipi per rappresentare la Corte/100 Archetypes to Represent the Court* (Torino: Volumina, 2007).
Gregory, Kate and Andrea Witcomb, 'Beyond Nostalgia: The Role of Affect in Generating

Historical Understanding at Heritage Sites', in Simon Knell, Suzanne MacLeod and Sheila Watson (eds), *Museum Revolutions: How Museums Change and Are Changed* (London and New York: Routledge, 2007), pp. 263–75.

Greenaway, Peter, *100 Objects to Represent the World* (Stuttgard: Verlag Gerd Hatje, 1992).

Greenaway, Peter, *The Stairs 1: Geneva, the Location* (London: Holberton, 1994).

Greenaway, Peter and Elisabeth Schweeger (eds), *The Stairs 2: Munich Projection* (London: Merrell Holberton, 1995).

Greub, Suzanne and Thierry Greub (eds), *Museums in the Twenty-First Century: Concepts, Projects, Buildings* (Munich: Prestel, 2006).

Griffith, David W., 'Some Prophecies: Film and Theatre, Screenwriting, Education', in Harry M. Geduld (ed.), *Focus on D. W. Griffith* (Englewood Cliffs, NJ: Prentice-Hall, 1971), pp. 34–5.

Griffiths, Alison, '"Automatic Cinema" and Illustrated Radio: Multimedia in the Museum', in Charles R. Acland (ed.), *Residual Media* (Minneapolis: University of Minnesota Press, 2007), pp. 69–95.

Griffiths, Alison, 'Film Education in the Natural History Museum: Cinema Lights Up the Gallery in the 1920s', in Marsha Orgeron, Devin Orgeron, and Dan Streible (eds), *Learning with the Lights Off* (New York: Oxford University Press, 2012), pp. 124–44.

Griffiths, Alison, '"Journey for Those Who Can Not Travel": Promenade Cinema and the Museum Life Group', *Wide Angle*, 18, 3, 1996, pp. 53–84.

Griffiths, Alison, 'Media Technology and Museum Display: A Century of Accommodation and Conflict', in David Thorburn and Henry Jenkins (eds), *Rethinking Media Change. The Aesthetics of Transition* (Cambridge, MA: MIT Press, 2003), pp. 375–89.

Griffiths, Alison, *Shivers Down Your Spine. Cinema, Museums and the Immersive View* (New York: Columbia University Press, 2008).

Griffiths, Alison, *Wondrous Difference. Cinema, Anthropology, and Turn of the Century Visual Culture* (New York: Columbia University Press, 2002).

Groys, Boris, 'Media Art in the Museum', *Last Call*, 2, 1, 2001, <http://www.belkin.ubc.ca/_archived/lastcall/past/pages2/page2.html> (last accessed 30 September 2018).

Groys, Boris, 'The Struggle Against the Museum; or, The Display of Art in Totalitarian Space', in Daniel J. Sherman and Irit Rogoff (eds), *Museum Culture: Histories, Discourses, Spectacles* (Mineapolis: University of Minnesota Press, 1994), pp. 144–62.

Guerin, Frances and Roger Hallas, 'Introduction', in Frances Guerin and Roger Hallas (eds), *The Image and the Witness: Trauma, Memory and Visual Culture* (London and New York: Wallflower, 2007), pp. 1–20.

Guerin, Frances and Roger Hallas (eds), *The Image and the Witness: Trauma, Memory and Visual Culture* (London and New York: Wallflower, 2007).

Gunning, Tom, 'Attractions: How They Came into the World', in Wanda Strauven (ed.), *The Cinema of Attractions Reloaded* (Amsterdam: Amsterdam University Press, 2006), pp. 31–40.

Gunning, Tom, 'The Cinema of Attractions. Early Film, its Spectator and the Avant-Garde', in Wanda Strauven (ed.), *The Cinema of Attractions Reloaded* (Amsterdam: Amsterdam University Press, [1986] 2006), pp. 381–8.

Gunning, Tom, 'Fantasmagorie et fabrication de l'illusion: pour une culture optique du dispositif cinématographique', *Cinémas*, 14, 1, 2003, pp. 67–89.

Gunning, Tom, 'The Transforming Image: The Roots of Animation in Metamorphosis and Motion', in Suzanne Buchan (ed.), *Pervasive Animation. An AFI Film Reader* (London and New York: Routledge, 2013), pp. 52–69.

Gunning, Tom, 'The World as Object Lesson: Cinema Audiences, Visual Culture and the St. Louis World's Fair, 1904', *Film History*, 6, 4, 1994, pp. 422–44.

Hansen, Miriam, *Babel and Babylon: Spectatorship in American Silent Film* (Cambridge, MA: Harvard University Press, 1991).

Hediger, Vinzenz and Patrick Vonderau (eds), *Films that Work: Industrial Film and the Productivity of Media* (Amsterdam: Amsterdam University Press, 2009).

Hein, Hilde, *The Museum in Transition: A Philosophical Perspective* (Washington, DC: Smithsonian Institution Press, 2000).

Henning, Michelle, 'Legibility and Affect: Museums as New Media', in Sharon MacDonald and Paul Basu (eds), *Exhibition Experiments* (London: Blackwell Publishing, 2007), pp. 25–46.

Henning, Michelle (ed.), *Museum Media – The International Handbooks of Museum Studies* (New York: Wiley Blackwell, 2015).

Henning, Michelle, *Museums, Media and Cultural Theory* (Maidenhead: Open University Press, 2006).

Historial Charles de Gaulle, *Dossier de presse* (Paris: Historial Charles de Gaulle, 2008), http://www.culture.gouv.fr/culture/actualites/conferen/albanel/dphistorial08.pdf> (last accessed 30 September 2018).

Hooper-Greenhill, Eilean, *Museums and the Interpretation of Visual Culture* (London and New York, Routledge: 2000).

Hooper-Greenhill, Eilean, *Museums and the Shaping of Knowledge* (London and New York, Routledge: 1992).

Hoskins, Andrew and Amy Holdsworth, 'Media Archaeology in/of the Museum', in Michelle Henning (ed.), *Museum Media* (New York: Wiley Blackwell, 2015), pp. 23–41.

Houston, Penelope, *Keepers of the Frame: The Film Archives* (London: British Film Institute, 1994).

Hughes, Catherine, *Museum Theatre: Communicating with Visitors through Drama* (Portsmouth, NH: Heinemann, 1998).

Huhtamo, Erkki and Jussi Parikka, *Media Archaeology. Approaches, Applications, and Implications* (Berkeley and Los Angeles: University of California Press, 2011).

Huyssen, Andreas, *Present Pasts: Urban Palimpsests and the Politics of Memory* (Stanford: Stanford University Press, 2003).

Huyssen, Andreas, *Twilight Memories: Marking Time in a Culture of Amnesia* (London and New York: Routledge, 1995).

In Flanders Fields Museum, *Educational Package* (Ieper, 2012).

'Imperial Institute', *Museums Journal*, 26, 5, 1926, p. 139.

Imperial Institute, *Annual Report 1926* (London: Imperial Institute, 1927).

Imperial Institute, *Annual Report 1927* (London: Imperial Institute, 1928).

Imperial Institute, *Annual Report 1929* (London: Imperial Institute, 1930).

Imperial Institute, *Annual Report 1930* (London: Imperial Institute, 1931).

Imperial Institute, *Bulletin of The Imperial Institute*, 34, 1936.

Imperial War Museum, *Annual Report 1986–1988* (London: HMSO, 1988).

Imperial War Museum, *Eighteenth Annual Report of the Imperial War Museum, 1934–1935* (London: HMSO, 1935).

Imperial War Museum, *Eightieth Annual Report of the Imperial War Museum, 1924–1925* (London: HMSO, 1925).

Imperial War Museum, *Eleventh Annual Report of the Imperial War Museum, 1927–1928* (London: HMSO, 1928).

Imperial War Museum, *Fourth Annual Report of the Imperial War Museum, 1920–1921* (London: HMSO, 1921).

Imperial War Museum, *Second Report of the Imperial War Museum, 1918–1919* (London: HMSO, 1919).
Imperial War Museum, *Seventeenth Annual Report of the Imperial War Museum, 1933–1934* (London: HMSO, 1934).
Imperial War Museum, *Sixth Annual Report of the Imperial War Museum, 1922–1923* (London: HMSO, 1923).
Imperial War Museum, *Tenth Annual Report of the Imperial War Museum, 1926–1927* (London: HMSO, 1927).
Imperial War Museum, *Third Annual Report of the Imperial War Museum 1919–1920* (London: HMSO, 1920).
Imperial War Museum, *Thirteenth Annual Report of the Imperial War Museum, 1929–1930* (London: HMSO, 1930).
Imperial War Museum, *Twelfth Annual Report of the Imperial War Museum, 1928–1929* (London: HMSO, 1929).
Imperial War Museum, *Twentieth Annual Report of the Imperial War Museum, 1937–1938* (London: HMSO, 1938).
Imperial War Museum, *Twenty-first Annual Report of The Director-General to the Board of Trustees, 1938–1939* (London: HMSO, 1939).
Imperial War Museum North (IWM North), *Accessible and Easy to Read Guide* (Manchester: Imperial War Museum North, s.d).
Imperial War Museum North (IWM North), *Your Visit Learning Resources. The Big Picture Show: Introduction 'Children and War', 'Weapons of War' and 'Why War?'* (Manchester: Imperial War Museum North, 2013).
Johnson, Christopher D., *Memory, Metaphor, and Aby Warburg's Atlas of Images* (Ithaca and New York: Cornell University Press, 2012).
Jameson, Fredric, *Postmodernism, or the Cultural Logic of Late Capitalism* (Durham, NC and London: Duke University Press, 1990).
Jameson, Fredric, *Signatures of the Visible* (London and New York: Routledge, 1990).
Johnstone, Paul, 'Museums and Television', *Museums Journal*, 64, 3, 1964, pp. 242–8.
Kalay, Yehuda E., Thomas Kvan and Janice Affleck (eds), *New Heritage. New Media and Cultural Heritage* (London and New York: Routledge, 2008).
Kaplan, Flora E. S., 'Making and Remaking National Identities', in Sharon Macdonald (ed.), *A Companion to Museum Studies* (Oxford: Blackwell Publishing, 2006), pp. 152–69.
Kaplan, Flora E. S. (ed.), *Museums and the Making of Ourselves: The Role of Objects in National Identity* (London and New York: Leicester University Press, 1994).
Katzive, David, 'Museums Enter the Video Generation', *Museum News*, January 1973, pp. 20–4.
Kavanagh, Gaynor, 'Museum as Memorial: The Origins of the Imperial War Museum', *Journal of Contemporary History*, 23, 1, 1988, pp. 77–97.
Kidd, Jenny, *Museums in the New Mediascape: Transmedia, Participation, Ethics* (London and New York: Routledge, 2016).
Kim, Jessica, 'Modern Museum Techniques: projectiondesign® Helps Visitors Better Comprehend the Stories of First World War', *AVING. Global News Network*, 20 February 2013, <http://us.aving.net/542089> (last accessed 30 September 2018).
'Kinema Films for Posterity', *Museums Journal*, 14, 10, 1915, pp. 336–7.
King, Margaret J., 'Never Land or Tomorrow Land?', *Museum International*, XLIII, 1, 1991, pp. 5–8.
Kirby, Lynne, *Parallel Tracks: The Railroad and Silent Cinema* (Durham, NC and London: Duke University Press, 1997).

Kirshenblatt-Gimblett, Barbara, *Destination Culture: Tourism, Museums and Heritage* (Berkeley: University of California Press, 1998).
Kissiloff, William, 'How to Use Mixed Media in Exhibits', *Curator*, 12, 2, 1969, pp. 83–95.
Kittler, Friedrich, *Discourse Networks 1800/1900* (Stanford: Stanford University Press, [1985] 1990).
Kotler, Neil, and Philip Kotler, *Museum Strategy and Marketing: Designing Missions, Building Audiences, Generating Revenue and Resources* (San Francisco: Jossey-Bass, 1998).
LaCapra, Dominick, *Writing History, Writing Trauma* (Baltimore and London: Johns Hopkins University Press, 2001).
'La cinématographie au service des Musées et des Monuments d'art', *Mouseion*, 25–6, 1934, pp. 156–160.
Landsberg, Alison, *Prosthetic Memory: The Transformation of American Remembrance in the Age of Mass Culture* (New York: Columbia University Press, 2004).
Lebart, Luce, 'Archiver les photographies fixes et animées: Matuszewski et l'"internationale documentaire"', in Magdalena Mazaraki (ed.), *Boleslas Matuszewski/Écrits cinématographiques* (Paris: Cinémathque française/AFRHC, 2006), pp. 47–66.
Leeder, Murray, 'Introduction', in Murray Leeder (ed.), *Cinematic Ghosts: Haunting and Spectrality From Silent Cinema to the Digital Era* (New York and London: Bloomsbury, 2015), pp. 1–14.
Leighton, Tanya (ed.), *Art and the Moving Image. A Critical Reader* (London: Tate/Afterall, 2008).
Levi, Pavle, *Cinema by Other Means* (Oxford and New York: Oxford University Press, 2012).
Lewis, Amanda, 'L.A. Museum of the Holocaust's Tree of Testimony Tells Survivors' Stories Through Video Art', *LA Weekly*, 23 April 2012, <http://www.laweekly.com/publicspectacle/2012/04/23/la-museum-of-the-holocausts-tree-of-testimony-tells-survivors-stories-through-video-art> (last accessed 30 September 2018).
Linsday, Harry, 'Visual Instruction at the Imperial Institute', *Museums Journal*, 36, 6, 1936, pp. 289–93.
Lindsay, Vachel, *The Art of the Moving Picture* (New York: Modern library, [1915] 2000).
Lissitzky, El, 'Exhibition Rooms', in Sophie Lissitzky-Küppers (ed.), *El Lissitzky: Life, Letters, Texts* (London: Thames & Hudson, [1926] 1968), pp. 366–7.
Lissitzky, El, *Union der Sozialistischen Sowjet-Republiken: Katalog des Sowjet-Pavillons auf der Internationalen Presse-Ausstellung Köln 1928* (Köln: M. Dumont Schauberg, 1928).
Lissitzky-Küppers, Sophie (ed.), *El Lissitzky: Life, Letters, Texts* (London: Thames & Hudson, 1968).
Löffer, Petra 'Ghosts of the City: A Spectrology of Cinematic Spaces', *communication +1*, 4, <http://scholarworks.umass.edu/cpo/vol4/iss1/9> (last accessed 30 September 2018).
Longair, Sarah and John McAleer (eds), *Curating Empire. Museums and the British Imperial Experience* (Manchester: Manchester University Press, 2012).
Lovey, Dianna, 'Museum av: Cultural Affairs', *Audio Visual Communications*, 13, 1979, pp. 12–18, 92.
Lowe, Edwin E., 'The Cinema in Museums', *Museums Journal*, 29, 10, 1930, pp. 342–7.
Luckhurst, Roger, 'The Contemporary London Gothic and the Limits of the "Spectral Turn"', *Textual Practice*, 13, 3, 2002, pp. 527–46.
Lugon, Olivier, 'Dynamic Paths of Thought. Exhibition Design, Photography and Circulation in the Work of Herbert Bayer', in François Albera and Maria Tortajada (eds), *Cinema Beyond Film: Media Epistemology in the Modern Era* (Amsterdam: Amsterdam University Press, 2010), pp. 117–44.
Lugon, Olivier, 'Entre l'Affiche et le monument, le photomural dans les années 1930', in

Olivier Lugon (ed.), *Exposition et médias: photographie, cinéma, télévision* (Lausanne: L'Age d'Homme, 2012), pp. 79–123.

Macdonald, Sharon, 'Expanding Museum Studies: An Introduction', in Sharon Macdonald (ed.), *A Companion to Museum Studies* (Oxford: Blackwell Publishing, 2006), pp. 1–12.

Macdonald, Sharon (ed.), *A Companion to Museum Studies* (Oxford: Blackwell Publishing, 2006).

Macdonald, Sharon and Helen Rees Leahy (eds), *The International Handbooks of Museum Studies* (New York: Wiley Blackwell, 2015), 4 volumes.

MacLeod, Suzanne, Jocelyn Dodd, and Tom Duncan, 'New Museum Design Cultures: Harnessing the Potential of Design and "Design Thinking" in Museums', *Museum Management and Curatorship*, 30, 4, 2015, pp. 314–41.

Malík, M., 'Principles of Automation in Museum Exhibitions', *Curator*, 6, 3, 1963, pp. 247–68.

Malraux, André, *Museum without Walls* (London: Secker and Warburg, [1947] 1965).

Mannoni, Laurent, *The Great Art of Light and Shadow: Archaeology of the Cinema* (Exeter: University of Exeter Press, [1994] 2000).

Martin, David, 'Making Movies', *Museum Practice*, Winter 2006, pp. 46–8.

Matuszewski, Bolesław, 'A New Source of History', in Bolesław Matuszewski, *A New Source of History. Animated Photography: What It Is, What It Should Be* (Warsaw: Filmoteka Narodowa, [1898] 1999), pp. 25–30.

Matuszewski, Bolesław, 'Animated Photography: What It Is, What It Should Be', in Bolesław Matuszewski, *A New Source of History. Animated Photography: What it is, What it Should Be* (Warsaw: Filmoteka Narodowa, [1898] 1999), pp. 33–65.

Maule, Rosanna (ed.), 'Representational Technologies and the Discourse on Early Cinema's Apparatus/Les Technologies de représentation et le discours sur le dispositif cinématographique des premiers temps', *Cinéma & Cie. International Film Studies Journal*, special issue, 3, 2003.

McCann Morley, Grace L., 'Présentation des expositions éducatives', *Museum*, V, 2, 1952, pp. 80–6.

McCarthy, Conal (ed.), *Museum Practice* (New York: Wiley Blackwell, 2015).

McClusky, Frederick D., 'Place of Moving Pictures in Visual Education', *University of Illinois Bulletin*, XX, 46, 1923, pp. 3–11.

McLean, Kathleen, 'Do Museum Exhibitions Have a Future?', *Curator*, 50, 1, 2007, pp. 109–21.

McLuhan, Marshall, *The Gutenberg Galaxy: The Making of Typographic Man* (Toronto: University of Toronto Press, 1962).

McLuhan, Marshall, *Understanding Media: The Extensions of Man* (New York: McGraw-Hill, 1964).

McLuhan, Marshall, Harley Parker and Jacques Barzun, *Exploration of the Ways, Means, and Values of Museum Communication with the Viewing Public* (New York: Museum of the City of New York, 1969).

Message, Kylie and Andrea Witcomb (eds), *Museum Theories* (New York: Wiley Blackwell, 2015).

Metz, Christian, *The Imaginary Signifier: Psychoanalysis and the Cinema* (Bloomington: Indiana University Press, [1977] 1982).

Michalka, Matthias (ed.), *X-Screen. Film Installation and Actions in the 1960s and 1970s* (Köln: Walther König, 2004).

Michaud, Philippe-Alain (ed.), *Le Mouvement des images* (Paris: Centre Georges Pompidou, 2006).

Miller, Robert C., 'A Scientific Museum's Experiment in Television', *Museum*, V, 4, 1952, pp. 248–59.

'Ministry of Information: Films and Projectors', *Museums Journal*, 41, 2, 1941, p. 32.

'Ministry of Information Films in Museums and Art Galleries', *Museums Journal*, 42, 1, 1942, p. 4.
Mintz, Ann, 'That's Edutainment', *Museum News*, 73, 6, 1994, pp. 32–5.
Moholy-Nagy, László, 'Lichtrequisit einer elektrischen Bühne / Installation lumineuse d'une scne électrique / Lighting Requisite for an Electric Stage', *Die Form*, 5, 11–12, 1930, pp. 297–8.
Moholy-Nagy, László, *Painting, Photography, Film* (Cambridge, MA: MIT Press, [1925] 1969).
Morettin, Eduardo, 'Universal Exhibitions and the Cinema: History and Culture', *Revista Brasileira de História*, 31, 61, 2011, pp. 231–49.
Mumford, Lewis, *Technics and Civilization* (New York: Harcourt, Brace and Co., 1934).
'"Museum of Art" to be Made Available in 34 Languages', *Business Screen*, 19, 5, 1958, p. 23.
'Museums and Movies', *Museums Journal*, 29, 10, 1930, pp. 334–51.
Mumford, Lewis, *The Culture of Cities* (San Diego, New York and London: Harvest/HBJ, [1938] 1970).
Nead, Lynda, 'The Artist's Studio: The Affair of Art and Film', in Angela Dalle Vacche (ed.), *Film, Art, New Media. Museum without Walls?* (Basingstoke: Palgrave Macmillan, 2012), pp. 23–7.
Nead, Lynda, *The Haunted Gallery: Painting, Photography, Film c.1900* (New Haven and London: Yale University Press, 2007).
Nichols, Bill, *Introduction to Documentary* (Bloomington: Indiana University Press, [2001] 2010).
Noordegraaf, Julia, *Strategies of Display. Museum Presentation in Nineteenth- and Twentieth-Century Visual Culture* (Rotterdam: NAi-Museum Boijmans van Beuningen, 2004).
Noordegraaf, Julia, Cosetta G. Saba, Barbara Le Maître and Vinzenz Hediger (eds), *Preserving and Exhibiting Media Art: Challenges and Perspectives* (Amsterdam: Amsterdam University Press, 2013).
Ockman, Joan, 'The Road Not Taken: Alexander Dorner's Way Beyond Art', in Robert E. Somol (ed.), *Autonomy and Ideology: Positioning an Avant-Garde in America* (New York: Monacelli, 1997), pp. 80–120.
O'Doherty, Brian, *Inside the White Cube: The Ideology of the Gallery Space* (Berkeley and Los Angeles: University of California Press, 1976).
Orgeron, Marsha, Devin Orgeron and Dan Streible (eds), *Learning with the Lights Off* (New York and Oxford: Oxford University Press, 2012).
Paci, Viva, *La Machine à voir. A propos de cinéma, attraction, exhibition* (Lille: Presses Universitaires du Septentrion, 2012).
Païni, Dominique, *Le temps exposé. Le cinéma de la salle au musée* (Paris: L'Etoile and Cahiers du cinéma, 2002).
Païni, Dominique and Guy Cogeval (eds), *Hitchcock et l'Art: coïncidences fatales* (Paris: Centre Pompidou and Milan: Fondazione Mazzotta, 2000).
Pardo, Jordi, 'Audiovisual Installations as a Strategy for the Modernisation of Heritage Presentation Spaces', *AVICOM -Cahiers d'etude*, 5, 1998, pp. 17–21.
Parikka, Jussi, *What is Media Archaeology?* (Cambridge: Polity Press, 2012).
Parr, Albert E., 'Some Basic Problems of Visual Education by Means of Exhibits', *Curator*, 5, 1, 1962, pp. 36–44.
Parr, Albert E., 'The Arrogance of Artlessness', *Curator*, 6, 3, 1963, pp. 240–3.
Parr, Albert E., 'The Time and Place for Experimentation in Museum Design', *Curator*, 1, 4, 1958, pp. 36–40.
Parry, Ross (ed.), *Museums in a Digital Age* (London and New York: Routledge, 2010).
Parry, Ross and Andrew Sawyer, 'Space and the Machine. Adaptive Museums, Pervasive

Technology and the New Gallery Environment', in Suzanne MacLeod (ed.), *Reshaping Museum Space. Architecture, Design, Exhibitions* (London and New York: Routledge, 2005), pp. 39–52.

Pascoe, David, *Peter Greenaway: Museums and Moving Images* (London: Reaktion Books, 1997).

Pearce, Susan, *Interpreting Objects and Collections* (London and New York: Routledge, 1994).

Peeren, Esther, *The Spectral Metaphor. Living Ghosts and the Agency of Invisibility* (Basingstoke: Palgrave Macmillan, 2014).

Pickford, John, 'Making the Churchill Museum', <http://www.cassonmann.co.uk/publications/making- the-churchill-museum, last visit 7 march 2015> (last accessed 30 September 2018).

Pine, Joseph and James H. Gilmore, *The Experience Economy: Work Is Theater & Every Business a Stage* (Boston, MA: Harvard Business School Press, 1999).

Pine, B. Joseph and James H. Gilmore, 'Museums & Authenticity', *Museum News*, May–June 2007, pp. 76–80, 92–3.

Postman, Neil, 'Love Your Machine', *Museum International*, XLIII, 1, 1991, p. 9.

'Problèmes d'organisation des musées ethnographiques', *Mouseion: revue internationale de muséographie*, 10, 1, 1930, pp. 61–3.

Rader, Karen A. and Victoria E. M. Cain, *Life on Display: Revolutionizing U.S. Museums of Science and Natural History in the Twentieth Century* (Chicago and London: University of Chicago Press, 2014).

Radford, Thomas, 'From A to V.', *Museum News*, 52, 5, 1974, pp. 36–40.

Ramsey, Grace Fisher, *Educational Work in Museums of the United States. Development, Methods and Trends* (New York: The HW Wilson Company, 1938).

'Réunion de la Commission consultative d'experts de l'Office International des Musées (8 et 9 Février 1929)', *Mouseion*, 7, 1929, pp. 76–84.

Richter, Hans, *Filmgegner von Heute - Filmfreunde von Morgen* (Berlin: H. Reckendorf, 1929).

Ricœur, Paul, *Memory, History, Forgetting* (Chicago and London: University of Chicago Press 2004).

Riou, Florence, 'Le Cinéma à l'Exposition internationale de 1937: un média au service de la recherche scientifique', *1895. Revue d'Histoire du Cinéma*, 58, 2009, pp. 30–55.

Rivire, Georges Henri, *UNESCO Regional Seminar on the Educational Role of Museums. Rio de Janeiro, Brazil 7–30 September 1958. Report* (Paris: UNESCO, 1960).

Rjasanzew, Igor, 'El Lissitzky und die "Pressa" in Köln 1928', in Jürgen Scharfe (ed.), *El Lissitzky* (Halle: Staatliche Galerie Moritzburg, 1982), pp. 72–81.

'Road to Victory: A Procession of Photographs of the Nation at War', *The Bulletin of the Museum of Modern Art*, special issue, 9, 5–6, 1942.

Roberts, Lisa C., *From Knowledge to Narrative: Educators and the Changing Museum* (Washington, DC: Smithsonian Institution Press, 1997).

Rosen, Phil (ed.), *Narrative, Apparatus, Ideology* (New York: Columbia University Press, 1986).

Royoux, Jean-Christophe, 'Cinéma d'exposition: l'espacement de la durée', *Art Press*, 262, 2000.

Royoux, Jean-Christophe, 'Pour un cinéma d'exposition. Retour sur quelques jalons historiques', *Omnibus*, 20, 1997.

Rydell, Robert W., 'World Fairs and Museums', in Sharon Macdonald (ed.), *A Companion to Museum Studies* (Oxford: Blackwell Publishing, 2006), pp. 135–51.

Rydell, Robert W., *World of Fairs: The Century-of-Progress Expositions* (Chicago and London: University of Chicago Press, 1993).

Samson, Denis, 'La Trame narrative, le multimédia et l'Exposition Universelle', in V.V. A. A.,

La Science en scne (Paris: Presse de l'Ecole Normale Supérieure-Palais de la Découverte, 1996), pp. 121–34.

Sarkar, Bhaskar, and Janet Walker (eds), *Documentary Testimonies: Global Archives of Suffering* (London and New York: Routledge, 2009).

Scandiffio, Theresa, *'Better'n Any Circus That Ever Come To Town': Cinema, Visual Culture And Educational Programming At Chicago's Field Museum Of Natural History* (PhD dissertation, Chicago: University of Chicago, 2008).

Schnapp, Jeffrey T., 'Unlevel Crossings', in Studio Terragni, Jeffrey T. Schnapp, Film Work, and Gruppe Gut Gestaltung (eds), *Tunnel REvision: Le Gallerie di Piedicastello = The Trento Tunnels* (Trento: Fondazione Museo storico del Trentino, 2010), pp. 24–8.

Schoener, Allon, 'An Art Museum's Experiment in Television', *Museum*, V, 4, 1952, pp. 239–44.

Schorr, Thomas, *Die Film und Kinoreformbewegung und die deutsche Filmwirtschaft* (PhD dissertation, Munich: Universität der Bundeswehr, 1990).

Schubert, Karsten, *The Curator's Egg* (London: Ridinghouse, 2000).

Sconce, Jeffrey, *Haunted Media. Electronic Presence from Telegraphy to Television* (Durham, NC and London: Duke University Press, 2000).

Searle, John, *Speech Acts: An Essay in the Philosophy of Language* (Cambridge: Cambridge University Press, 1969).

Serrell, Beverly, 'The Abraham Lincoln Presidential Library and Museum. The Civil War in Four Minutes', *Curator*, 49, 1, January 2006, pp. 105–8.

Shandler, Jeffrey, *Holocaust Memory in the Digital Age* (Stanford: Stanford University Press, 2017).

Shannon, Joseph, 'The Icing Is Good but the Cake Is Rotten', *Museum News*, 52, 5, 1974, pp. 29–34.

Shaw, Robert P., *Exhibition Techniques: A Summary of Exhibition Practice Based on Surveys Conducted at the New York and San Francisco World Fairs of 1939* (New York: New York Museum of Science and Industry, 1940).

Shaw, Robert P., 'Visualizing the Industrial Exhibit', *Business Screen*, 1, 3, 1938, pp. 30, 33, 46.

Shearman, John, *Only Connect...: Art and the Spectator in the Italian Renaissance* (Washington, DC: The National Gallery of Art and Princeton: Princeton University Press, 1992).

Shenker, Noah, *Reframing Holocaust Testimony* (Bloomington: Indiana University Press, 2016).

Slide, Anthony, *Nitrate Won't Wait. A History of Film Preservation in the United States* (Jefferson, NC: McFarland & Company, 1992).

Smallcombe, W. A., 'Films in Museums', *Museums Journal*, 44, 10, 1945, p. 207.

Smither, Roger and David Walsh, 'Unknown Pioneer: Edward Foxen. Cooper and the Imperial War Museum Film Archive, 1919–1934', *Film History*, 12, 2, 2000, pp. 187–203.

Spigel, Lynn, *TV by Design: Modern Art and the Rise of Network Television* (Chicago and London: University of Chicago Press, 2008).

Spock, Daniel, 'Lincolns in Latex: Exploring Lincoln's Legacy at the Abraham Lincoln Library and Museum', *Curator*, 49, 1, 2006, pp. 95–104.

Staniszewski, Mary Anne, *The Power of Display. A History of Exhibition Installations at the Museum of Modern Art* (Cambridge, MA: MIT Press, 1998).

Steinorth, Klaus (ed.), *Internationale Ausstellung des Deutschen Werkbundes Film und Foto: Stuttgart, 1929* (Stuttgart: Deutsche Verlags-Anstalt, 1979).

Stemmrich, Gregor, 'White Cube, Black Box and Grey Areas: Venues and Values', in Tanya Leighton (ed.), *Art and the Moving Image. A Critical Reader* (London: Tate/Afterall, 2008), pp. 430–43.

Stewart, Susan, 'Prologue: From the Museum of Touch', in Marius Kwint, Christopher Breward, Jeremy Aynsley (eds), *Material Memories* (Oxford: Berg, 1999), pp. 17–37.

Stier, Oren Baruch, *Committed to Memory. Cultural Mediations of the Holocaust* (Ameherst-Boston: University of Massachusetts Press, 2003).
Stoichita, Victor I., *The Pygmalion Effect: From Ovid to Hitchcock* (Chicago and London: University of Chicago Press, 2008).
Strauven, Wanda, 'Early Cinema's Touch(able) Screens: From Uncle Josh to Ali Barbouyou', *NECSUS: European Journal of Media Studies*, 2, 2012, <http://www.necsus-ejms.org/early-cinemas-touchable-screens-from-uncle-josh-to-ali-barbouyou/> (last accessed 30 September 2018).
Strauven, Wanda, 'Media Archaeology: Where Film History, Media Art, and New Media (Can) Meet', in Noordegraaf, Julia, Cosetta G. Saba, Barbara Le Maître and Vinzenz Hediger (eds), *Preserving and Exhibiting Media Art: Challenges and Perspectives* (Amsterdam: Amsterdam University Press, 2013), pp. 59–79.
Strauven, Wanda (ed.), *The Cinema of Attractions Reloaded* (Amsterdam: Amsterdam University Press, 2006).
Studio Azzurro, 'From Museums as Collections to Museums as Narration', in Studio Azzurro (ed.), *Musei di narrazione. Percorsi interattivi e affreschi multimediali/Museums as Narration. Interactive Experiences and Multimedia Frescoes* (Cinisello Balsamo: Silvana Editoriale, 2011), pp. 22–35.
Studio Azzurro, 'Museo audiovisivo della Resistenza', in Studio Azzurro (ed.), *Musei di narrazione. Percorsi interattivi e affreschi multimediali/Museums as Narration. Interactive Experiences and Multimedia Frescoes* (Cinisello Balsamo: Silvana Editoriale, 2011), pp. 55–7.
Studio Azzurro, 'Progettare musei, liberare menti', in UOS Centro Studi e Ricerche ASL Roma and Studio Azzurro, *Museo laboratorio della mente – Portatori di storie. Da vicino nessuno è normale* (Cinisello Balsamo: Silvana Editoriale, 2012), pp. 18–45.
Studio Azzurro (ed.), *Studio Azzurro. Immagini sensibili* (Cinisello Balsamo: Silvana Editoriale, 2006).
Survey of Situation Regarding Non-Theatrical Cinematograph Apparatus and Films (London: British Film Institute, 1934).
Sutton, Gloria, *The Experience Machine: Stan VanDerBeek's Movie-Drome and Expanded Cinema* (Cambridge, MA: MIT Press, 2015).
Taillibert, Christel, *L'Institut International du Cinematographe Educatif: regards sur le role du cinema educatif dans la politique internationale du fascisme italien* (Paris: L'Harmattan, 1999).
Taylor, Diana, *The Archive and the Repertoire: Performing Cultural Memory in the Americas* (Durham, NC and London: Duke University Press, 2003).
'The Dramagraph', *Museums Journal*, 31, 1, 1931, pp. 23–5.
'The Imperial Institute', *Bulletin of the Imperial Institute*, II, 1904, pp. 1–6.
'The Imperial Institute Exhibition Galleries', *Museums Journal*, 26, 8, 1927, pp. 193–8.
'The Mannheim Conference on Museums as Places of Popular Culture', *Museums Journal*, 3, 4, 1903, pp. 105–9.
Thomas, Selma and Ann Mintz (eds), *The Virtual and the Real: Media in the Museum* (Washington, DC: American Association of Museums, 1998).
Treleani, Matteo, *Qu'est-ce que le patrimoine numérique? Une sémiologie de la circulation des archives* (Lormont: Le Bord de l'Eau, 2017).
Trodd, Tamara (ed.), *Screen/Space. The Projected Image in Contemporary Art* (Manchester: Manchester University Press, 2011).
Trope, Alison, 'Le Cinéma pour le Cinéma: Making Museums of the Moving Image', *The Moving Image*, 1, 1, 2001, pp. 29–67.
Tschichold, Jan, 'Display that Has Dynamic Force, Exhibition Stands Designed by El Lissitzky', *Commercial Art*, 10, 1931, pp. 21–6.

Tupitsyn, Margarita, 'Back to Moscow', in Margarita Tupitsyn (ed.), *El Lissitzky. Beyond the Abstract Cabinet. Photography, Design, Collaboration* (New Haven: Yale University Press and Hanover: Sprengel Museum, 1999), pp. 25–51.

UNESCO, *Convention for the Safeguarding of the Intangible Cultural Heritage 2003*, <http://portal.unesco.org/en/ev.php-URL_ID=17716&URL_DO=DO_TOPIC&URL_SECTION=201.html/> (last accessed 30 September 2018).

UOS Centro Studi e Ricerche ASL Roma and Studio Azzurro, *Museo laboratorio della mente – Portatori di storie. Da vicino nessuno è normale* (Cinisello Balsamo: Silvana Editoriale, 2012).

UOS Centro Studi e Ricerche ASL Roma and Studio Azzurro (eds), *Museo Laboratorio della Mente* (Cinisello Blasamo: Silvana Editoriale, 2010).

Uroskie, Andrew V., *Between the Black Box and the White Cube: Expanded Cinema and Postwar Art* (Chicago and London: University of Chicago Press, 2014).

Urry, John and Jonas Larsen, *The Tourist Gaze 3.0* (London: Sage, 2011).

Valéry, Paul, 'The Problem of Museums', in Paul Valéry, *The Collected Works of Paul Valéry*, vol. 12 (New York: Pantheon Books, [1923] 1960), pp. 202–7.

Van Assche, Christine, Catherine David and Raymond Bellour (eds), *Passages de l'image. Films, vidéos, images de synthèse* (Paris: Centre Georges Pompidou, 1990).

Vergo, Peter (ed.), *The New Museology* (London: Reaktion Books, 1989).

Violi, Patrizia, 'Spectacularizing Trauma: The Experientialist Visitor of Memory Museums', *Versus. Quaderni di studi semiotici*, 119, July–December 2014, pp. 51–70.

Virilio, Paul, 'The Third Window: An Interview with Paul Virilio', in Cynthia Schneider and Brian Wallis (eds), *Global Television* (Cambridge, MA: MIT Press, 1988), pp. 185–197.

VV. AA., *Agnès Varda. L'Ile et elle. Regards sur l'exposition* (Paris: Fondation Cartier, 2006).

Wainwright, Clive and Charlotte Gere, 'The Making of the South Kensington Museum II: Collecting Modern Manufactures: 1851 and the Great Exhibition', *Journal of the History of Collections*, 14, 1, 2002, pp. 25–43.

Walton Smith, F. G., 'Planet Ocean: Applying Disneyland Techniques at a Science Museum', *Curator*, 25, 2, 1982, pp. 121–30.

Warburg, Aby, *Der Bilderatlas: Mnemosyne*, edited by Martin Warnke and Claudia Brink (Berlin: Akademie Verlag, 2000).

Ward, Janet, *Weimar Surfaces: Urban Visual Culture in 1920s Germany.* (Berkeley: University of California Press, 2001).

Warner, Marina, *Phantasmagoria: Spirit Visions, Metaphors, and Media into the Twenty-first Century* (Oxford: Oxford University Press, 2008).

Wasson, Haidee, 'Big, Fast Museums/Small, Slow Movies: Film, Scale, and the Art Museum', in Charles R. Acland and Haidee Wasson (eds), *Useful Cinema* (Durham, NC and London: Duke University Press, 2011), pp. 178–204.

Wasson, Haidee, 'Every Home an Art Museum: Mediating and Merchandising the Metropolitan', in Charles R. Acland (ed.), *Residual Media* (Minneapolis: University of Minnesota Press, 2007), pp. 158–85.

Wasson, Haidee, *Museum Movies: The Museum of Modern Art and the Birth of Art Cinema* (Berkeley, Los Angeles and London: University of California Press, 2005).

Wasson, Haidee, 'The Other Small Screen: Moving Images at New York's World Fair, 1939', *Canadian Journal of Film Studies*, 21, 1, 2012, pp. 81–103.

Watson, Sheila, 'Emotions in the History Museum', in Andrea Witcomb and Kylie Message (eds), *Museum Theory – The International Handbooks of Museum Studies* (New York: Wiley Blackwell, 2013), pp. 283–302.

W. E. S, 'The Cinema and the Museum', *Museums Journal*, 55, 12, 1956, pp. 301–2.

Wieviorka, Annette, *The Era of the Witness* (Ithaca and New York: Cornell University Press, 2006).
Williams, Paul, 'Memorial Museums and the Objectification of Suffering', in Janet C. Marstine (ed.), *The Routledge Companion to Museum Ethics: Redefining Ethics for the Twenty-First Century Museum* (London and New York: Routledge, 2011), pp. 220–35.
Williams, Paul, *Memorial Museums: The Global Rush to Commemorate Atrocities* (Oxford and New York: Berg, 2007).
Witcomb, Andrea, 'Interactivity: Thinking Beyond', in Sharon Macdonald (ed.), *A Companion to Museum Studies* (Oxford: Blackwell Publishing, 2006), pp. 353–61.
Witcomb, Andrea, *Re-Imagining the Museum. Beyond the Mausoleum* (London and New York: Routledge, 2003).
Witkovsky, Matthew S. (ed.), *Avant-Garde Art in Everyday Life: Early Twentieth-Century European Modernism* (Chicago and New Haven: Art Institute of Chicago and Yale University Press, 2011).
Witteborg, Lothar P., 'Curator Look at "Expo 58"', *Curator*, 1, 4, pp. 41–8.
Witteborg, Lothar P., 'Design Standards in Museum Exhibits', *Curator*, 1, 1, 1958, pp. 29–41.
Wonders, Karen, *Habitat Dioramas. Illusions of Wilderness in Museums of Natural History* (Uppsala: Almqvist & Wiksell, 1993).
Worsley, Giles, 'A Globe Ripped to Pieces', *The Daily Telegraph*, 29 June 2002, <http://www.telegraph.co.uk/culture/art/3579471/A-globe-ripped-to-pieces.html> (last accessed 30 September 2018).
Youngblood, Gene, *Expanded Cinema* (New York: P. Dutton & Co., 1970).

Index

Abraham Lincoln Presidential Library and Museum, 76–7
Abstract Cabinet, 47–8; *see also* Lissitzky, El
Albera, François, 49
American Museum of Natural History, 8, 9, 25n, 30, 67–8
Ang, Ien, 99
archival footage, 33–4, 37, 82–5, 92, 98, 118, 119, 120, 125, 126, 127
Arnold-de Simine, Silke, 7–8, 80n, 99, 100–1
assemblage, 5
Audiovisual Museum of Resistance, 125–6
audio-visual reconstructions, 33, 74–5, 78, 86–7, 96–100, 112

Balsom, Erika, 3, 115–16, 122n
Baudry, Jean-Louis, 5, 13n
Bayer, Herbert, 46, 49–50, 51–2, 106, 113n
Bellour, Raymond, 3, 122n, 137
Beneš, Josef, 66, 68
Bennett, Tony, 52, 105
Billing, Scott, 100
black box, 3, 58n, 65, 115
Boni, Federico, 92, 130
Bottomore, Stephen, 19
BRC Imagination Arts, 76–7
British Film Institute, 41
British Museum, 19
Bruno, Giuliana, 113, 133–4

Cain, Victoria E. M., 53–4
Canudo, Ricciotto, 1
Casetti, Francesco, 2, 5, 122n
Chicago Museum of Science and Industry, 52
Churchill Museum, 83–5
cinema
   artists' cinema, 3, 101, 138
   cinema of exhibition, 3
   other cinema, 3, 122n
   othered cinema, 3, 115, 122n

theatres in museums, 28–9, 34, 62, 119–21
   see also dispositif
Commission on Educational and Cultural Films, 21
Connolly, Maeve, 3, 101, 115
Cummings, Carlos, E., 53, 54

Day, Will, 1, 12n, 30, 35, 39
de Jong, Steffi, 8
Deleuze, Gilles, 5
De Rosa, Miriam, 133
Derrida, Jacques, 94, 95, 99
diorama *see* panorama at the Imperial Institute
dispositif, 46
   cinematic *dispositif*, 2, 3, 9, 79, 138
   cinematic *dispositif* and museum exhibition, 5–6, 46, 105, 117–18, 137–8
   'classic' cinematic *dispositif* (viewing situation inside the movie theatre), 2–3, 9, 13n, 29, 50, 58n, 117, 137
   definition, 5–6, 13n
   see also assemblage, dispositive
dispositive, 5, 13n; *see also dispositif*
Dockstader, Frederick, 66
Dramagraph, 30
Dubois, Philippe, 3
Durand, Jacques, 62

education
   and/vs entertainment in museums and great exhibitions, 11, 23, 27, 53, 54, 67, 68, 101, 124–5
   role of cinema in, 20–1, 22, 33–4
Eisenstein, Sergei, 49, 50, 79, 105
Elsaesser, Thomas, 9–10, 101
Elwes, Catherine, 6
entertainment
   and audio-visuals in museums and great exhibitions, 54, 56, 67, 101, 116

entertainment (*cont.*)
  and/vs education in museums and great exhibitions *see* education
  museums and entertainment venues, 23, 24, 67, 75–6, 116
  Mutoscopes as entertainment devices, 35–6
epidiascope, 30
Exhibition of Mechanical Aids to Learning, 21, 40
experience
  economy, 75
  in museums, 75–80

Fagalay, William, 66
ffoulkes, Charles (Major), 35–7, 39, 40
Field Museum of Natural History, 25n, 52
Film und Foto Exhibition, 49; *see also* Lissitzky, El
Fontanille, Jacques, 84
Foucault, Michel, 5, 10
Foxen Cooper, Edward, 32, 36, 37, 39
Fredy, Morgan, 18
Furse, William T., 27–8, 29

Galleries of Piedicastello (Trento Tunnels), 106–9
Gance, Abel, 120
Gardner, George S., 67–8
Gaudreault, André, 79, 102
ghosts
  as a conceptual metaphor, 91–2, 112, 129
  in contemporary art, 101
  in contemporary museums, 91, 101–2, 108, 109, 129–30, 138
  in early cinema, 91
  witnesses as ghosts, 95, 96–100
  see also Phantasmagoria, spectre
Gilmore, James H., 75
Godard, Jean-Luc, 2
Greenaway, Peter, 110–13
Gregory, Kate, 77
Griffith, David W., 25n
Griffiths, Alison, 8–9, 10–11, 25n, 30
Groys, Boris, 100
Gunning, Tom, 79, 102, 109

Hein, Hilde, 78
Henning, Michelle, 7, 23
Historial Charles de Gaulle, 84–5, 119–21, 138
Hooper-Greenhill, Eilean, 73, 78
Huyssen, Andreas, 75–6

ICOM (International Council of Museums), 61, 62, 74
IMAX, 8, 86, 116, 120
immersion, 7, 8, 63, 67, 69n, 74–5, 77, 78, 80, 85, 86, 96, 101, 107, 108, 120, 121, 134, 138
Imperial Institute, 27–9, 33
Imperial War Museum (IWM)
  cinema theatre, 34
  establishment, 31, 33
  film collection, 31–4
  First World War Galleries, 85–6, 86–7, 101
  Mutoscopes, 35–40, 42, 78, 82, 83, 124, 137–8
Imperial War Museum North (IWM North)
  Big Picture Show, 4, 117–19, 138
In Flanders Fields Museum, 82–3, 96–100, 138
interactivity, 7, 8, 75, 76, 77, 78, 84, 92, 96, 117, 120, 121, 124–35

Jameson, Frederic, 84, 112

Kendall, J. Murray (Captain), 35
Kissiloff, William, 65
Kotler, Neil, 75
Kotler, Philip, 75

LaCapra, Dominick, 96
Landsberg, Alison, 77–8
Langlois, Henry, 1
Leeder, Murray, 91
Leicester Museum, 29–30
Levi, Pavle, 48
Libeskind, Daniel, 116
L'île et elle exhibition, 2
Lindsay, Vachel, 20–1
Lissitzky, El, 46, 47–9, 50
Los Angeles Museum of the Holocaust
  Tree of Testimony installation, 88–9
  World That Was installation, 126–7
Lowe, Edwin E., 27, 29–31, 38, 40
Lugon, Olivier, 46, 47, 65, 105–6

McCann Morley, Grace L., 55
McClusky, Frederick D., 20
McLean, Kathleen, 11
McLuhan, Marshall, 63–5, 69–70n
magic lantern slides, 33
  and contemporary museums, 100
  in lectures and shows, 3, 21, 22, 30
  in museums, 22, 30, 33
Malevich, Kazimir, 23

Index

Malík, M., 66
Mallet-Stevens, Robert, 1
Marinetti, Filippo Tommaso, 23
Martinitt and Stelline Museum, 101
Matuszewski, Bolesław, 18–19, 20, 23, 32
media archaeology, 9–10
Metropolitan Museum of Art (New York), 25n
modernist museum, 3, 100
Moholy-Nagy, László, 46, 49–51, 120, 123n
montage, 48, 49, 82, 85–6, 87, 105, 106, 107, 108, 113, 117, 121, 126, 127, 137
Moussinac, Léon, 1
Moy, Mr, 35, 36, 39, 40
multimedia displays, 50–1, 64–8
Mumford, Lewis, 17–18, 23
museum
  and popular audience, 21–3
  and theme parks, 68, 75–6
  and world fairs, 53–5, 62
  studies, 6–8, 63, 77–8
Museum Laboratory of the Mind, 127–35, 138
Museum of Modern Art (MoMA), 8, 51
  Road to Victory exhibition, 106
Museum of the City of New York, 63, 64–5, 85
Mutoscopes
  British Biograph, 35–6
  in museums, 40–2
  see also Imperial War Museum

Nead, Lynda, 91
New York Museum of Science and Industry, 52, 55–7, 138

Paci, Viva, 79
Païni, Dominique, 106
Palazzo Ducale in Gubbio, 101–2
panorama, 2, 8, 52
  at the Imperial Institute, 27–8
Parker, Harley, 63–5, 69n
Parr, Albert E., 63
Parry, Ross, 79
Paul, Robert, 19
Peopling the Palaces installation, 110–13
Pepper's Ghost, 100
Phantasmagoria, 10, 91, 109
  and contemporary art, 101
  in contemporary museums, 100–2, 109
Pickford, John, 83–4
Pine, Joseph, 75
Pressa Exhibition, 48–9; *see also* Lissitzky, El

Rader, Karen A., 53–4
Radford, Thomas, 77
relocation, 122n
Ricœur, Paul, 88, 89, 94
Robertson (Etienne-Gaspard Robert), 101, 102n
Room of the Present, 49–51; *see also* Moholy-Nagy, László

San Diego Museum of Man, 52
Scandiffio, Theresa, 25n
Schnapp, Jeffery, 107, 109
Science Museum London, 1, 9, 29, 30, 35, 38, 52
Shannon, Joseph, 67
Shaw, Robert P., 53, 54–7
Shearman, John, 93–5
Smither, Roger, 32, 40
spectres
  spectral nature of moving images, 18, 91, 99, 100, 111, 128–30, 138
  spectral turn in social sciences, 91–2, 127, 130
  see also ghosts
Steichen, Edward, 106
Stewart, Susan, 124
Strauven, Wanda, 124–5
Studio Azzurro, 4, 127, 131, 132; *see also* Museum Laboratory of the Mind

The Art in French Cinema exhibition, 1
Trento Tunnels *see* Galleries of Piedicastello

UNESCO, 61–2, 74
USC Shoah Foundation Institute for Visual History and Education, 87–8, 89
useful cinema, 9

Valéry, Paul, 23
Varda, Agnès, 2
Venaria Reale *see Peopling the Palaces* installation
video testimonies, 74, 75, 78–9, 82, 87–9, 92–6, 125–6, 130, 132–5, 138
Violi, Patrizia, 77
Virtual Archaeological Museum Herculaneum, 86
Voyage(s) en utopie exhibition, 2

Walsh, David, 32, 40
Ward, Janet, 46
Wasson, Haidee, 8, 9, 25n, 43n, 54–5
Watson, Sheila, 77

white cube, 3
Widespread Museum of Resistance, Deportation, War, Rights and Freedom, 92–6, 126, 138
Williams, Paul, 75, 80n

Witcomb, Andrea, 77
Wonders, Karen, 86
Wright Gilbert, 66

Youngblood, Gene, 117, 120

EU representative:
Easy Access System Europe
Mustamäe tee 50, 10621 Tallinn, Estonia
Gpsr.requests@easproject.com